DATE DUE

A

CHRIST AND CULTURE REVISITED

Christ and Culture Revisited

D. A. CARSON

WILLIAM B. EERDMANS PUBLISHING COMPANY

GRAND RAPIDS, MICHIGAN / CAMBRIDGE, U.K.

Published 2008 by

Wm. B. Eerdmans Publishing Co.

2140 Oak Industrial Drive N.E., Grand Rapids, Michigan 49505 /

P.O. Box 163, Cambridge CB3 9PU U.K.

Printed in the United States of America

13 12 11 10 09 08   7 6 5 4 3 2

Library of Congress Cataloging-in-Publication Data

Carson, D. A.

Christ and culture revisited / D. A. Carson.

p.   cm.

Includes bibliographical references and indexes.

ISBN 978-0-8028-3174-3 (cloth: alk. paper)

1. Christianity and culture.

2. Niebuhr, H. Richard (Helmut Richard), 1894-1962. Christ and culture.

I. Title.

BR115.C8C333   2008

261 — dc22

2007046554

www.eerdmans.com

This one is gratefully dedicated

to

Scott and Cathy

Contents

—◦◦◦—

Preface

—◦◦◦—

Four considerations impelled me to write this book.

First, ever since Pentecost Christians have had to think through the nature of their relationships with others. Christians soon multiplied in number and across an amazing number of racial and social barriers, constituting a church, a fellowship, a body, that transcended the established categories of empire, ethnicity, language, and social status. Even within the pages of the New Testament, Christians are told both to view government as something ordained by God and to view at least one particular government as representative of antichrist. The earliest reported squabbles *within* the church turned in part on cultural differences, on perceived injustices in the distribution of services to different language groups. Beyond the pages of the New Testament, even a casual knowledge of the history of the church discloses an incredible diversity of situations in which Christians have found themselves: persecuted and reigning, isolated and dominant, ignorant and well educated, highly distinguishable from the surrounding culture and virtually indifferentiable from it, impoverished and wealthy, evangelistically zealous and evangelistically dormant, social reformers and supportive of the social *status quo,* hungry for heaven and hoping it won't arrive too soon. All of these polarized possibilities reflect diverse *cultural* self-understanding. Inevitably, in most generations Christians have pondered what their attitudes *ought* to be. Mine is merely one more voice in this long chain of Christian reflection.

The second thing that has impelled me to write this book is as contemporary as the first reason is universal. Today's instantaneous communications mean that with only minimum effort Christians become aware of the extraordinarily diverse cultural settings in which other Christians find themselves. We find out about Christians in Sierre Leone, the poorest country on earth; we also find out about Christians in Hong Kong and New York City. We watch the church multiplying in Latin America, out in the open, and watch it multiplying in China, in some measure underground. We witness the remarkable loss of Christian consensus almost everywhere in Western Europe, and see the numbers of Christians exploding in the Ukraine and in Romania. We read of Christians being arrested in Iran, beheaded in Saudi Arabia, and butchered by the hundreds of thousands in southern Sudan, while observing the opulence of some Christian surroundings in Dallas and Seoul. We sit with semi-literate brothers and sisters in Christ in a village of Papua New Guinea who are learning to read for the first time, and we cannot forget that their grandparents were headhunters; we sit with presidents of Christian seminaries and universities, responsible for wisely dispensing many tens of millions of dollars every year. In the past, it was easier to speak out of one's own culture without reference to the cultures of others, but essays that are so narrowly focused today either seem out-of-date or they self-consciously target only one culture — they make no pretensions to a wider vision. Many of the most thoughtful essays and books written by Christians in the past to unpack the relationship between believers-living-in-a-broader-culture and unbelievers-within-the-broader-culture reflected the specificity of the author's cultural location. Dietrich Bonhoeffer is not going to sound quite like Bill Bright, and most reasonable people will admit that their own experiences have a fair bit to do with their respective theological emphases, not least those touching on the relationships between Christians and unbelievers. If Abraham Kuyper had grown up under the conditions of the killing fields of Cambodia,[1] one suspects his view of the relationship between Christianity and culture would have been

---

1. See especially Don Cormack, *Killing Fields, Living Fields* (London: Monarch, 1997).

significantly modified. Even the sweeping cultural analysis of H. Richard Niebuhr, about which I'll say much more, though it trawls through history to enrich the study, is transparently the stance of a mid-twentieth-century Westerner steeped in the heritage of what liberal Protestantism then was. Today, however, the sheer diversity of Christian experience is forced on our attention as never before. We become so suspicious of glib analyses that seem to be true in one cultural situation and patently irrelevant elsewhere, that we attempt only local analysis. But I shall argue that something important, something transcendent, is lost by this failure of nerve.

The third impetus is the "advisee group" — what some institutions call "small group" or "chaplaincy group" or "formation group" — at Trinity Evangelical Divinity School for which Scott Manetsch and I have shared responsibility during the last few years. This group continues to be one of my constant joys in life, not only for the privilege of working with Scott, but also because of all the relationships that have been formed, and, in measure, shaped, by that group. A couple of years ago, we worked through a short unit on Christians and culture. Inevitably, one of the starting points for the discussion was the classic work by Richard Niebuhr. The discussion that erupted at that time prompted me to do some more work and put down on paper a few things I had been thinking about for some time.

Finally, an invitation from the Faculté libre de théologie évangélique at Vaux-sur-Seine, just outside Paris, to give some lectures at one of their theological colloquia served as the incentive to start writing up my notes. The first two chapters of this book were presented at Vaux. I want to express my profound thanks to Émile Nicole and the other members of the faculty, and not least to my old friend Henri Blocher, for the warmth of their welcome and the acuteness of their interaction. I should add that although I was reared in French and can still speak it pretty fluently, I have lived outside the French-speaking world for so many decades that I do not trust myself to write polished French. I am therefore profoundly grateful to Pierre Constant, a former (and highly gifted) doctoral student at Trinity, for giving the French form of these chapters whatever grace they display.

Even though Niebuhr's *Christ and Culture* is more than fifty years old, it is difficult, at least in the English-speaking world, to ignore him.

His work, for good and ill, has shaped much of the discussion. Even the celebrated distinctions of earlier scholars — such as Weber's distinction between "church" and "sect," in which the church sets itself up as part of the culture while the sect sets itself up as something over against the culture — have been mediated to many people through Niebuhr's volume. On the other hand, during the last half-century, many debates have raged over the very meaning of "culture." Disenchanted by the arrogance of some Enlightenment assumptions, many writers have questioned those assumptions, raising a raft of new questions about how Christians — or any other religious group, for that matter — should think of themselves with respect to the surrounding culture, when they themselves cannot escape being part of that culture.

My own effort in this book begins by summarizing Niebuhr, since Niebuhr has become an icon to which everyone refers, though few today still read him closely. Apart from some initial evaluation of Niebuhr on his own terms, I then try to lay out the rudiments of a responsible biblical theology that any Christian will want to acknowledge, and begin to show how these turning points in the history of redemption must shape Christian thinking about the relationships between Christ and culture (chaps. 1 and 2). The structures generated by such biblical theology are robust enough to allow the many differing emphases within Scripture to find their voices, so that to speak of different "models" of the Christ-and-culture relationship begins to look misleading. Such reflection requires more probing, not only with respect to current debates over "culture" and "postmodernism" (chap. 3), but also with respect to some of the dominant cultural forces of our time (chap. 4). One of the dimensions of this ongoing debate is the relation between church and state (chap. 5). Here I have sketched the very different cultural stances associated with the notion of separation of church and state found in France and in the United States, with glances at a few other countries, so that we can more clearly detect the kinds of cultural spectacles we inevitably bring to the task of reading Scripture, and how even the application of the balance of Scripture will almost inevitably shift in different cultures. The final chapter raises a selection of perennial temptations Christians face as they work through these issues. It is a modest attempt to forge a stable and flexible stance that is immune to various siren calls.

A number of people have read the manuscript and made helpful suggestions. I am indebted to Mark Dever, Tim Keller, Andy Naselli, Bob Priest, Michael Thate, and Sandy Willson. Thanks go as well to Jim Kinney of Baker Book House, who gave me galley copies of two books that were not yet published so I could benefit from them in my own work. Andy Naselli's customary energy and attention to detail were in rich display in the compilation of the indexes. And finally, I am thankful to the folk at Eerdmans for seeing this work safely and efficiently through the press.

Soli Deo gloria.

D. A. CARSON
Trinity Evangelical
Divinity School

ONE

How to Think about Culture:
Reminding Ourselves of Niebuhr

—⟨⟨⟨⟩⟩⟩—

Before plunging into this subject, we had better find some agreement as to what we mean by "culture."

Not very long ago, "culture" commonly referred to what is now meant by "high culture." For instance, we might have said, "She has such a cultured voice." If a person read Shakespeare, Goethe, Gore Vidal, Voltaire, and Flaubert, and listened to Bach and Mozart while reading a slender volume of poetry, all the while drinking a mild Chardonnay, he was cultured; if he read cheap whodunits, Asterix, and Eric Ambler — or, better yet, did not read at all — while drinking a beer or a Coke, all the while listening to ska or heavy metal and paying attention to the X-Box screen with the latest violent video game, he was uncultured. But this understanding of "culture" must, sooner or later, be challenged by those who think of "high" culture as a species of elitism, as something intrinsically arrogant or condescending. For them, the opposite of "high culture" is not "low culture" but "popular culture," with its distinct appeal to democratic values. But even the appeal to "popular culture" is not very helpful for our purposes, because it appeals to only one part of "culture": presumably there are various forms of "unpopular culture" out there too.

Today, "culture" has become a fairly plastic concept that means something like "the set of values broadly shared by some subset of the human population." That's not bad, but doubtless the definition could be improved by a bit of tightening. Probably the most important seminal definition, arising from the fields of intellectual history and cultural anthropology, is that of A. L. Kroeber and C. Kluckhohn:

> Culture consists of patterns, explicit and implicit, of and for behavior acquired and transmitted by symbols, constituting the distinctive achievement of human groups, including their embodiment in artifacts; the essential core of culture consists of traditional (i.e., historically derived and selected) ideas and especially their attached values; culture systems may, on the one hand, be considered as products of action, on the other hand as conditioning elements of further action.[1]

Not a few other definitions say something similar. Brief and to the point is the one-liner definition of Robert Redfield: "shared understandings made manifest in act and artifact."[2] The widely cited definition offered by Clifford Geertz combines succinctness and clarity: "[T]he culture concept . . . denotes an historically transmitted pattern of meanings embodied in symbols, a system of inherited conceptions expressed in symbolic form by means of which men communicate, perpetuate, and develop their knowledge about and attitudes towards life."[3]

Doubtless the details of these definitions could be debated and refined; indeed, a significant minority of anthropologists and others are suspicious of the entire concept of culture.[4] The primary reason has

1. A. L. Kroeber and C. Kluckhohn, *Culture: A Critical Review of Concepts and Definitions* (New York: Random House, 1952), 357.

2. Cited by Richard A. Shweder, *Why Do Men Barbecue? Recipes for Cultural Psychology* (Cambridge: Harvard University Press, 2003), 10, which, despite its title, is a serious and insightful volume. I am indebted to Robert Priest for drawing the first chapter of that book to my attention. It offers one of the most helpful surveys of the current debate on the nature of culture of which I am aware. Cf. also Richard A. Shweder and Robert A. LeVine, *Culture Theory: Essays on Mind, Self, and Emotion* (Cambridge: Cambridge University Press, 1984).

3. Geertz, *The Interpretation of Cultures* (New York: Basic Books, 1973), 89.

4. Some of their views are conveniently summarized in Shweder, *Why Do Men Barbecue?* in the introductory chapter. For more detailed access to their theories, it is helpful to read the following (some of whom Shweder does not discuss): Antonio Gramsci, *Selections from the Prison Notebooks,* trans. Quinton Hoare and Geoffrey Nowell Smith (New York: International, 1971); Michel Foucault, *The Order of Things: An*

to do with confusion between what "culture" means and what "metanarrative" means. The critics offer two dominant arguments. *First,* they insist, we simply must reject the pretension that a metanarrative is possible: there is no big explanatory story that makes sense of all the little stories. And if we reject the notion of metanarrative, we cannot continue to talk about culture, since culture is bound up with universal or even transcendental assumptions. *Second,* all such discussions presuppose that we who are discussing culture somehow stand outside it, and that is impossible. For instance, any discussion between Christ (and thus Christianity) and culture is incoherent, since all forms of Christianity are inherently and unavoidably embedded in cultural expression. How can there be a dialogue with only one partner?

Some of these challenges I will attempt to address in the third chapter. This is not (yet) the place to probe the matter in any detail. It is enough for the moment to point out that my own use of "culture" will nestle comfortably in the domain of the definitions I've already provided, in particular the contribution of Geertz. These definitions presuppose that there are many cultures and make no pretensions about assigning transcendental value to any of them.[5] That all exemplifications of faith, Christian and otherwise, are necessarily expressed within forms that are cultural cannot reasonably be denied. What that means for the dialogue is still to be worked out.

That brings me to the nub of the issue I want to address.

Archaeology of the Human Sciences (New York: Vintage Books, 1970); Foucault, *The Archaeology of Knowledge* (repr. London: Routledge, 2002); Raymond Williams, *Marxism and Literature* (Oxford: Oxford University Press, 1977); Terry Eagleton, *Ideology: An Introduction* (London: Verso, 1991); Eagleton, *The Idea of Culture* (Oxford: Blackwell, 2000); Edward Said, *Culture and Imperialism* (New York: Random House, 1997).

5. Here I am parting company from many older treatments, which, despite their heuristic value, subtly assume some notion or other of "high" culture. For instance, in one of his last works, T. S. Eliot, *Notes Towards the Definition of Culture* (New York: Harcourt, Brace and Company, 1949), asserts that the word "culture" has three different associations, "according to whether we have in mind the development of an *individual,* of a *group* or *class,* or of a *whole society*" (p. 19; italics his). His thesis is that the culture of the individual is dependent upon the culture of the group, which is itself dependent upon the culture of the whole society. But observe his terminology: he is thinking of the "development" of an individual, group, or society; he readily speaks of "achieving" culture (p. 20). Under the dominant definitions most commonly deployed today, belonging to or being part of a culture is unavoidable.

The Contemporary Challenge

In the move from the old covenant to the new, the locus of the covenant people passed from the covenant-nation to the international covenant-people. That inevitably raised questions about the relationships this people should have with the people around them who were *not* part of the new covenant. In political terms, Christians had to work through the relationship between the church and the state, between the kingdom of God and the Roman Empire. Somewhat different answers were called up by different circumstances: contrast, for instance, Romans 13 and Revelation 19. But the issues the church faced by being an international community claiming ultimate allegiance to a kingdom not of this world were much more than governmental. They also had to do with whether Christians should participate in socially expected customs when those customs had religious overtones (e.g., 1 Corinthians 8), with styles of governance (e.g., Matthew 20:20-28), with an array of relational expectations (e.g., Philemon; 1 Peter 2:13–3:16), with the challenge of persecution (e.g., Matthew 5:10-12; John 15:18–16:4; Revelation 6), and much more.

All of these dynamics changed with the Constantinian settlement, of course — but that does not mean that from the beginning of the fourth century, the tensions were all resolved and the debates silenced. The challenge of how to respond to official persecution obviously declined in the Empire after the accession of Constantine, but other questions had to be thought through. For instance, just war theory, articulated in pagan form by Cicero, took on distinctively Christian forms once believers faced increasing responsibilities of political leadership.[6] "Give back to Caesar what is Caesar's, and to God what is God's," the Master had said (Mark 12:17), and unpacking that utterance, in the context of the entire corpus of New Testament documents, was unlikely to achieve stable resolution in a generation or two. In the political arena alone, Christians produced masses of literature as they attempted to work out appropriate relations between Christ and culture.[7]

6. In brief compass, cf. D. A. Carson, *Love in Hard Places* (Wheaton: Crossway, 2002), 108-44, esp. 143.

7. Beyond all praise is the work of Oliver O'Donovan and Joan Lockwood

Yet it is not my intention to treat the history of these debates, except to note in passing that we must never fall into the trap of supposing that we are the first generation of Christians to think about these things. My focus is on how we should be thinking about the relations between Christ and culture *now,* at the beginning of the twenty-first century. We have the same biblical texts that earlier generations of Christians thought their way through, of course, but our reflections are shaped by six unique factors.

(1) Especially in the Anglo-Saxon world, discussion of these matters cannot ignore the programmatic analysis of H. Richard Niebuhr. I shall return to him in a moment.

(2) We live at a time when diverse voices are clamoring for the right to dictate what the relationships between Christ and culture *ought* to be.

(3) Owing to modern communication technology and to immigration patterns that have made many megalopolises around the world into extraordinary centers of multiculturalism, debates rage regarding what is "cultural" in "multicultural."

(4) This in turn has precipitated debates over the relative merits of one culture over another, or, alternatively put, over whether one ever has the right to affirm the superiority of one culture over another. That in turn, of course, feeds into debates over religious claims, since religions, too, under the definition of "culture" already given, are necessarily forms of cultural expression. What gives a religion, any religion, the right to claim its own superiority or even uniqueness?

(5) In much of the Western world, though not, by and large, elsewhere, confessional Christianity is in serious decline. That means the inherited *status quo* in most Western countries cannot continue unquestioned. We are forced to think through, yet again, what the relationship between Christ and culture ought to be.

(6) The actual history of tensions between church and state varies enormously from state to state in the Western world and beyond,

---

O'Donovan, eds., *From Irenaeus to Grotius: A Sourcebook in Christian Political Thought* (Grand Rapids: Eerdmans, 1999).

making it difficult to make generalizations, or even discuss examples, without numerous caveats. For instance, the now-proverbial "wall of separation" between church and state colors all debates in the United States, yet there is no similar wall, though there are similar freedoms, in the United Kingdom. In France, the "laïcité française" is in part a function of a deeply rooted historical anticlericalism that finds no parallel, until very recently, in, say, the Scandinavian countries or the United States.

Most of these points will be explored later, but it is worth expanding a few of them here, so as to clarify the challenges we face. We must not overlook the sheer diversity of the voices that constitute this challenge. In much of the Western world, despite the fact that Christianity was one of the forces that shaped what the West became (along with the Enlightenment, and a host of less dominant powers), culture is not only moving away from Christianity, it is frequently openly hostile toward it. Christianity can be tolerated, provided it is entirely private: Christian belief that intrudes itself into the public square, especially if it is trying to influence public policy, is most often taken, without examination, as *prima facie* evidence for bigotry and intolerance. In most of the Western world, this sneering condescension has become dominant in many public organs only within the last quarter-century or so — though obviously it advanced farther, faster, and earlier in deeply anti-clerical countries like France and in distinctly secular countries like Australia than in countries with a once-strong national church like England or with a pronounced Bible belt like America. Even in the latter two cases, the strength of the assault depends on both geography and social location: it is strong in the north of England, the Pacific Northwest, and the New England states of the United States, and in segments of the culture such as the media and the institutions of tertiary education.

Meanwhile, in some ways the world has become *more* furiously religious.[8] In the Western world, more so in Europe than in North

---

8. Small wonder that some scholars comment on the decline of atheism: see, for instance, Alister McGrath, *The Twilight of Atheism: The Rise and Fall of Disbelief in the Modern World* (New York: Doubleday, 2004).

America, this is experienced in terms of rising numbers of Muslims — a trend that is bound to continue, granted the fact that the birth rate of the more traditional European population is not sufficiently high to maintain itself in a single European country. And, of course, all of us who live in large urban centers necessarily interact nowadays with Hindus, Sikhs, and even animists, as well as with secularists. As the new slogan puts it, "Nobody is leaving anyone else alone and isn't ever again going to." The multiplicity of religious claims is here to stay, and governments are going to have to get used to it. The urgency of thinking afresh about Christ and culture is becoming more acute.[9]

Inevitably, Christians respond in various ways. Some advocate one form or another of withdrawal. Others want to gain more access to the media. Still others put forth valiant efforts to influence government and pass appropriate legislation. Some, whether consciously or unconsciously, develop a two-tier mentality, one for Christians and church functions, and one for the broader cultural encounters that take up most of the rest of the week. Still others think little about these matters but simply want to get on with evangelism and church planting.

Both the rising hostility in the West toward Christianity and the responses Christians offer make certain assumptions as to what the relationship between Christ and culture ought to be. So also do the competing voices of other religions. For instance, if we are to adapt the labeling approach of Niebuhr, we might call the strongest hostility "Culture over Christ." Alternatively, where strong voices insist that religion, including the Christian religion, ought to be restricted to purely private matters, then what is being said, of course, is that Christ and culture belong in separate spheres, the former private and the latter public. When some Christian voices hold up the model of Abraham Kuyper, whom we shall think about later, they have clearly moved into the "Christ above culture" paradigm (what Niebuhr further specifies to be the "conversionist" model). Richard Bauckham sees two opposing dangers. On the one hand, some Christians attempt to embed their faith in the culture, and run the risk "of dissipat-

---

9. This is one of the central themes of David Herbert, *Religion and Civil Society: Rethinking Public Religion in the Contemporary World* (Aldershot: Ashgate, 2003).

ing Christianity into something indistinguishable from other options in Western culture."[10] On the other hand, some retreat so far from engagement with the world that they scarcely engage directly with it, creating for themselves an alternative rationality, largely defensive in posture, which Bauckham identifies with "fundamentalism."[11]

Even when no theoretical position is formally adopted, a theoretical position is usually presupposed. When practical advice is given to Christians by firm voices that articulate one heritage or another, some sort of relationship between Christ and culture is *invariably* assumed. Whether anyone in that tradition has systematically thought about this larger relationship is another matter. To take some examples: (1) Nancy Pearcey claims that when the "total truth" of the gospel is articulated and defended, Christianity is liberated from its cultural captivity,[12] which in this case is predominantly tied to American forms of postmodernism. (2) Stassen and Gushee advocate a form of kingdom pacifism.[13] (3) Another work, a collection of essays preserving diverse points of view, worries over the impact of globalization, and the diverse ways in which America rules over an "empire."[14] Meanwhile, (4) Gorringe's "theology of culture" is essentially an attempt to ground a fairly left-wing socialism in Christian theology.[15]

At the moment, I am neither criticizing nor defending any of these stances. I am merely pointing out that every one of them presupposes some sort of relationship between Christ and culture, even though that relationship is usually not *directly* addressed.

That brings us, then, to the place where we must remind our-

---

10. Richard Bauckham, *God and the Crisis of Freedom: Biblical and Contemporary Perspectives* (Louisville: Westminster John Knox, 2002), 54.

11. Bauckham, *God and the Crisis of Freedom,* 54-55.

12. *Total Truth: Liberating Christianity from Its Cultural Captivity* (Wheaton: Crossway, 2004). I have always found "total" to be a rather strange adjective to modify "truth."

13. Glen H. Stassen and David P. Gushee, *Kingdom Ethics: Following Jesus in Contemporary Context* (Downers Grove: InterVarsity, 2003).

14. Wes Avram, ed., *Anxious about Empire: Theological Essays on the New Global Realities* (Grand Rapids: Brazos, 2004). Cf. Chalmers Johnson, *The Sorrows of Empire: Militarism, Secrecy, and the End of the Republic* (New York: Owl Books, repr. 2004).

15. See especially T. J. Gorringe's *Furthering Humanity: A Theology of Culture* (Aldershot: Ashgate, 2004).

selves of Niebuhr's useful taxonomy of the possibilities. I shall try to describe the options he lays out for us as carefully as I can. I will attempt a little evaluation as I proceed, but most of the evaluation will await the next two chapters.

H. Richard Niebuhr

Niebuhr offers us five options, each option taking up a chapter, the five being enveloped by a lengthy introduction and a "concluding unscientific postscript." The purpose of the book, Niebuhr writes,

> is to set forth typical Christian answers to the problem of Christ and culture and so to contribute to the mutual understanding of variant and often conflicting Christian groups. The belief which lies back of this effort, however, is the conviction that Christ as living Lord is answering the question in the totality of history and life in a fashion which transcends the wisdom of all his interpreters yet employs their partial insights and their necessary conflicts.[16]

The problem is not new. Christians had to confront it during the days of the Roman Empire. In certain important respects, the Empire was tolerant: the vast array of religions and customs were not only tolerated but encouraged. Christianity's insistence that Jesus alone is Lord (however nonpolitical Christians were at the beginning of the Christian era) was simultaneously despised and seen as a threat. As then, so today: strong voices assert that "all consideration of the claims of Christ and God should be banished from the spheres where other gods, called values, reign" (9).

If he is going to talk about "Christ and culture," Niebuhr must provide reasonably clear definitions of both "Christ" and "culture," and so he devotes several pages to each. He is fully aware that every understanding of "Christ" is at best partial; no one confession says every-

---

16. H. Richard Niebuhr, *Christ and Culture* (New York: Harper Torchbooks, 1951), 2. Hereafter, page references to this book will be given parenthetically in the text.

thing, thereby capturing the objective truth, the essence of Jesus Christ. Nevertheless, he insists, "If we cannot say anything adequately, we can say some things inadequately. . . . Though every description is an interpretation, it can be an interpretation of the objective reality. Jesus Christ who is the Christian's authority can be described, though every description falls short of completeness and must fail to satisfy others who have encountered him" (14). However disparate or complementary these descriptions may be, Jesus "can never be confused with a Socrates, a Plato or an Aristotle, a Gautama, a Confucius, or a Mohammed, or even with an Amos or Isaiah" (13). This prepares the way for Niebuhr to talk about the strengths and weaknesses, as he sees them, of the liberal Christ, the existentialist Jesus, and so forth, and in particular of the various virtues that Christians cherish as they think of Christ — faith, hope, obedience, humility, and others. In short, Niebuhr wishes to be broadly comprehensive, accepting as "Christ" the various portraits of Jesus Christ found in dominant strands of Christendom.

Niebuhr's approach to what "Christ" means in his title "Christ and Culture" prompts two initial reflections. *First,* for him, "Christ" is not infinitely plastic. He includes no fundamentalist Arians, for instance, such as Jehovah's Witnesses; nor does he include the Mormon Jesus. Nevertheless, the sweep of the interpretations of "Christ" that he embraces is doubtless too broad, if one is trying to limit oneself to the forms of confessional Christianity that explicitly and self-consciously try to live under the authority of Scripture. As a result, certain elements of his understanding of the possibilities of the relationship between Christ and culture should, I think, be ruled out of court, where they are decisively shaped by a frankly sub-biblical grasp of who Christ is. Obviously, I shall have to return to this point. *Second,* Niebuhr is fully aware that all human understanding is necessarily both partial and interpretative — or, to use the contemporary category, all human knowledge is necessarily perspectival. Human finiteness, let alone human fallenness, warrants this assessment. Postmoderns, especially American postmoderns, tend to give the impression that every thinker who came before them, not least those nasty moderns, were all under the delusion that genuine human knowing was absolutist. Quite frankly, this assessment of modernism is, in many cases, a caricature: modernist though he is, Niebuhr is thoroughly aware that human knowledge is partial and perspectival. Yet he wisely avoids the extreme postmodern position that concludes that knowledge of the objective is impossible. We may say some true things inadequately, even if we cannot say anything adequately, that is, with the knowledge of omniscience, with omniperspective. Despite the calumnies of many postmoderns, Niebuhr is not the only modern who is conscious of human limitations.[17]

Turning to what he understands by "culture" (29-39), Niebuhr wants to avoid the technical debates of anthropologists. The culture with which we are concerned, he says, "is not a particular phenomenon but the general one, though the general thing appears only in particular forms, and though a Christian of the West cannot think about the problem save in Western terms" (31). Then he writes:

> What we have in view when we deal with Christ and culture is that total process of human activity and that total result of such activity to which now the name *culture,* now the name *civilization,* is applied in common speech. Culture is the "artificial, secondary environment" which man superimposes on the natural. It comprises language, habits, ideas, beliefs, customs, social organization, inherited artifacts, technical processes, and values. This "social heritage," this "reality sui generis," which the New Testament writers frequently had in mind when they spoke of "the world," which is represented in many forms but to which Christians like other men are inevitably subject, is what we mean when we speak of culture. (31; italics his)

Moreover, although Niebuhr refuses to speak of the "essence" of culture, he is prepared to describe some of its chief characteristics: it is

---

17. Here, for instance, is Brooke Foss Westcott, writing more than a century ago, criticizing the sort of "history" that von Ranke and others embraced: "There is undoubtedly at present a strong feeling in favour of realistic, external, history; but it may reasonably be questioned whether this fashion of opinion will be permanent, and it is obviously beset by many perils. Realistic history often treats only of the dress and not of the living frame, and it can never go beyond the outward circumstances of an organisation which is inspirited by one vital power" (*The Gospel According to St. John: The Greek Text with Introduction and Notes* [Grand Rapids: Baker, repr. 1980], cxii).

always social (i.e., it is bound up with human life in society), it is human achievement (presupposing purposiveness and effort), it is bound up with a world of values which, dominantly, are thought to be for "the good of man" (32-35). Again, culture in all its forms and varieties is concerned with the "temporal and material realization of values" (36). And so, since the achievement of these values is accomplished "in transient and perishing stuff, cultural activity is almost as much concerned with the *conservation of values* as with their realization" (36; italics his).

As with Niebuhr's definition of Christ, so with his definition of culture: we must engage in a little preliminary evaluation before we can proceed. Niebuhr's definition of culture embraces "ideas" and "beliefs" as well as customs, social organization, inherited artifacts, and the like. On the face of it, if culture embraces ideas, beliefs, values, customs, and all the rest, it is hard to see how it can avoid embracing Christianity — in which case, once again, it is difficult to see how it is possible to analyze the relation between Christ and culture, when, under this definition, Christ appears to be embraced by culture. Niebuhr survives this problem by restricting culture to the domain of the "temporal and material realization of values," and by associating "culture" with what the New Testament means by "world": that is, by "culture" he means something like "culture-devoid-of-Christ." Then, as the discussion progresses and he works out what the relationship between Christ and culture might be, that culture might, for instance, be "transformed" by Christ, so that it is no longer "culture-devoid-of-Christ" but now something that it was not before: "culture-transformed-by-Christ." The slipperiness of the "culture" terminology is palpable.

What is becoming obvious is that Niebuhr is not so much talking about the relationship between Christ and culture, as between two sources of authority as they compete within culture, namely Christ (however he is understood within the various paradigms of mainstream Christendom) and every other source of authority divested of Christ (though Niebuhr is thinking primarily of secular or civil authority rather than the authority claimed by competing religions). If we do not recognize that the polarities Niebuhr sets up are along such lines, the rest of his elegant discussion simply becomes incoherent. Our task now, however, is to try to understand his fivefold paradigm in his own terms, before we think it through afresh, so for the time being I will retain his use of the terminology.

(1) Christ against Culture

That Niebuhr's understanding of what "Christ" and "culture" mean lies along the line of competing authority claims is strikingly illustrated in his summary of the first paradigm: "The first answer to the question of Christ and culture we shall consider is the one that uncompromisingly affirms the sole authority of Christ over the Christian and resolutely rejects the culture's claims to loyalty" (45). This stance is found in the book of Revelation, where it is made all the more acute because Christians are threatened with persecution. But it is also forcefully depicted in 1 John. Despite its profound elaboration of "the doctrine of love" (46) — it is this Epistle which declares, "God is love" (1 John 4:8, 16) — nevertheless "the central interest of the writer . . . is quite as much the Lordship of Christ as the idea of love" (46). Loyalty to this Christ has entailments in the doctrinal, moral, and social realms. Moreover, "[t]he counterpart of loyalty to Christ and the brothers is the rejection of cultural society; a clear line of separation is drawn between the brotherhood of the children of God and the world" (46-48).

Nevertheless, this "Christ against culture" stance is still not in its most radical form, since John also takes it for granted "that Jesus Christ has come to expiate the sins of the world" (49). Tertullian states it in radical fashion: Christians constitute a "third race," different from Jews and Gentiles, and called to live a way of life quite separate from culture. Indeed, Niebuhr avers, Tertullian

> replaces the positive and warm ethics of love which characterizes the First Letter of John with a largely negative morality; avoidance of sin and fearsome preparation for the coming day of judgment seem more important than thankful acceptance of God's grace in the gift of his Son. (52)

Inevitably, then, "Tertullian's rejection of the claims of culture is correspondingly sharp" (52). And the worst thing in the culture is pagan religion, especially as it reflects idolatry, polytheism, false beliefs and rites, sensuality, and commercialization. But this religion touches everything in the ancient world, so that for the Christian, political life must be shunned, and so also military service, philosophy, and the arts. Of course, learning is important for the believer, so "learning literature is allowable for believers" (55, citing *On Idolatry* x), but not teaching it, since teaching it enmeshes the teacher in commending the literature, with the result that one ends up commending and affirming "the praises of idols interspersed therein" (55).

Of course, Tertullian cannot be quite as consistent in this "Christ against culture" position as he seems, for he rejects the charge that Christians are "useless in the affairs of life," for, as he points out,

> we sojourn with you in the world, abjuring neither forum, nor shambles, nor bath, nor booth, nor inn, nor weekly market, nor any other places of commerce. . . . We sail with you, and fight with you, and till the ground with you; and in like manner we unite with you in your traffickings — even in the various arts we make public property of our works for your benefit. (53, citing *Apology* xlii)

Nonetheless, as Niebuhr points out, this "is said in defense," while when he admonishes believers, Tertullian's counsel is primarily to "withdraw from many meetings and occupations" (53).

Niebuhr traces the same impulse through the *Rule of St. Benedict*, through some Mennonite groups (he does not mention them, but in North America one automatically thinks of the Amish), and the early Quakers. In some detail, he takes us through the later writings of Leo Tolstoy. But Niebuhr insists that all these are merely "illustrations of the type": one finds similar groups "among Eastern and Western Catholics, orthodox and sectarian Protestants, millenarians and mystics, ancient and medieval and modern Christians" (64). It really does not matter whether these groups understand their own significance in mystical or apocalyptic terms. The type is found equally in monasteries and in a Lutheran Kierkegaard. I suppose that today we would add that this position is also found in Stanley Hauerwas.

Niebuhr muses that this position is both "necessary" and "inadequate" (65-76). The stance is often heroic, principled, morally stalwart, and uncompromising. Historically, the monasteries helped to conserve and transmit the Western cultural tradition, while Quakers and Tolstoyans, "intending to abolish all methods of coercion, have helped to reform prisons, to limit armaments, and to establish international organizations for the maintenance of peace through coercion" (67). The position is inevitable:

> The relation of the authority of Jesus Christ to the authority of culture is such that every Christian must often feel himself claimed by the Lord to reject the world and its kingdoms with their pluralism and temporalism, their makeshift compromises of many interests, their hypnotic obsession by the love of life and the fear of death. . . . If Romans 13 is not balanced by 1 John, the church becomes an instrument of state, unable to point men to their transpolitical destiny and their suprapolitical loyalty; unable also to engage in political tasks, save as one more group of power-hungry or security-seeking men. (68)

Yet however inevitable, the position is inadequate. The most radical Christians inevitably make use of the culture, or parts of the culture. "In almost every utterance Tertullian makes evident that he is a Roman, so nurtured in the legal tradition and so dependent on philosophy that he cannot state the Christian case without their aid" (69-70). Similarly, Tolstoy is intelligible only as a nineteenth-century Russian. In all of our confession of Christ, we are using words, and words are culturally embedded, even words like "Christ" and "Logos" and "love." When Tertullian commends modesty and patience, he is partly indebted to Stoic categories; when Tolstoy speaks of nonresistance, it is impossible not to discern the influence of Jean-Jacques Rousseau. "The difference between the radicals and the other groups is often only this: that the radicals fail to recognize what they are doing, and continue to speak as though they were separated from the world" (76).

Niebuhr finds four theological problems with this position. (a) There is a tendency in such radical movements to use "reason" to refer to the methods and content of knowledge within the "culture," and "revelation" to refer to their own Christian faith. Unfortunately, however, "[t]hey cannot solve their problem of Christ and culture without recognizing that distinctions must be made both with respect to the reasoning that goes on outside the Christian sphere and to the knowledge that is present in it" (78). (b) These radicals give the impression that sin abounds in the culture, while light and piety attach themselves to Christians. But this fails to wrestle adequately with the sin that is found among Christians, as it fails to recognize the "common grace" (though that is not Niebuhr's expression) amply demonstrated in the world. (c) This position often seeks to defend itself with new laws, new rules of conduct, that are so unbending and so precise that grace itself seems demoted to a second or third tier. (d) Above all, the "knottiest theological problem" with this position, according to Niebuhr, is "the relation of Jesus Christ to the Creator of nature and Governor of history as well as to the Spirit immanent in creation and in the Christian community" (80-81). This is in part a Trinitarian challenge; even more, it is the temptation to convert "their ethical dualism into an ontological bifurcation of reality" (81) that ends up in Montanism, in the inner light of Quakerism, in Tolstoy's spiritualism.

(2) The Christ of Culture

This second position is adopted by people who hail Jesus as the Messiah of their society, the one who fulfills its best hopes and aspirations. They are Christians "not only in the sense that they count themselves believers in the Lord but also in the sense that they seek to maintain community with all believers. Yet they seem equally at home in the community of culture" (83). They do not seek Christ's sanction for everything in their culture, but only for what they find to be the best in it; equally, they tend to disentangle Christ from what they judge to be barbaric or outmoded Jewish notions about God and history. "Sociologically they may be interpreted as nonrevolutionaries who find no need for positing 'cracks in time' — fall and incarnation and judgment and resurrection" (84).

In the early centuries of the Christian church, they are best exemplified by the Gnostics. Although its most notable leaders were in time condemned by the church, "[t]he movement represented by Gnosticism has been one of the most powerful in Christian history." "It sees in Christ not only a revealer of religious truth but a god, the object of religious worship; but not the Lord of all life, and not the son of the Father who is the present Creator and Governor of all things" (88-89).

Although Gnosticism died out in time,[18] the "Christ of culture" position was further developed after the Constantinian settlement, in the rise of "so-called Christian civilization" (89). In the medieval period, Abélard is the best exemplar, even though his thought was far removed from Gnosticism. Formally, Abélard merely quarrels with the church's way of stating the faith; in reality, "he reduces it to what conforms with the best in culture. It becomes a philosophic knowledge about reality, and an ethics for the improvement of life" (90). It was within this framework that Abélard offered the moral theory of the atonement

> as an alternative not only to a doctrine that is difficult for Christians as Christians but to the whole conception of a once-and-for-all act of redemption. Jesus Christ has become for Abélard the great moral teacher who in all that he did in the flesh . . . had the intention of our instruction, doing in a higher degree what Socrates and Plato had done before him. (90)

If in medieval culture "Abélard was a relatively lonely figure," since the eighteenth century "his followers have been numerous, and what was heresy became the new orthodoxy." Niebuhr is referring, of course, to what he calls "culture-Protestantism." Its defenders "interpret Christ as a hero of manifold culture" (91). Both John Locke, with his *The Reasonableness of Christianity,* and Immanuel Kant, with his *Religion within the Limits of Reason,* belong here. So also does Thomas Jefferson, who could write, "I am a Christian in the only sense in which he [Jesus Christ] wished any one to be" (cited on 91-92), after cutting up the New Testament so as to preserve only the bits that commended themselves to him. Niebuhr lines up Schleiermacher, Emer-

18. Some argue, of course, that it has returned in some modern forms of "spirituality" and of "new age" theology. Inevitably, there are both parallels and discontinuities. See, for instance, Peter Jones, *The Gnostic Empire Strikes Back: An Old Heresy for the New Age* (Phillipsburg: P & R, 1992).

son, F. D. Maurice, and others in this camp, but devotes principal attention to Albrecht Ritschl. After all, Ritschl's theology "had two foundation stones: not revelation and reason, but Christ and culture" (95). Ritschl achieved the reconciliation of Christ and culture that he wished, largely by appealing to his understanding of the kingdom of God. The kingdom "denotes the association of mankind — an association both extensively and intensively the most comprehensive possible — through the reciprocal moral action of its members, action which transcends all merely natural and particular considerations" (cited on 98). By this understanding of the kingdom, then, Jesus becomes the Christ of culture in both senses: "as the guide of men in all their labor to realize and conserve their values, and as the Christ who is understood by means of nineteenth-century cultural ideas" (98).

Niebuhr sees considerable strengths in this heritage. It has attracted many people to Jesus, precisely because it does not make him seem as alien as the first position does. Moreover, Niebuhr asserts,

> [t]he cultural Christians tend to speak to the cultured among the despisers of religion; they use the language of the more sophisticated circles, of those who are acquainted with the science, the philosophy, and the political and economic movements of their time. They are missionaries to the aristocracy and the middle class, or to the groups rising to power in a civilization. (104)[19]

Moreover, Jesus himself, though he was more than a prophet, nevertheless "like an Isaiah showed concern for the peace of his own city" (105). Though to him nothing was as important as one's "soul," yet he not only forgave their sins but healed the sick as well.

> For the radical Christian the whole world outside the sphere where Christ's Lordship is explicitly acknowledged is a realm of equal darkness; but cultural Christians note that there are great differences among the various movements in society; and by observing these they not only find points of contact for the mission of the church, but also are enabled to work for the reformation of

19. One cannot help but note that when he here speaks of "the cultured," Niebuhr has retreated to a "high" use of the term, away from his own working definition.

18

the culture. The radicals reject Socrates, Plato, and the Stoics, along with Aristippus, Democritus, and the Epicureans; tyranny and empire seem alike to them; highwaymen and soldiers both use violence; figures carved by Phidias are more dangerous temptations to idolatry than those made by a handy man; modern culture is all of one piece, individualistic and egoistic, secularistic and materialistic. The cultural Christian, however, understands that there are great polarities in any civilization; and that there is a sense in which Jesus Christ affirms movements in philosophy toward the assertion of the world's unity and order, movements in morals toward self-denial and the care for the common good, political concerns for justice, and ecclesiastical interests in honesty in religion. (106)

At the same time, Niebuhr can identify theological and other objections to this position. Cultural Christians are often assailed, not only by the orthodox, but by outsiders: pagan writers criticized Christian Gnostics, and both John Dewey and Karl Marx rejected Christian liberalism. They suspect that what is to them a compromised position will weaken the purity of their paganism, or of their liberalism, or of their Marxism — just as, from the other side, the orthodox suspect that these cultural Christians have sacrificed too much of what is essential to Christianity. Indeed, it is hard to deny that they "take some fragment of the complex New Testament story and interpretation, call this the essential characteristic of Jesus, elaborate upon it, and thus reconstruct their own mythical figure of the Lord." What this fragment is turns out, inevitably, to be "something that seems to agree with the interests or the needs of their time. . . . Jesus stands for the idea of spiritual knowledge; or of logical reason; or of the sense for the infinite; or of the moral law within; or of brotherly love" (109). I suspect that we could add today that Jesus stands for inclusion, for tolerance, for spirituality. Further, these cultural Christians have no firm grasp of "Christian views of sin, of grace and law, and of the Trinity" (112). For instance, they do not grasp how endemic sin is, how it corrupts not only all human beings but all of human nature. Theirs is a moralism that understands little of grace, because it understands little of the need for grace. And God himself easily becomes redefined:

"Gnostics need more than a Trinity, liberals less. All along the line the tendency in the movement is to identify Jesus with the immanent divine spirit that works in men" (114).

(3) Christ above Culture

Unlike the "Christ against culture" position, and unlike the "Christ of culture" position, this stance, "Christ above culture," Niebuhr understands to be the majority position in the history of the church. But it surfaces in three distinct forms, which constitute the three final entries in his fivefold typology.[20]

Niebuhr calls these three, together, "the church of the center" (117). At the heart of this stance is a creedal point:

> One of the theologically stated convictions with which the church of the center approaches the cultural problem is that Jesus Christ is the Son of God, the Father Almighty who created heaven and earth. With that formulation it introduces into the discussion about Christ and culture the conception of nature on which all culture is founded, and which is good and rightly ordered by the One to whom Jesus Christ is obedient and with whom he is inseparably united. Where this conviction rules, Christ and the world cannot be simply opposed to each other. Neither can the "world" as culture be simply regarded as the realm of godlessness; since it is at least founded on the "world" as nature, and cannot exist save as it is upheld by the Creator and Governor of nature. (117-18)

Despite this starting point, the church of the center also holds to strong convictions "about the universality and radical nature of sin," and about "the primacy of grace and the necessity of works of obedience" (118-19), even though there are highly divergent understandings of how these things work out. Granted these commonalities, however, there are three groups: the synthesists, the dualists, and the conversionists. At this juncture Niebuhr focuses exclusively on the synthesists.

20. Niebuhr's breakdown is a bit confusing. It may help some to think of the last three of his five types as: (3) Christ above culture: synthesist type; (4) Christ above culture: dualist type; (5) Christ above culture: conversionist/transformationist type.

Synthesists seek a "both-and" solution. They maintain the gap between Christ and culture that the cultural Christian never takes seriously and that the radical does not even try to breech — yet they insist that Christ is as sovereign over the culture as over the church. "We cannot say, 'Either Christ or culture,' because we are dealing with God in both cases. We must not say, 'Both Christ and culture,' as though there were no great distinction between them; but we must say, 'Both Christ and culture,' in full awareness of the dual nature of our law, our end, our situation" (122). That is what is presupposed in Jesus' utterance, "Render to Caesar the things that are Caesar's and to God the things that are God's" (Matthew 22:21, as cited on 123). That is also why we are to be subject to the governing authorities, for there is no authority apart from what God himself has instituted (Romans 13).

Synthetic answers were attempted by Justin Martyr. The first great representative of this type, however, is Tertullian's contemporary, Clement of Alexandria. For instance, in discussing the rich, he can, on the one hand, appeal to great Stoic virtues of thankful generosity, sounding at times like the quintessential cultural Christian. But he goes farther, and gently "issues a clear Christian call to respond to the love of the self-impoverished Lord" (124). Yes, a Christian must be a good person, in accordance with the standards of "a good culture," but Christ invites people to attain more, and gives them grace to achieve it: love of God for his own sake. "This sort of life is not of this world, and yet the hope of its realization and previsions of its reality fill present experience." Thus Clement's Christ "is not against culture, but uses its best products as instruments in his work of bestowing on men what they cannot achieve by their own efforts" (127).

But perhaps the most important synthesist is Thomas Aquinas, who "represents a Christianity that has achieved or accepted full social responsibility for all the great institutions" (128). Thomas understood that Christ is far above culture, and never tried "to disguise the gulf that lies between them" (129). Yet he manages to combine without confusing "philosophy and theology, state and church, civic and Christian virtues, natural and divine laws, Christ and culture" (130). Niebuhr seeks to demonstrate this in the way in which Thomas "sought to synthesize the ethics of culture with the ethics of the gospel" (130) and in his theory of law (135). No less importantly,

"Thomas' synthesis was not only an intellectual achievement but the philosophical and theological representation of a social unification of Christ and culture" (137). Even though that unification was promptly broken by the stresses of the fourteenth century, and further torn apart by the Reformation and the Renaissance, it marked a comprehensiveness of synthesis one is hard pressed to find again in later times. None of this should be despised: "Man's search for unity is unconquerable, and the Christian has a special reason for seeking integrity because of his fundamental faith in the God who is One" (141). Others have of course insisted on the importance of social and civil institutions, but what "distinguishes the synthesist of Thomas' sort is his concern to discover the bases of right in the given, created nature of man and his world" (142).

But Niebuhr is not blind to the problems of the synthesist version of Christ above culture. Christians of the other groups "will point out that the enterprise in and of itself must lead into an error," for the effort to bring Christ and culture, grace and works, God's work and human work, the temporal and the eternal, all into one neat system, is bound to lead "to the absolutizing of what is relative, the reduction of the infinite to a finite form, and the materialization of the dynamic." Moreover, all such syntheses are themselves culturally conditioned. For instance, "[t]he hierarchical view of natural order in Thomas Aquinas is historical and medieval" (145). Moreover, Thomas, as has often been observed, "lacked historical understanding" (196). Further, the passion to synthesize "leads to the institutionalization of Christ and his gospel" (146). Indeed, however much they profess the contrary, the synthesists simply "do not in fact face up to the radical evil present in all human work" (148). And that brings us to the next section.

(4) Christ and Culture in Paradox

This is the second of the groups that belong to the "Christ above culture" pattern. The first were synthesists; these are dualists.

For the dualists, the fundamental issue in life is not the line that must be drawn between Christians and the pagan or secular world, but between God and all humankind — or, "since the dualist is an existential thinker — between God and us; the issue lies between the righteousness of God and the righteousness of self." If we are to think about Christ and culture, we must begin with reminding ourselves of what Christ came to do: he came to effect "the great act of reconciliation and forgiveness" that has been undertaken by this Christ (150). Sin is in us; grace is in God. In one sense, this group is much like the first, those who hold to the "Christ against culture" position. But in that position, there is a tendency to put the strongest emphasis on the distinction between "them" and "us"; in this dualist position, by contrast, we are all lost, we are all sinners. "Human culture is corrupt; and it includes all human work, not simply the achievements of men outside the church but also those in it, not only philosophy so far as it is human achievement but theology also, not only Jewish defence of Jewish law but also Christian defence of Christian precept" (153). To understand dualists, Niebuhr asserts, we must see that they are not passing judgment on other human beings, but on all, including themselves. If they speak of the corruption of reason, they include their own.

> The other thing that must be kept in mind is that for these believers the attitude of man before God is not an attitude man takes in addition to other positions, after he has confronted nature, or his fellow men, or the concepts of reason. It is the fundamental and ever-present situation; though man is forever trying to ignore the fact that he is up against God, or that what he is up against when he is "up against it" is God. (153)

"Hence the dualist joins the radical Christian in pronouncing the whole world of human culture to be godless and sick unto death. But there is this difference between them: the dualist knows that he belongs to that culture and cannot get out of it, that God indeed sustains him in it and by it; for if God in His grace did not sustain the world in its sin it would not exist for a moment." And thus the dualist "cannot speak otherwise than in what sound like paradoxes" (156). Those paradoxes spill over into law and grace, into divine wrath and divine mercy, and the dualist cannot evaluate culture without thinking of these ongoing paradoxical realities.

Niebuhr argues that there are few clear-cut, consistent dualists (as he has described them), but he finds the dualist *motif* in Paul, a motif which is then taken in a rather different direction by Marcion, and preserved in a more direct line of succession in Augustine, and powerfully in Luther. Yet this is still a subset of the "Christ above culture" paradigm:

> Christ deals with the fundamental problems of the moral life; he cleanses the springs of action; he creates and recreates the ultimate community in which all action takes place. But by the same token he does not directly govern the external actions or construct the immediate community in which man carries on his work. On the contrary, he sets men free from the inner necessity of finding special vocations and founding special communities in which to attempt to acquire self-respect, and human and divine approval. He releases them from monasteries and the conventicles of the pious for service of their actual neighbors in the world through all the ordinary vocations of men.
>
> More than any great Christian leader before him, Luther affirmed the life in culture as the sphere in which Christ could and ought to be followed; and more than any other had discerned that the rules to be followed in the cultural life were independent of Christian or church law. Though philosophy offered no road to faith, yet the faithful man could take the philosophic road to such goals as were attainable by that way. . . . The education of youth in languages, arts, and history as well as in piety offered great opportunities to the free Christian man; but cultural education was also a duty to be undertaken. "Music," said Luther, "is a noble gift of God, next to theology. I would not change my little knowledge of music for a great deal." Commerce was also open to the Christian, for "buying and selling are necessary. . . ." Political activities, and even the career of the soldier, were even more necessary to the common life, and were therefore spheres in which the neighbor could be served and God could be obeyed. (174-75)

The tensions in all this, Niebuhr asserts, are the tensions of a dialectic thinker trying to face reality. "Living between time and eternity, between wrath and mercy, between culture and Christ, the true

24

Lutheran finds life both tragic and joyful. There is no solution of the dilemma this side of death" (178).

Niebuhr provides two or three examples of post-Luther dualists, including Kierkegaard, and then he mentions the two most common indictments with which the other groups charge them: dualism tends to lead Christians toward (a) antinomianism, and (b) cultural conservatism. The reason for the latter, it is alleged, is that dualists focus on "only one set of the great cultural institutions and sets of habits of their times — the religious" (188). The result is that they tend to leave other matters — matters of political justice, say, or an institution like slavery — unchanged.

And that brings us to Niebuhr's final category.

(5) Christ the Transformer of Culture

This is the third subcategory under the "Christ above culture" pattern. The other two were the synthesist and the dualist; this one is the conversionist. And it is vital to understand that Niebuhr is not thinking so much of individual conversion (though doubtless that is to some extent included) as of the conversion *of the culture itself.*

> The conversionists' understanding of the relations of Christ and culture is most closely akin to dualism, but it also has affinities with the other great Christian attitudes. That it represents a distinct *motif,* however, becomes apparent when one moves from the Gospel of Matthew and the Letter of James through Paul's epistles to the Fourth Gospel, or proceeds from Tertullian, the gnostics, and Clement to Augustine, or from Tolstoy, Ritschl, and Kierkegaard to F. D. Maurice. The men who offer what we are calling the conversionist answer to the problem of Christ and culture evidently belong to the great central tradition of the church. Though they hold fast to the radical distinction between God's work in Christ and man's work in culture, they do not take the road of exclusive Christianity into isolation from civilization, or reject its institutions with Tolstoyan bitterness. Though they accept their station in society with its duties in obedience to their Lord, they do

not seek to modify Jesus Christ's sharp judgment of the world and all its ways. In their Christology they are like synthesists and dualists; they refer to the Redeemer more than to the giver of a new law, and to the God whom men encounter more than to the representative of the best spiritual resources in humanity. . . .

What distinguishes conversionists from dualists is their more positive and hopeful attitude toward culture. (190-91)

This more positive stance toward culture, Niebuhr writes, is grounded in three theological convictions: (a) While the dualist tends to think of God's act of creation as merely the *mise-en-scène* of God's mighty act of redemption in the cross and resurrection of Christ, conversionists rest more weight on the creation. Although creation is not permitted to overpower redemption, or be overpowered by it, creation is not only the setting for redemption, but the sphere in which God's sovereign, ordering, work operates. (b) While dualists are sometimes in danger of treating matter, or even human selfhood, as intrinsically evil, with the result that they tend "to think of the institutions of culture as having largely a negative function in a temporal and corrupt world" (193), the conversionist insists the fall is "moral and personal, not physical and metaphysical, though it does have physical consequences" (194). (c) The conversionist adopts "a view of history that holds that to God all things are possible in a history that is fundamentally not a course of merely human events but always a dramatic interaction between God and men" (194). Indeed, the conversionist has a somewhat stronger "realized" component to his or her eschatology than do most other Christians: "For the conversionist, history is the story of God's mighty deeds and of man's responses to them. He lives somewhat less 'between the times' and somewhat more in the divine 'Now' than do his brother Christians. The eschatological future has become for him an eschatological present" (195).

Niebuhr finds this motif especially strong in the Fourth Gospel. Without the Logos, nothing has been created; the world that he made is his home. "John could not say more forcefully that whatever is is good." For this evangelist, "natural birth, eating, drinking, wind, water, and bread and wine are . . . not only symbols to be employed in dealing with the realities of the life of the spirit but are pregnant with spiritual meaning" (197). The "world" is simultaneously "the totality of creation and especially of humanity as the object of God's love," it is "also used to designate mankind in so far as it rejects Christ, lives in darkness, does evil works, is ignorant of the Father, rejoices over the death of the Son" (198). But John does not provide us with any abstract doctrine of sin; rather, he illustrates it, while refusing to define it (199). Within this framework, the gift of God provided through Christ is "eternal life," but the eschatology of the Fourth Gospel is so realized that this life is substantially enjoyed now, with all that means for all of human existence and culture.

Niebuhr concedes, "We are prevented from interpreting the Fourth Gospel as a wholly conversionist document, not only by its silence on many subjects but also by the fact that its universalistic note is accompanied by a particularist tendency" (204). The same sort of tension is found, Niebuhr avers, in the second-century Letter to Diognetus. But it is in Augustine and other leaders of the fourth century that "[t]he expectation of universal regeneration through Christ emerges" rather more clearly — though here, too, there is no unqualified universalism (i.e., a completely conversionist understanding) because of these theologians' need to contend on two fronts. They had to stand "against the anticulturalism of exclusive Christianity, and against the accommodationism of culture-Christians" (206). For Augustine, Niebuhr insists,

> Christ is the transformer of culture . . . in the sense that he redirects, reinvigorates, and regenerates that life of man, expressed in all human works, which in present actuality is the perverted and corrupted exercise of a fundamentally good nature; which, moreover, in its depravity lies under the curse of transiency and death, not because an external punishment has been visited upon it, but because it is intrinsically self-contradictory. (209)

The moral virtues human beings develop in perverse cultures are not so much displaced by new virtues at conversion, as converted by love. Converted people, the citizens of the holy City of God, who "live according to God in the pilgrimage of this life, both fear and desire, and grieve and rejoice. And because their love is rightly placed, all these affections of theirs are right" (*City of God* xiv.9, cited on 214). Yet Augustine does not carry this conversionist program to its logical conclusion; he does not "actually look forward with hope to the realization of the great eschatological possibility, demonstrated and promised in the incarnate Christ — the redemption of the created and corrupted human world and the transformation of mankind in all its cultural activity" (215). Instead, he leaps to "the eschatological vision of a spiritual society, consisting of some elect human individuals together with angels, living in eternal parallelism with the company of the damned" (216). Niebuhr finds this step very difficult to understand, and inconsistent with what he takes to be Augustine's dominant conversionist stance.

Calvin, Niebuhr writes, is similar, making the same move as Augustine. Wesley is in the same tradition, but strengthens his conversionist heritage by becoming the exponent of perfectionism. But the culmination of this line of development is in F. D. Maurice, who is, according to Niebuhr, "above all a Johannine thinker" (220). Maurice sees every person to be in Christ, and the culmination of human destiny is such cultural conversion that ultimately the prayer of Jesus in John 17 is fulfilled: we all become one, even as the Father and the Son are one.

> What made Maurice the most consistent of conversionists, however, was the fact that he held fast to the principle that Christ was king, and that men were therefore required to take account of him only and not of their sin; for to concentrate on sin as though it were actually the ruling principle of existence was to be enmeshed in still further self-contradiction. (224)

Indeed, Maurice took issue with German and English Evangelicals on precisely this ground (224). Niebuhr quotes Maurice, "I am obliged to believe in an abyss of love which is deeper than the abyss of death: I dare not lose faith in that love. I sink into death, eternal death if I do. I must feel that this love is compassing the universe. More about it I cannot know" (cited on 226).

Although Niebuhr never explicitly aligns himself with any of the five patterns he treats in his volume, what is striking about this fifth paradigm is that he offers no negative criticism whatsoever. Most scholars understand Niebuhr thus to be bestowing his approval.

*   *   *

Thus we come to Niebuhr's "Concluding Unscientific Postscript." We need not follow all of his thought here; it takes us a bit far afield from his own fivefold paradigm. But it is worth picking up two points. *First,* Niebuhr argues that his study could be extended indefinitely, if it explored a host of other Christian leaders — not only theological thinkers, but a vast array of "political, scientific, literary and military examples of loyalty to Christ in conflict and adjustment to cultural duties." He is thinking of "Constantine, Charlemagne, Thomas More, Oliver Cromwell and Gladstone, Pascal, Kepler, Newton, Dante, Milton, Blake and Dostoievsky [*sic*], Gustavus Adolphus, Robert E. Lee and 'Chinese' Gordon — these and many more." One marvels at a few names that have been omitted, such as Abraham Kuyper, perhaps, and Abraham Lincoln, Wilberforce, and Shaftesbury. Nevertheless, Niebuhr's point is that it is impossible to say, "This is the Christian answer" (231).

Second, while there is no single theoretical answer, Niebuhr holds that there must be movement "from insight to decision" (233), as each believer reaches his or her own "final" conclusion. These decisions are relative in at least four ways. "They depend on the partial, incomplete, fragmentary knowledge of the individual; they are relative to the measure of his faith and his unbelief; they are related to the historical position he occupies and to the duties of his station in society; they are concerned with the relative values of things" (234). Yet even this relativity must be worked out in the context of "faith in the absolute faithfulness of God-in-Christ" (239).

It is hard to overestimate the influence of Niebuhr's fivefold template, especially in the English-speaking world.[21] Our next steps

21. Many scores of books and essays could be adduced. Even today, when a number of voices are insisting that Niebuhr needs to be revised (see chap. 3, below), social studies continue to appeal to the Niebuhr taxonomy. For instance, when David W. Jones (*Reforming the Morality of Usury: A Study of the Differences That Separated the Protestant Reformers* [Lanham: University Press of America, 2004]) argues that the dif-

must be to evaluate it, both on its own terms and in the light of biblical theology (chap. 2). At that point we shall bring to bear more recent discussion of culture and related concepts (chap. 3).

---

ferent approaches to usury adopted by the various Protestant Reformers are related to the respective *cultural* location of the Reformers, it is Niebuhr's typology of culture that shapes his discussion.

TWO

Niebuhr Revised:
The Impact of Biblical Theology

—ง/ง/ง—

In this chapter I set myself two primary tasks: first, offer a preliminary critique of Niebuhr in general terms, largely utilizing his own categories; second, evaluate briefly how his typology might change if it were to take into account a robust biblical theology. The next chapter will probe a little more deeply some of the problems with Niebuhr's definition of "culture" already mentioned in chapter 1, and wrestle with the epistemological shifts in many forms of Western culture that play their part in looking for a more adequate typology.

A Preliminary Critique of Niebuhr

The Strengths and Weaknesses of Niebuhr's Comprehensiveness

One of the reasons Niebuhr has been so influential is that his analysis embraces Catholics and Protestants, East and West, examples from the Fathers, the Middle Ages, the Reformation, and the modern period, conservatives and liberals, mainstream believers (whatever they are in any period), and sectarians. From our perspective at the beginning of the twenty-first century, the only significant component that is missing is the voice of the contemporary church in the Two-Thirds world. In all fairness, however, anyone who reads him sympathetically can pretty well guess where Niebuhr would place most of these voices, without substantially revising his fivefold paradigm. One cannot fairly blame Niebuhr for writing fifty years ago. So we reflect, with gratitude, on his comprehensiveness.

At the same time, however, it is hard to avoid the conclusion that Niebuhr's comprehensiveness is also a deadly weakness. Implicitly he deploys *some* criteria to eliminate from consideration movements that he judges beyond the pale — whether Arians (and their modern counterparts), Mormons, or the more wild-eyed sects (one thinks, for instance, of the followers of Thomas Münzer). Yet he does not eliminate any branch of "Christian" Gnosticism, nor any wing of "Christian" liberalism. Why not? What these two have in common is their numerical strength during their respective periods of dominance. Is that a sufficient reason to account them Christian? Moreover, Niebuhr has clearly bought into historical reconstructions of these two periods that were rather common in academic circles when he wrote, but which are in fact often (and rightly) called into question.

Owing not least to the influence of Walter Bauer,[1] many scholars have come to accept the view that there was no distinction between what we now call orthodoxy and what we now call heterodoxy (or heresy) until well into the second century. In other words, both "orthodoxy" and "heterodoxy" were originally valid options within nascent Christianity. Accept that view, and Gnosticism has as much claim to validity as what came to be called orthodoxy. Writing at a time when the long shadow cast by Bauer swept over most academic theological reflection in the Western world, Niebuhr simply assumes this stance. But nowadays Bauer's position, though still popular in some circles,[2] has become more and more difficult to defend. Full-blown Gnosticism is a second-century development. It is parasitic on first-century theology, rather than coeval with it. Many have responded to Bauer's

---

1. *Rechtgläubigkeit und Ketzerei im ältesten Christentum* (Tübingen: Mohr Siebeck, 1934). The book was published in English three and a half decades later: *Orthodoxy and Heresy in Earliest Christianity* (Philadelphia: Fortress, 1971).

2. For instance, it shows up in Bart Ehrman's *Lost Christianities: The Battles for Scriptures and Faiths We Never Knew* (Oxford: Oxford University Press, 2003), where the claims are extravagant and the interaction with literature critical of this thesis is virtually ignored.

book with detailed and penetrating criticism.[3] For instance, noting that Bauer's title claims to address what takes place in "earliest Christianity," even though he examines only the second century, I. Howard Marshall opts for the cheeky title, "Orthodoxy and Heresy in Earlier Christianity."[4]

The point to recall is that the New Testament writers themselves distinguish between orthodoxy and heresy, both in early writings (e.g., Galatians 1:8-9; 2 Corinthians 11:3-4) and later writings (e.g., 1 John). And when Gnosticism did develop and grow strong, its theological emphases, though they were in line with a lot of contemporary thought in the broader culture, were far removed from central biblical "givens." In short, Gnosticism has neither the credentials nor the profile to warrant inclusion in a book of this sort (unless, of course, one is also willing to include Arians, Nestorians, Mormons, and so forth).

Similarly for liberal theology, which is one form of what Niebuhr calls "culture Christianity": transparently, Niebuhr is not talking about what C. S. Lewis would call "mere Christians," some of whom happen to hold some more-or-less liberal positions on this detail or that economic policy. "Sociologically," Niebuhr says of them, "they may be interpreted as nonrevolutionaries who find no need for positing 'cracks in time' — fall and incarnation and judgment and resurrection."[5] Indeed, they reject "the whole conception of a once-and-for-all act of redemption."[6] This is pretty fundamental stuff. If that is what liberal Christianity is, then Machen, though he wrote three-

---

3. To cite only the most recent of the competent critics, see Paul Trebilco, "Christian Communities in Western Asia Minor into the Early Second Century: Ignatius and Others as Witnesses Against Bauer," *Journal of the Evangelical Theological Society* 49 (2006): 17-44.

4. *Themelios* 2/1 (1976): 5-14. See further H. E. W. Turner, *The Pattern of New Testament Truth: A Study in the Relations between Orthodoxy and Heresy in the Early Church* (London: A. R. Mowbray & Co., 1954); Daniel J. Harrington, "The Reception of Walter Bauer's *Orthodoxy and Heresy in Earliest Christianity* during the Last Decade," *Harvard Theological Review* 77 (1980): 289-99; Michel Desjardins, "Bauer and Beyond: On Recent Scholarly Discussions of Αἵρεσις in the Early Christian Era," *The Second Century* 8 (1991): 65-82.

5. H. Richard Niebuhr, *Christ and Culture* (New York: Torchbooks, 1951), 84.

6. Niebuhr, *Christ and Culture,* 90.

quarters of a century ago, was surely right: liberalism is not another denomination or any other kind of legitimate option within Christianity. Rather, it is another religion.[7] Moreover, although Niebuhr insists that since the eighteenth century Abélard's followers "have become more numerous, and what was heresy became the new orthodoxy,"[8] his judgment on this matter looks less compelling today. Certainly liberal theology (I continue to use his category) was on the ascendancy during the eighteenth, nineteenth, and twentieth centuries, at least in academic circles, but until the twentieth century it did not capture the majority of people in most denominations. And now, at the beginning of the twenty-first century, classic liberal theology looks more and more outmoded. It still embraces more than its share of scholars, of course, but its denominations are shrinking, its influence in the culture is declining, and its most extreme and vociferous proponents — the Jesus Seminar, for instance — simply look silly. Worldwide, people in the "liberal Christian" heritage make up only a tiny percentage of those who call themselves "Christians." Apparently, then, liberal Christianity and Gnostic Christianity have this in common: for a while, both seemed to sweep everything in front of them, such that if orthodoxy is measured by popularity rather than by some measure of commitment to conform to God's self-disclosure in Scripture and in his Son, they constituted the new orthodoxy. And both will be left on the ash pit of history.

To digress for a moment, this observation, though defensible, doubtless cries out for more nuance. As Henri Blocher has pointed out, there yet remain many flourishing liberal congregations.[9] More importantly, Blocher points out, when publishers, not least in Europe, seek authors to write manuals of religion or introductions to religious ethics, they almost always approach those in the liberal tradition. Certainly the faculties of theology and religion in universities find their loyalties in that same tradition. Worse, at least one wing of evangelicalism is constantly tempted in this direction. Nevertheless, several qualifications demand to be heard.

7. J. Gresham Machen, *Christianity and Liberalism* (Grand Rapids: Eerdmans, 1923).

8. Niebuhr, *Christ and Culture*, 91.

9. "Discerner au sein de la culture," *Théologie Évangélique* 4/2 (2005): 49.

(1) By "classic liberal theology" I do not refer to every form of unbelief that has some vague connection with Christianity. I refer to that form of unbelief that is entirely happy to set aside the great turning points of redemptive history (including the incarnation and the atoning death and resurrection of Jesus Christ) while remaining convinced that Christianity has something invaluable to offer to humankind, something worth articulating and defending, something that liberal theology understands that neither "fundamentalists" nor outsiders can grasp. Classic liberal theologians seek to reshape the elementary components of historic Christian confessionalism to fit into a "contemporary" framework, convinced that this is the only way to preserve all that is good in Christianity. By contrast, many scholars today adopt "liberal" stances, insofar as these stances set aside the turning points in the Bible's story line, but by and large these contemporary scholars are much more hesitant about insisting on the intrinsic value of the "Christianity" they defend. The classic devout liberal scholar is a gradually dying breed, replaced by a scholar who is no less liberal but much less devout. This is part and parcel of the increased polarization that dominates much Western culture. This new liberalism is often more strongly informed by pluralism, and so it is prepared to think of "Christ in culture" only in the sense that we may also happily discern "Allah in culture," "Buddha in culture," a generalized "spirituality in culture," and so forth.

(2) European perceptions, not least French European perceptions, are invariably going to be a bit different from North American perceptions. The reasons are many, and some of them will be teased out in chapter 5 of this book. At the moment, it is worth reflecting on the fact that in the United States there are now more M.Div. students in seminaries belonging to some branch or other of the evangelical tradition than in all other seminaries combined, and that the best of the confessional seminaries are as academically tough as anything put forward by traditional liberal seminaries and theological faculties.

(3) Others have similarly noted the connection between a somewhat fading classic liberal theology and Niebuhr's "Christ of culture" option. For instance, David Wells sharply criticizes open theism for

"flirting with the old, discredited Christ-of-culture position which brought Liberal Protestants to such a sorry end."[10]

Getting back to the issue at hand, in Niebuhr's analysis, Gnosticism and liberalism constitute the major proponents of the second of his five patterns, namely, "the Christ of culture." If sober reflection commends the conclusion that neither is a Christian movement in any sense worthy of the adjective "Christian,"[11] then not much is left of this second category. Whether it is salvageable in any sense remains to be seen.

In any case, it appears that by his attempt at comprehensiveness Niebuhr has saddled himself with at least one pattern that is not well based. Should we perhaps envisage a fourfold rather than a fivefold scheme?

Niebuhr's Handling of Scripture

One of the attractive features of Niebuhr's work is his effort to ground most of his five patterns in the Scriptures themselves, before he sweeps through history on his hunt for people and movements that exemplify, in whole or in part, each of these five. In this endeavor to ground his patterns in the Bible, he is less than successful with the second: the "Christ of culture" pattern pays scant attention to Scripture and then leaps to the two dominant movements, Gnosticism and liberalism, that are themselves least grounded in Scripture. By this I mean that these movements detach themselves from the great turning points in the Bible's story line.

---

10. Wells, *Above All Earthly Pow'rs: Christ in a Postmodern World* (Grand Rapids: Eerdmans, 2005), 248.

11. I hasten to add that this is *not* to suggest that no useful insights or helpful scholarship emerged from either movement. The gifts and blessings of common grace are everywhere. Liberal theology, for instance, has stimulated much penetrating thought on what "history" is (a question of no small importance to a religion that claims to be grounded in a *historical* revelation) and has left a substantial corpus of philology, to cite but two examples. It is simply to say that any movement whose structure of thought depends on sidestepping the great turning points of redemptive history, including fall, incarnation, atonement, resurrection, and final judgment, is not usefully thought of as Christian.

But there are other elements to his handling of Scripture that are less than satisfactory. Most notable, perhaps, is his reading of the Fourth Gospel in defense of his fifth pattern, "Christ the transformer of culture." When John tells us that all things were made by the Logos, and apart from him nothing was made that has been made (John 1:1-3), Niebuhr infers, "John could not say more forcefully that whatever is is good."[12] But surely it would be more accurate to infer, "John could not say more forcefully that whatever the Logos *originally* made was good." For these affirmations serve, in John's argument, as a setup to expose the depravity of the world. It is precisely because the world was made by the Logos that the world's disowning of the Logos is shown in its ugliest light: "He was in the world, and though the world was made through him, the world did not recognize him" (1:10). Thus we are back to the awfulness of the rebellion which Niebuhr finds more prevalent in the "Christ against culture" pattern and in the dualist pattern ("Christ and culture in paradox"). Indeed, when John asserts that "God so loved the world that he gave his one and only Son" (3:16), we are invited to admire God's love, not because the world is big or diverse or beautiful or created, but because the world is so bad.[13]

Niebuhr's assertion that for this evangelist "natural birth, eating, drinking, wind, water, and bread and wine are . . . not only symbols to be employed in dealing with the realities of the life of the spirit but are pregnant with spiritual meaning"[14] is simultaneously true and misleading. It is true, of course, but in exactly the same way that the other evangelists use symbols, including references to the birds of the air and the flowers of the field. One could even say that it is true for references to thieves: Jesus will return like a thief in the night, which presumably does not refer to the thief's motives or greed or wickedness, but to the unexpectedness of his arrival. So Niebuhr's claim is true, at least at some superficial level. Yet it is misleading: in Niebuhr, the metaphorical use of elements in nature is then quietly linked to realized eschatology, so utterly realized that what Niebuhr wants, in

12. Niebuhr, *Christ and Culture*, 197.
13. See discussion in D. A. Carson, *The Difficult Doctrine of the Love of God* (Wheaton: Crossway, 2000).
14. Niebuhr, *Christ and Culture*, 197.

37

the ideal, is such a transformationist approach to culture that every-thing gradually gets better by the grace of the gospel. True, John's Gospel is eschatologically more realized than some other New Testa-ment documents, but his ultimate hope is not in the progressive transformation of the world but in the final cataclysm: Jesus is going away to prepare a place so that his followers may join him (John 14), and when he returns the Son of Man will open the graves of all, precip-itating a resurrection to life and a resurrection to condemnation (John 5:28-29). Jesus will raise his own people from the dead on the last day (John 6:39-40).

Of course, Niebuhr is a sufficiently careful reader of texts that even after he has milked the Fourth Gospel for all that he can take out of it — more in fact than is there — he finally concedes (as we have seen), "We are prevented from interpreting the Fourth Gospel as a wholly conversionist document, not only by its silence on many sub-jects but also by the fact that its universalistic note is accompanied by a particularistic tendency."[15] Just so. But then one must ask whether the conversionist paradigm, at least in the ideal form in which Niebuhr wishes it would exist, is *ever* found in Scripture. The most that Niebuhr can claim is that there are universalistic strands or mo-tifs in the Bible. Out of these he has constructed his fifth pattern, even though he is forced to concede that the New Testament document most conducive to this line of thought cannot be taken to support it, at least in its pure form, because it is too "particularistic" — and, we should add, too much enmeshed in futurist eschatology and in a com-prehensive vision of the rebellion and idolatry of the "world." More-over, the greatest post–New Testament exemplars of this fifth pattern are, according to Niebuhr, Augustine and Calvin, until we arrive at F. D. Maurice. Augustine and Calvin are disappointing to Niebuhr be-cause they do not follow the conversionist pattern all the way; F. D. Maurice turns out to be the hero, because he allows the conversionist pattern to take him into universalism — not on the ground that any New Testament document supports this line, but on the ground of what Maurice asserts he is "obliged" to believe in.[16] Insofar as this

15. Niebuhr, *Christ and Culture*, 31.
16. See above, p. 28.

stance has any biblical warrant whatsoever, it is in line with a universalistic strand or motif that sometimes emerges, even though there is no New Testament document that adopts this stance, for even a book like John's Gospel will not allow this ostensible universalistic strand to control the entire presentation, since it also displays "particularistic" tendencies.[17]

Methodologically, then, it is hard to see how this fifth pattern escapes the criticism that Niebuhr himself levels against various forms of liberal theology. Liberal theologians, he asserts, often fasten on one strand of biblical teaching about Jesus, invariably the strand that they find most appealing, and then make that the whole. In his fifth pattern, Niebuhr has fallen into the same trap: he wants the conversionist paradigm, the only one for which he offers no criticism, to prevail, even though in its pure form he finds it neither in any New Testament document, nor in any great figure of church history until F. D. Maurice, who finally justifies it, not on the ground of the balance of Scripture or the balance of any Scriptural document, but on his absolutizing of one motif. But one wonders if this motif has been rightly understood — that is, in line with what the New Testament writers had in mind — when it is made to stand in sharp contradiction of what else they wrote. And thus we are forced to wonder, by the same token, if Niebuhr's fifth pattern, at least in the pure form that Niebuhr prefers, has any real warrant for itself at all, save in the liberal theology of F. D. Maurice.

As we shall see, there is more to be said for this fifth pattern than there is for the second, but there is very little to be said for it in the absolute form in which Niebuhr wants it to exist and triumph.

Niebuhr's Assignment of Historical Figures

One of the attractive features of Niebuhr's work is his crisp discussion of many historical figures. The way these figures align with each of Niebuhr's five patterns, however, is sometimes problematic. Niebuhr

17. For a convenient history of universalism in the heritage of Christendom, see Richard Bauckham, "Universalism: A Historical Survey," *Themelios* 4/2 (1979): 48-54.

frankly tells us, more than once, that his five patterns are idealizations, and that in reality people and movements are likely to pick and choose — to merge disparate elements from two or more of these paradigms. At some point, however, one begins to wonder if the discrete patterns are the best way of thinking about the relations between Christ and culture, if in most instances the historical figures prefer mixtures.

It is not just that Augustine and Calvin do not follow the conversionist ideal to its conclusion, but that Tertullian is not quite consistent in his adoption of the "Christ against culture" paradigm, while Justin Martyr and Clement of Alexandria are not consistent in their pursuit of the synthesist pattern, and so forth. Indeed, some figures show up in two or three patterns: F. D. Maurice appears both as a witness to the "Christ of culture" paradigm and as the best embodiment of the conversionist pattern ("Christ as transformer of culture"). One begins to wonder whether, at least in some cases, the discrete patterns rarely subsist in pure forms, and perhaps ought not do so. Is it possible that a merging of patterns sometimes brings greater fidelity to the biblical revelation than adopting any of the patterns in its purest form?

We can get at this same point another way, as follows.

Niebuhr and Canon

Niebuhr's appeal to Scripture for most of his five patterns, his "typical Christian answers," is a commendable attempt to ground his configuration in the foundation documents of the Christian faith. We have already seen that the attempt fails in certain respects: Niebuhr's second pattern is certainly found in historical movements, but these movements are of doubtful Christian authenticity and have no warrant in the Bible. The fifth pattern, "Christ the transformer of culture," is found in restricted forms in the New Testament, but certainly not in the strong form Niebuhr would like to see adopted.

But the issue transcends the individual cases. At stake are two quite different views as to how the canon should function.

(1) Niebuhr's view, a view that is still quite common in some academic circles, is that the Bible in general, and the New Testament in

particular, provides us with a number of discrete paradigms. We are being faithful to Scripture so long as we align our choices with any one of these paradigms, or perhaps even with some combination of them. The canon's "rule" is thus not so much in the totality of the canon's voice, as in providing the boundaries of the allowable paradigms.[18] Frequently these paradigms are identified with scholarly conceptions of discrete early Christian movements: the Johannine community, the Pauline churches, the Matthean community, and so forth. In the strongest form of the argument, these disparate communities are hermetically sealed off from one another, except for fragmentary crossovers that are sometimes detectable in literary dependence of one New Testament document on another (e.g., Does James know Matthew? Has John borrowed from Mark? And therefore does John's community know anything about Mark's community?). Thus Niebuhr finds Galatians and 1 John to be fine exemplars of the "Christ against culture" pattern, and the Fourth Gospel to be a fine exemplar (though perhaps not fine enough!) of the "Christ transforming culture" pattern (i.e., the conversionist model).

(2) Alternatively, Christians recognize the diversity of the Bible in general, and of the New Testament in particular, but insist that the Bible *as a whole* constitutes the canon — and this canon's "rule" lies in the totality of the canon's instruction, not in providing a boundary to possible options. Those who defend this position — and it is the historic position of Christian theology — try to take pains to avoid "flattening" the Scriptures. They fully recognize the differences of literary genres in the Bible (e.g., letter, discourse, gospel, fable, parable, proverb, apocalyptic, lament, song, genealogy, history, prophetic oracle), and therefore also the different ways in which these literary forms make their rhetorical appeal.[19] They understand that there are changes across the covenants: after all, most Christians today are not seventh-day Sabbatarians, concerned to eat only kosher food, and ea-

18. Hence, for example, James D. G. Dunn (*Unity and Diversity in the New Testament: An Inquiry into the Character of Earliest Christianity* [Philadelphia: Westminster, 1977], 376) asserts that the New Testament "canonizes the diversity of Christianity."

19. Cf. Kevin J. Vanhoozer, "The Semantics of Biblical Literature: Truth and Scripture's Diverse Literary Forms," in *Hermeneutics, Authority and Canon,* ed. D. A. Carson and John D. Woodbridge (Grand Rapids: Zondervan, 1986), 42-104.

ger to see a temple reconstructed on Mount Zion so they can offer the sacrifice of bull and goat on Yom Kippur. Exactly *how* the different parts of Scripture cohere has always been a matter of considerable dispute: answers vary along numerous axes, from the fourfold method of medieval interpretation, to dispensationalism in its various forms, to covenant theology, to Lutheranism, and so forth. Yet historic confessional Christianity has insisted that once such matters have been resolved, at least to the satisfaction of a particular Christian group, so that we see how the Bible hangs together, we may talk about what the Bible "says," not just about what one part of the biblical tradition says. Moreover, while such Christians will recognize that New Testament writers have differing agendas and emphases (Mark is not exactly like Luke), that different New Testament writers deploy individual vocabularies and styles (each writer has his own "idiolect," the linguists say), and different New Testament books lay theological emphasis and ethical priority in quite different places (Romans does not read like Hebrews), yet nevertheless God himself stands behind these books. It is now widely recognized that in the first century, Christians did not speak of "the Gospel *of* Matthew," "the Gospel *of* Mark," and so on; rather, they spoke of the one gospel, the gospel of Jesus Christ, *according to* Matthew, Mark, Luke, and John.[20] Similarly across the New Testament corpus: read sympathetically, the rich diversities are mutually complementary, and, without for a moment weakening the attention that must be paid to historical peculiarities, the *canonical* function of the text demands that we listen to all of these voices and integrate them appropriately.

These two views of the canon are quite distinct — and they have an immediate bearing on our topic. Recall that Niebuhr appeals to Galatians as a stellar example of the "Christ against culture" pattern. But the same apostle Paul who wrote Galatians also wrote Romans 13, which is certainly a great deal less confrontational. Over against Romans 13, the book of Revelation holds up a massive confrontation

20. See, for instance, Martin Hengel, *The Four Gospels and the One Gospel of Jesus Christ: An Investigation of the Collection and Origin of the Canonical Gospels* (Harrisburg: Trinity Press International, 2000); Ronald A. Piper, "The One, the Four and the Many," in *The Written Gospel*, ed. Markus Bockmuehl and Donald A. Hagner (Cambridge: Cambridge University Press, 2005), 254-73.

between Christ and Satan, between the new Jerusalem and Babylon, between the bride of Christ and the great whore — in short, between Christ and culture. Are we to assume that the Paul who wrote Romans 13 would disavow Revelation if he found himself in John the seer's position? Would he disallow his own epistle to the Galatians? Assuming that the same John wrote both 1 John and the Fourth Gospel, was he thinking of two disparate paradigms for the relation between Christ and culture when he wrote the two books, one espousing "Christ against culture" and the other providing some support for "Christ the transformer of culture"?

This is not the place to offer a detailed defense of the second view of the function of the canon. Nevertheless, I hold that it is the only one that can be sustained, and certainly it is the one with the longest and best credentials. Assuming that it is right, then surely another modification of the Niebuhr fivefold paradigm is called for. We should not think of each pattern in Niebuhr's fivefold scheme as warranted by individual documents in the New Testament, such that we have the option to pick and choose which pattern we prefer, assured that all are equally encompassed by the canon that warrants them individually. Rather, we should be attempting a holistic grasp of the relations between Christ and culture, fully aware, as we make our attempt, that peculiar circumstances may call us to emphasize some elements in one situation, and other elements in another situation.

Shall we tell Christians in southern Sudan to adopt a different paradigm of Christ-and-culture relations than Christians in Washington, D.C., and vice versa? Shall we tell them that the Bible sets forth several discrete patterns, and they can choose the pattern that seems best to them? Or do we seek to work out a more comprehensive vision, a canon-stipulated vision, of what such relations should be (recognizing, of course, how imperfect all syntheses are), while insisting that the outworking of that comprehensive vision is sufficiently rich and flexible to warrant appropriate diversity in outworking in these two very different cultural contexts?[21]

21. Cf. Lesslie Newbigin, *The Gospel in a Pluralist Society* (Grand Rapids: Eerdmans, 1989), 38: "[T]he Christian story provides us with . . . a set of lenses, not something for us to look at, but for us to look through."

The Non-negotiables of Biblical Theology

I have several times referred to the necessity of incorporating into our thinking about the relations between Christ and culture some account of the great turning points of redemptive history. This is not only a negative criterion, but a positive one — that is, it is not just that the dismissal of such realities as creation, fall, incarnation, Jesus' death and resurrection, the coming of the Spirit, and the final judgment and consummation, places one outside the Christian camp, but that it is important to think through the *positive* bearing of these realities on the topic. To put the matter more personally: on the one hand, however loyal one judges oneself to be to Jesus, it is difficult to see how such loyalty is a mark of *Christian* thought if the Jesus so invoked is so domesticated and selectively constructed that he bears little relation to the Bible. But on the other hand, there is a need to spell out the bearing of these epochal events on how we *should* think about the relations between Christ and culture.

Before developing the argument, two preliminary observations are called for.

(1) "Biblical theology" has become a highly disputed expression.[22] Some use it to refer to the theology of individual biblical books or corpora (e.g., the theology of Matthew, the theology of Paul). Others use it to refer to the theology of the Bible when the Bible is studied diachronically, over against systematic theology, which tends to be organized topically, synchronically. As subsets of this latter category, there are two further refinements. When some hear the expression "biblical theology," they think of how various themes can be traced right through the Bible, or through large parts of it. These

---

22. For a summary and assessment of the expression and of the discipline to which it refers, see D. A. Carson, "New Testament Theology," in *Dictionary of the Later New Testament and Its Developments,* ed. Ralph P. Martin and Peter H. Davids (Downers Grove: InterVarsity, 1997), 797-814. For more extended discussion, see many entries in T. D. Alexander, Brian S. Rosner, D. A. Carson, and Graeme Goldsworthy, eds., *New Dictionary of Biblical Theology* (Leicester/Downers Grove: InterVarsity, 2000); and especially James Barr, *The Concept of Biblical Theology: An Old Testament Perspective* (Minneapolis: Fortress, 1999), along with the essay by Robert W. Yarbrough, "James Barr and the Future of Revelation in History in New Testament Theology," *Bulletin for Biblical Research* 14 (2004): 105-26.

themes constitute the ligaments that hold the canon together: rest, temple, sacrifice, priesthood, kingdom, covenant, and so forth. Others reflect on what I have called "the great turning points in redemptive history." Of course, those who are committed to studying the Bible phenomenologically and who deny that there is one God behind the whole thing doubt that biblical theology in the latter senses is possible. It always results, they say, in a flattening of the lush diversity that makes up the Bible. For our purposes in the present inquiry, we shall leave them in their doubt, and survey some of these great turning points.[23]

(2) Perhaps it does not need to be said, but the following paragraphs are the merest sketch. My only defense for covering such important and complicated material so quickly is that something is gained by talking about all these pieces at the same time and hinting, as I go along, at their bearing on any Christian discussion of culture. Indeed, as I shall make clear in the final section of this chapter, it is the commitment to think about all of them at the same time that preserves us from forging very different patterns of the relationships between Christ and culture, and commends one complex reality that can nevertheless be worked out in highly different contexts.

Creation and Fall

God made everything, and he made it good. He made human beings in his image and likeness. Our common parentage (cf. Acts 17:26-28) speaks against slavery, mutual degradation, and repulsive notions of

---

23. I should add that the number of turning points is necessarily disputed, as the term is somewhat ambiguous. The matter is resolved, not on some theoretical basis, but on the basis of scale: one can examine an object from far away and from much closer up, forcing the scale to change. Moreover, the turning points briefly surveyed in what follows have been chosen in part for their obvious bearing on discussion of the relations between Christ and culture. Perhaps I should add that there have been penetrating critiques of Niebuhr from the perspective of a more traditionally structured systematic theology, none more penetrating than that of John Frame in the second chapter of his *Christ and Culture: Lectures Given at the Pensacola Theological Institute, July 23-27, 2001,* accessed on 5 March 2007 at http://www.thirdmill.org/newfiles/joh_frame/Frame.Apologetics2004.ChristandCulture.pdf.

"half-human, half-ape." Creation is what grounds all human account-ability to God our Maker: we *ought* to delight in him, to serve him, to trust him, to obey him, not only because he is perfectly good, but be-cause he made us for himself and sustains us, and therefore we *owe* him. The glories of that original creation continue to testify to God's existence and power; they continue to evoke awe and wonder, even if their present ordering includes death and disaster.

That God made us embodied beings says something important about our intrinsic nature, and anticipates the culmination of every-thing at the other end of history: we are made to know and love and enjoy God in the context of embodied existence, and will one day know and love and enjoy God in the context of resurrected embodied existence. Moreover, as God's image bearers we have peculiar respon-sibilities toward the rest of the created order — responsibilities of governance and care, as we recognize our oneness with the created or-der and our distinguishing place within it.

We are not only a created race but a fallen race. The fall is not merely the breaking of some arbitrary rule. It is the rebellion of the creature against the Creator; it is the appalling commitment to try to usurp the Creator's place. The astonishingly arrogant and futile cry, "I will be God!" in reality issues not only in death, but in the destruction of every relationship. Death itself is multifaceted: we die to God, we die physically (as the ghastly repeated refrain of the genealogy of Gen-esis 5 makes plain: "and then he died"), we die the second death. Con-sumed by our own self-focus, we desire to dominate or manipulate others: here is the beginning of fences, of rape, of greed, of malice, of nurtured bitterness, of war.

Yet the heart of all this evil is idolatry itself. It is the de-godding of God. It is the creature swinging his puny fist in the face of his Maker and saying, in effect, "If you do not see things my way, I'll make my own gods! I'll *be* my own god!" Small wonder that the sin most fre-quently said to arouse God's wrath is not murder, say, or pillage, or any other "horizontal" barbarism, but idolatry — that which de-thrones God. That is also why, in every sin, it is God who is the most of-fended party, as David himself well understood: "Against you, only, have I sinned and done what is evil in your sight; so you are right in your verdict and justified when you judge" (Psalm 51:4). Jesus well understood that the first commandment is to love God with heart and soul and mind and strength (Mark 12:28-34; cf. Deuteronomy 6). It follows that the first sin is a failure to love God with heart and soul and mind and strength. It is the sin that is always committed when any other sin is committed. The second commandment is to love one's neighbor as oneself. It is only the second, because what makes sin most heinous in the first place is its offensiveness to God: he is always the most offended party. Moreover, the second commandment is grounded in the first. The words that Jesus quotes from Leviticus 19:18 make this clear: "Love your neighbor as yourself. *I am the* LORD." Experience confirms the witness of Scripture: we cannot long sin against God without sinning against God's image-bearers, and if in measure we do love God, we will love those who bear his image (an insight that 1 John repeatedly substantiates).

The consequences of the fall are universal and devastating because they are first and foremost revolt against the Almighty. We must be reconciled to God, for he is the One who now stands against us — not now only our Creator, but our Judge. The drama of the entire story line of the Bible turns on our persistent alienation from God. Scan the entire Old Testament: What is it that characteristically evokes God's wrath? It is, quite simply, idolatry — all that degrades God or diminishes God or de-gods God or replaces God. And since God is the sovereign Judge, human beings must finally be reconciled to him or be lost. The New Testament Scriptures place similar emphasis on the wrath of God, and insist that the only thing that spares us from destruction under this wrath is the death of God's own Son. " 'He himself bore our sins' in his body on the cross, so that we might die to sins and live for righteousness" (1 Peter 2:24). The alternatives are absolute: "Whoever believes in the Son has eternal life, but whoever rejects the Son will not see life, for God's wrath remains on them" (John 3:36). The wretched fact is that we were by nature deserving of wrath (Ephesians 2:3). This wrath is described as "blazing fire," when Jesus himself "will punish those who do not know God and do not obey the gospel of our Lord Jesus. They will be punished with everlasting destruction and shut out from the presence of the Lord" (2 Thessalonians 1:7-9). Because of the things that constitute us idolaters, "God's wrath comes on those who are disobedient" (Ephesians 5:6). Our only hope lies in

Christ: he "redeemed us from the curse of the law by becoming a curse for us" (Galatians 3:13). The glory of the good news is that the very God who stands over against us in wrath, and justly so, stands over against us in love, because he is that kind of God: "[B]ecause of his great love for us, God, who is rich in mercy, made us alive with Christ even when we were dead in transgressions — it is by grace you have been saved" (Ephesians 2:4-5).

As the Bible's story line unfolds, sin's wretched dimensions become clearer and clearer. Sin can be seen not only as idolatry and as the archetypal hubris, but also as the transgression of law that God lays down. It weaves its own web of corruption and its entailments, as God gives his creatures over to their own desires. Sin is social: although it is first and foremost defiance of God, there is no sin that does not touch the lives of others. Even secret sins of the heart and mind adversely affect others, since by subtly changing me, they change my relations with others. Secretly nurtured lust, for instance, soon affects a man's or a woman's relations with the spouse and with other human beings. That is one reason why God's judgment is poured out on people to the third and fourth generations of those who hate God (Exodus 20:5): sin is social. Judgment comes not only in the death of every generation, but in the sweeping condemnation of the flood (Genesis 7–8), in the repeated cycles of war, pestilence, and famine (e.g., Judges, the exile), and ultimately in hell itself, about which Jesus says so much. Sin is so warping that it corrodes every facet of our being, our wills and affections, our view of others and thus our relationships, our bodies and our minds. Sinners incur guilt, yet they need more than forgiveness and reconciliation to God (though never less), since the results of sin are so pervasive: they also need regeneration and transformation.

Yet the fall does not have the last word. Already in Genesis 3, there are signs of hope. God himself pursues the rebels; God himself promises them offspring that will one day crush the serpent's head; God himself clothes them to hide their nakedness. It comes as enormous relief to discover that this God is not only the jealous God who punishes "the children for the sin of the parents to the third and fourth generation" of those who hate him (for sin, as we have seen, has massive social ramifications), but he is also the God who shows "love to a thousand generations of those who love [him] and keep [his] commandments" (Exodus 20:6). Similarly, it comes as an enormous relief to recognize that, however odious and sweeping sin is, whether in personal idolatry or in its outworking in the barbarities of a Pol Pot or an Auschwitz, God intervenes to restrain evil, to display his "common grace" to and through all, so that glimpses of glory and goodness disclose themselves even in the midst of the wretchedness of rebellion. God still sends his sun and rain upon the just and the unjust; he still guides the surgeon's hand and gives strength to the person who picks up the garbage; the sunset still takes our breath away, while a baby's smile steals our hearts. Acts of kindness and self-sacrifice surface among every race and class of human beings, not because we are simple mixtures of good and evil, but because even in the midst of our deep rebellion God restrains us and displays his glory and goodness.

Perhaps I may be excused for introducing the testimony of one scholar who largely managed to escape the mesh of the classic theological liberalism in which he had been formed. P. T. Forsyth testifies:

> It also pleased God by the revelation of His holiness and grace, which the great theologians taught me to find in the Bible, to bring home to me my sin in a way that submerged all the school questions in weight, urgency, and poignancy. I was turned from a Christian to a believer, from a lover of love to an object of grace. And so, whereas I first thought that what the Churches needed was enlightened instruction and liberal theology, I came to be sure that what they needed was evangelization.[24]

Christians cannot long think about Christ and culture without reflecting on the fact that this is *God's* world, but that this side of the fall this world is simultaneously resplendent with glory and awash in shame, and that every expression of human culture simultaneously discloses that we were made in God's image and shows itself to be mis-shaped and corroded by human rebellion against God.

---

24. P. T. Forsyth, *Positive Preaching and the Modern Mind,* 3rd ed. (1949; Carlisle: Paternoster, 1998), 177. I am grateful to Graham Cole for drawing this passage to my attention.

Israel and the Law

It would be useful to devote space to the calling of Abraham and to the covenant that bears his name. Here lies exposed the sovereign gracious choice of God in calling out certain individuals, Abraham and Sarah, and through them a race and a nation, yet this particularity issues in the promise that through Abraham and his seed all the nations of the earth will be blessed. One might also usefully reflect on the strange role of Melchizedek (Genesis 14:18-20) — what he depicts of the idealized king-priest, and the place he holds in the trajectory through Psalm 110 and Hebrews 7.

Instead, we turn to the exodus, the constituting of the people of Israel as a nation, the giving of the law, the establishing of what would in time be referred to as "the old covenant," the entrance into the promised land. From the many facets of this nest of events on which we might focus, we select five:

(1) As in the call of Abraham, so here: God graciously chooses his own people (Deuteronomy 7; 10). In this instance, he rescues them, saves them from slavery, and constitutes them his own. But if Israel constitutes the locus of the people of God throughout most of the Old Testament, one cannot but recall as well God's mercy toward Nineveh (so Jonah), Isaiah's promise that one day even Israel's archetypical enemies, Assyria and Egypt, will become part of God's people (Isaiah 19:19-25; cf. Psalm 87), and Ruth's role in the line of the Davidic dynasty despite her own roots as a Moabitess.

(2) The law that God gives touches all of life, a way of saying, among other things, that God's people must remain God's people in every dimension of their existence. The law governs their morality, what they eat and drink, where they live, all their relationships, all their worship and ritual. It is surrounded by promises and threats of reprisals — and, in the event, becomes a way of showing that the people cannot long sustain themselves in obedience to this covenant's demands. What promises blessing and peace turns out, granted the waywardness of God's people, to multiply guilt, turning the fundamental idolatry into detailed transgression.

(3) Despite our penchant for thinking that the heart of the covenant is the moral law, much more space is devoted to the tabernacle,

the priesthood, the sacrificial system, and matters of individual and corporate ritual and praise. This should not surprise us: the crucial question is how guilty and soiled people become acceptable before God. God graciously provides an appropriate structure with mediators, sacrifices, and symbol-laden forms and patterns, both so as to ensure that the way into the Holy is never taken for granted and to make such access possible, while pointing forward to greater realities yet. Everything else flows from this; without this, all the other blessings are illusory. Indeed, the priestly structure is so foundational to the old covenant that if that structure were to change, the covenant itself would have to change (a point that the writer to the Hebrews well understands, Hebrews 7:11-28).

(4) Israel is constituted a *theocracy.* There is not a hint of a separation of "church" and "state" as we think of those categories — that is, of a separation between the "secular" rulers of the nation and the leaders of the "religious" community within the nation, which is more or less what we mean by separation of powers today.[25] Ancient Israel did distinguish between the role of king and the role of high priest, of course — a remarkable distinction, considering the fact that the ancient Near East favored priest-kings.[26] Yet all the Israelites together constituted the covenant people of God, and both king and high priest were charged with maintaining covenantal fidelity (and thus "religion") in a way quite different from what we find in the pages of the New Testament. There God stands behind Caesar, but Caesar has no particular responsibility to nurture the covenant people of God, and certainly not all the people in Caesar's sphere of rule belong to God's covenant people. In ancient Israel, God may have his agents through whom he rules his people — priest, king (from Saul on), and prophets to address both of them — but they act in his name and serve as his representatives in this tribal structure. Ideally, the entire Israelite culture was to reflect God's glory and reveal God's truth and God's character. A clash between God and culture under such a re-

25. An earlier draft of this chapter terminated the sentence just before the dash, which left it open to the obvious charge that my statement overlooked the obvious division of powers in ancient Israel between king and high priest. I am grateful to Henri Blocher for pointing out the lack of clarity, which then prompted additional lines.

26. As witness Melchizedek: Genesis 14:18-20; cf. Psalm 110.

gime could only mean that the people were distancing themselves from God in painful and odious ways. Such rebellion issued in cycles of judgment under the judges; ultimately, it issued in the exile. And still God's promises to restore his wayward people stood in line with the displays of grace that began at the fall.

(5) We must not forget that the story of the nation of Israel is itself embedded into the larger story of Abraham and his seed (a point made by Paul in Galatians 3), which is itself embedded into the still larger story of the creation and fall of the human race (a point made by Paul in Romans 1:18–3:32; 5:1-19).

We are constrained to reflect on the way these realities speak to how we should configure the relations between Christ and culture. Is this warrant for a theocracy? Why or why not?

Christ and the New Covenant

Here I must restrict myself to six observations:

(1) The incarnation of the eternal Word (John 1:1-18) grounds many exhortations in the New Testament. It is part of Jesus' supreme example of self-abnegation in service to others, preparatory to vindication (Philippians 2:5-11);[27] it is a necessary element of his self-identification with human beings, coming as he does to save *them,* and not fallen angels (Hebrews 2); it is the means by which he "tabernacles" with us (John 1:14) — he makes his dwelling with us, and becomes our tabernacle, our temple (2:19-22), our great meeting place between God and human beings. Here lies the ultimate "solution" to the strange language of texts like Isaiah 9: the promised one is simultaneously the long-awaited king in David's line and the one who is rightly called the Wonderful Counselor, the Mighty God, the Everlast-

---

27. This is rather different from saying that the incarnation becomes the foundational way we should think of doing mission ourselves, that is, in becoming "incarnated" in another culture. I understand what is being said, and what is being said is honorable and challenging. But such terminology is not without its problems: see the important discussion by Andreas J. Köstenberger, *The Missions of Jesus and the Disciples According to the Fourth Gospel: With Implications for the Fourth Gospel's Purpose and the Mission of the Contemporary Church* (Grand Rapids: Eerdmans, 1998).

ing Father, the Prince of Peace. Jesus is not presented merely as the one who brings his Father's message, the way Muhammad is presented in Islam as the final prophet who brings Allah's message; rather, in important ways, Jesus *is* the message, he *is* the Word, as well as bringing it.

(2) Jesus announces and inaugurates the kingdom of God. Although in one sense God is presented as the king of the universe, in another he is the king of Israel who mediates his sovereignty through his Davidic "son." Still, it is Yahweh himself who is the Great King, not just David and his heirs, and Jerusalem is the city of the Great King (Psalm 48). When Jesus inaugurates the long-awaited and long-predicted kingdom, "kingdom" carries diverse weight, depending on the context — or, as the specialists put it, "kingdom" becomes a tensive symbol that is decisively shaped by the surrounding contexts. Often "the kingdom of God" is best thought of as "the reign of God," for "kingdom" is far more commonly dynamic than static, rather more "kingdominion" or "reign" than "kingdom." In the New Testament, the kingdom comes with the baby who is born a king (Matthew 2). It also comes with the onset of Jesus' public ministry and the announcement of the dawning of the kingdom. It is displayed in the miracles and preaching of Jesus' disciples (Luke 10:1-24). In Jesus' parables, it can embrace good and evil, encompassing God's providential sovereignty, extending so far that it is the context in which both the wheat and the weeds grow (Mark 4); alternatively, it is highly restricted and becomes that subset of God's dynamic reign under which there is eternal life (John 3:3, 5). Jesus dies and rises again, and ascends to the right hand of the majesty on high, and in anticipation of this pronounces that all authority is his, in heaven and earth (Matthew 28:18): here, indeed, is his unqualified reign. As Paul puts it, all of God's sovereignty is mediated through Jesus (1 Corinthians 15:25-28). Nevertheless, his reign is at present contested; the day will come when it will never be contested again. The kingdom has already dawned; yet the kingdom is still to come, awaiting the return of the King.

This diversity of uses is among the reasons why we must constantly struggle with the tension inherent in them. The most important is the tension between the fact that the kingdom is already present ("realized" or "inaugurated" eschatology) and the promise that the kingdom will finally come at the end. In neither case is this kingdom a constitutional monarchy. Jesus raises to a superlative level anything that might be meant by "the divine right of kings." Indeed, in the consummation, every knee shall bow. Even now, to confess Jesus as "Lord" is to acknowledge the legitimacy of his sovereign claims, and to pledge to serve him. Further, the kingdom that Jesus has in view is no longer restricted to empirical Israel. Far from it: many will come from the east and the west and join Abraham and the other patriarchs in the kingdom, while the more obvious heirs are left outside (Matthew 8:10-12).

(3) It is not for nothing that the four canonical Gospels have been called passion and resurrection narratives with long introductions. That is the direction in which the plotline moves. To interpret them without primary reference to the cross and resurrection is simply irresponsible. Moreover, within the much larger framework of the canon, Jesus' death is tightly bound up with his "fulfillment" of the Old Testament sacrifices (especially those of Passover and Yom Kippur), and his resurrection vindicates him.

Jesus himself understands his death to provide a ransom for many (Mark 10:45; Matthew 20:28); his words of institution at the last supper demonstrate that he understands his death, the shedding of his blood and the breaking of his body, to be the ground of the remission of sins, as well as the inauguration of the new covenant. Small wonder that the apostle Paul insists his practice is to focus his preaching on the cross (1 Corinthians 2:1-5), which he understands as God's design to cancel sin and absorb the wrath, in the person of God's Son, that should have come to us (Romans 3:21-26). In similar vein, the apostle Peter sees in the cross both the model of self-sacrificing service to others, and the unique sacrifice in which Christ bore our sins in his own body on the cross (1 Peter 2:24). It takes an effort of will to hear the power of such claims today, because the phrases are so well known that they trip off our tongues and dance through our memories. But it was not so when the cross was such a symbol of curse and odium that men and women had to either write Jesus off as a God-damned malefactor or begin to glimpse what Christ Jesus bore in their behalf.

All of this, it must be said, is simply non-negotiable for any form of Christianity whatsoever that seeks its shape in the cruciform gospel. Insofar as any voice contests these fundamentals, as did both Jews and Greeks in the first century (1 Corinthians 1:18-25), it may receive high marks from the broader culture, not least when it despises the "folly" of the cross. But the foolishness of God is wiser than all the wisdom of human beings. Where there are competing authority claims on this sort of issue, Christians simply cannot afford to take their cues from the culture.

(4) That same death established the new covenant in Jesus' blood (Luke 22:20; 1 Corinthians 11:23-26). Just as the treatment of the kingdom moves it beyond the confines of empirical Israel, so the treatment of the new covenant established in Jesus' blood moves it beyond the old covenant established at Sinai.

(5) Jesus' death and resurrection, his being "lifted up" to the glory that he had with the Father before the world began, became the basis on which the Holy Spirit, the Paraclete, was bestowed by the Father and the Son on the new covenant community. In Paul's terminology, the Spirit is the down payment of the promised inheritance: here is a dimension of inaugurated eschatology that works out in limited but real measures of transformation, unity, revelation — in short, in experience of the presence and power of God. While the Holy Spirit convicts the world of sin (John 16:8-11), he constitutes the people of God under the new covenant — and this people, this blood-bought church, has a future as certain as the resolution and triumph of Christ: "I will build my church," the Master declared, "and the gates of death will not overcome it" (Matthew 16:18). Among the many entailments of the New Testament portraits of the church is this: the locus of the new covenant people of God is not in a nation — neither Israel nor any other nation — but in a transnational community made up of people from every tongue and tribe and people and nation. Of course, that fact does not overlook the common humanity that Christians enjoy with all others. Nevertheless it establishes the universal sphere of Christian witness — to all nations, all peoples, everywhere — while ensuring that this side of the consummation there will be ongoing tensions between the Christian community and all other communities. So once again, through another portal we approach the challenge of delineating the relations between Christ and culture.

(6) It is at this juncture that we must briefly reflect on Jesus' utterance, "Give back to Caesar what is Caesar's, and to God what is God's" (Matthew 22:21; Mark 12:17; Luke 20:25). The context is important. As a trap, some Pharisees and Herodians, in a strange mixing of bedfellows, ask Jesus whether or not it is lawful to pay the imperial tax to Caesar. If he replies in the affirmative, he risks alienating many in his Jewish audience, not only because they detested the Roman superpower, but also because the Emperor, whose image was on the coin, was worshiped as in some sense divine. If the coin by which this tax was paid was the denarius, it would have borne the head of Tiberius, the reigning Caesar, along with the words, in Latin, "Tiberius Augustus Caesar, Son of the Divine Augustus" *(TI CAESAR DIVI AVG F AVGVSTVS)*. To approve payment of such a tax, to such a lord, in such a medium, seemed tantamount to idolatry. On the other hand, if Jesus replies in the negative, he can be charged, by the Romans themselves, with inciting insurrection.

Jesus responds by asking for the relevant coin to be brought to him. He holds it up and asks the question, "Whose image is this? And whose inscription?" Inevitably, they respond with "Caesar's." That is when Jesus utters his famous dictum: "Give back to Caesar what is Caesar's, and to God what is God's."

At one level, then, Jesus' reply was a brilliant maneuver by which he evaded the trap and left his opponents speechless. But there are two further levels to his response that must be grasped if the bearing of Jesus' words on our topic is to be understood.

The *first* will be most clearly perceived when we recall that up to that point in history, religion and state were everywhere intertwined. This was true, of course, of ancient Israel: at least in theory, Israel was (as we have seen) a theocracy. Similarly in the pagan world: most of the gods of the people were necessarily the gods of the state. When the Romans took over some new territory, they arranged a god-swap: they adopted some of the local gods into their own pantheon and insisted that the locals take on some of the Roman gods. This had the effect of breaking down local allegiance to gods that were peculiarly theirs. If rebellion erupted, it would be less than clear on whose side the various gods were fighting. But nowhere was there a state that was divorced from all gods, what we would call a secular state, with state and religion occupying distinct, even if overlapping, spheres. But on the face of it, that is what Jesus is advocating. At very least, insofar as he envisages a transnational and transcultural community that is not identified with any one state, he anticipates the obligation to give to the Caesar that is in power whatever is his due.

We shall tease more of this out in the fifth chapter. Certainly this utterance of the Lord Jesus has been one of the roots, though not the only one, of long-standing and constantly evolving tensions between the church and the state across the centuries. Moreover, this way of looking at things is one of the most important features that differentiates Christianity and Islam. Islam has no body of tradition that enables it to distinguish between church and state. Indeed, the *ummah,* the people themselves, bound up with allegiance to Allah, are, in theory at least, more important than any state. But the state's role, finally, is to bow to the law of Allah.

Yet we must not think that Jesus' utterance warrants an absolute dichotomy between God and Caesar, or between church and state, or between Christ and culture. That brings up the *second* detail in the text that must be observed. When Jesus asks the question, "Whose image is this? And whose inscription?" biblically informed people will remember that *all* human beings have been made in the image and likeness of God (Genesis 1:26). Moreover, his people have the "inscription" of God's law written on them (cf. Exodus 13:9; Proverbs 7:3; Isaiah 44:5; Jeremiah 31:33). If we give back to God what has *his* image on it, we must all give ourselves to him.[28] Far from privatizing God's claim, that is, the claim of religion, Jesus' famous utterance means that God always trumps Caesar. We may be obligated to pay taxes to Caesar, but we owe everything, our very being, to God. "Whatever civil obligations Jesus' followers might have, they must be understood within the context of their responsibilities to God, for their duty to God claims their whole selves."[29]

---

28. This explanation has been set forth in readable form by David T. Ball, "What Jesus Really Meant by 'Render unto Caesar,'" *Bible Review* 19/2 (April 2003): 14-17, 52.

29. Ball, "What Jesus Really Meant by 'Render unto Caesar,'" 17. I cannot here go into an array of highly creative interpretations of this passage that do not stand up very well to close scrutiny — e.g., the Marxist reading of the passage undertaken by Alan H. Cadwallader, "In Go(l)d We Trust: Literary and Economic Currency Exchange in the Debate over Caesar's Coin (Mark 12:13-17)," *Biblical Interpretation* 14 (2006): 486-507.

Paul understands these realities. For when he insists that Christians should pay their taxes to Caesar, and, indeed, pay honor and respect and whatever else is due to the governing authorities (Romans 13:6-7), the authorities themselves do not enjoy an alternative or competing authority to that of God. How could they? They are *God's* servants (13:4); the authorities that exist have been established by God (13:1). Recognition of this point brings us to complex discussions about the nature of divine Providence, a discussion that must await later chapters. At this juncture, however, we recognize that with the coming of Jesus and the gospel, although Jesus himself has introduced a distinction between the authority of Caesar and the authority of God, related in part to the political reality that the locus of the people of God is not Caesar's state, or any other state, nevertheless Jesus does not concede that God and Caesar are parallel authorities. All that we have and are is God's. God never relinquishes his Godhood. Yet as soon as we have said this, we must remind ourselves that while Jesus affirms this truth, he is not surreptitiously reintroducing the theocracy of the state, or a medieval papal claim to be over states: the same Jesus also insists that Caesar, pagan and idolatrous Caesar, receive his due. Working some of these issues out is the task of the rest of this book.

A Heaven to Be Gained and a Hell to Be Feared

Even while it teaches us to be responsible people here and now, the New Testament repeatedly draws our attention to what comes after death, to what comes when Jesus returns. We are not to lay up treasure on earth, because everything here is merely temporal: moth and rust corrode, and thieves dig through and steal. What we lay up in heaven endures forever (Matthew 6:19-21). The culminating glory is a new heaven and a new earth, resurrection bodies, and the incessant joy of being always and forever in the presence of him who sits on the throne and of the Lamb (as the recurring phrase of the Apocalypse puts it); what must be feared and avoided at all costs is the second death (Revelation 20–22).

What this means is that the current relations between Christ and culture have no final status. They must be evaluated in the light of eternity. Further, this presupposes that as long as we remain in the inaugurated-but-not-yet-consummated kingdom, there will be no utopia.[30] Perfection, when it comes, will come with the consummation, with the return of Christ and the consummation of gospel blessings: there is no warrant, from a Christian point of view, to hunt for utopias elsewhere. But that means that in our present existence, even while we are afforded glimpses of the superlative glories and goodness of the consummation, even while by God's grace we live and serve in a community whose origin, authority, and mandate are not anchored in this world alone, we are not so naive as to think that we can bring in the consummation ourselves. It means that we live with tensions that will not finally be resolved until we live in the new Jerusalem.

Further Reflections on Niebuhr

To bring this chapter to a close, I must make four final observations.

(1) The biblical-theological points I have made in the previous section must control our thinking *simultaneously* and *all the time*. That is why I have called them "the *non-negotiables* of biblical theology." It will not do to adopt some configuration of a select few of them and on the basis of this configuration construct our pattern of what the relations between Christ and culture should be, and then call it *one* of the Christian options.

In some instances, at least, that is what Niebuhr has done. For instance, in his idealization of the "Christ the transformer of culture" model, he has simply left out the consummation. What he sees as a weakness in Augustine and Calvin suddenly becomes a strength: Augustine and Calvin are trying to integrate *all* the non-negotiables of biblical theology, which is precisely why they cannot adopt Niebuhr's "pure" form of the conversionist model. Of course, F. D. Maurice can adopt that model — but he is able to do so precisely because he is comfortable with abandoning some biblical-theological "givens."

Again, if we maximize the implications of the fall and maximize

---

30. See further chapter 6, below.

the uniqueness of the redeemed community, and then situate the result in the context of persecution, we generate the "Christ against culture" pattern. That is psychologically understandable. But is it helpful to think of it as *one of the options?* Would it not be better to remind ourselves of other complementary truths, such as the fact that God remains sovereign over the entire created order, that we ourselves are sinners constantly in need of grace so that we are never more than poor beggars telling others where there is bread, that the gospel transforms people such that they begin to function as salt and light in a world that is decaying and dark, that God's gifts of common grace are good gifts even when they are embedded in a culture dominantly characterized by rebellion against God, and that on the last day justice will not only be done, but will be seen to be done? In other words, if we see that this is the sweep of the whole, then there may be a place for emphasizing certain elements in the heritage of the "Christ against culture" pattern because of the existential realities of persecution. But even such persecuted Christians will not be so foolish as to think that their "take" on Christ and culture *is* the whole. To put the matter in a speculative, "what if" sort of way, would Tertullian have argued in exactly the same way if he had been transported to Rome in A.D. 325, or to Paris in 2005? In other words, is it not the part of wisdom to commend a more holistic reflection on the relations between Christ and culture, even while recognizing that certain elements in these relations may need special emphasis in concrete existential circumstances?

In short, it appears that some, and perhaps all, of Niebuhr's five patterns need to be trimmed in some way, by reflection on the broader realities of biblical-theological developments. When Lutherans and Calvinists adopt rather different perspectives on how music should or should not be used in the corporate praise of the people of God, is the best way of analyzing the difference one that says that Lutherans think of Christ and culture in paradox, and Calvinists think of Christ transforming culture? I doubt it. The word "culture" is being used in two different ways. In the "Christ and culture in paradox" pattern, "culture" is culture devoid of Christ, in which both the world and Christians are embedded. But where "culture" means something like that, Calvinists are no less convinced of human depravity than Lutherans. In the "Christ the transformer of culture" pattern, assigned by

Niebuhr to Calvin and his followers, there is an expectation that the presence and influence of Christians will make a difference in the world. Luther would say no less — and both Calvin and Luther would insist that such differences do not qualify anyone's acceptability before God. Theological differences continue to exist, of course. But by seeking to integrate *all* the non-negotiables of biblical theology into our reflections on these matters, and by observing different ways in which the vocabulary is sometimes used, we may wonder if the discrete patterns that Niebuhr lays out are sometimes so stylized as to mask the more foundational and undergirding biblical assumptions about Christ and culture.

I have just pointed out that Niebuhr's fifth category, the conversionist or "Christ the transformer of culture" pattern, *ought* not to be found in the pure form in which Niebuhr wants it to exist, because the pure form disowns some of the "givens" of biblical theology. Earlier I noted that his second category, the "Christ of culture" pattern, best exemplified in Gnostics and liberal theologians, abandons virtually all the great turning points of biblical theology. So should we abandon every vestige of Niebuhr's second pattern? Certainly we must do so if that pattern depends on abandoning so many biblical "givens." Nevertheless, a highly modified form of this "Christ of culture" pattern can be construed, one that does not abandon the elements of biblical theology. In his mercy, God leaves traces of himself and his ways in every culture. That is the point of some popular missiological accounts, such as Don Richardson's well-known *Peace Child:*[31] there are elements in any culture to which the gospel may legitimately appeal, even if (and here we leave Niebuhr behind) the adoption of the gospel will inevitably transform that culture in important ways.

(2) An analogy may help clarify this first point. Some theologians have identified different "models" of atonement theory that have been constructed across the history of the church, and have sought to ground each within the New Testament: the moral governance theory, for instance, or the substitutionary atonement theory, and so on. But this is *methodologically* flawed. When some historical figures have

---

31. *Peace Child* (Ventura: Regal Books, 1975).

sought to propound one "model" of the atonement *at the expense* of another, as we earlier witnessed with Abélard, there has usually been a larger theological agenda operating. But the wiser approach is to recognize that the foundational documents, the New Testament and other biblical documents, speak of the atonement in diverse and complementary ways. One should not so much speak of the differing, discrete "models" of the atonement, as of different aspects of the one atonement, trying to find out how these aspects cohere and relate to one another (as, for instance, in 1 Peter 2) and whether one aspect of the atonement rightly organizes or illumines or controls, and thus takes precedence over, the others.[32]

So also here. We will be wiser if we refrain from distinguishing discrete patterns or paradigms or models of the relations between Christ and culture, and think instead of wise integration, with different aspects of the whole clamoring for more attention from time to time. Better put, if for any reason we continue to think of different models of the relationship between Christ and culture, we must insist that they are not *alternative* models that we may choose to accept or reject. Rather, we shall ask in what sense they are grounded in the Scriptures and ponder their interrelations *within* the Scriptures, and how and when they should be emphasized under different circumstances exemplified *in* the Scriptures.

(3) That we insist on God's sovereignty over the entire created order, a sovereignty presupposed even in Jesus' utterance, "Give back to Caesar what is Caesar's, and to God what is God's," calls to mind another piece of unfinished business. For the reality of God's sovereignty reminds us that the categories "Christ" and "culture" are not mutually opposed in every respect. Postmoderns, whether Christians

---

32. There are plenty of other examples of readings of Scripture that are somewhere between hilarious and ludicrous, owing to the sad reality that the reading is detached from both the immediate and the canonical contexts. "Jesus as a Young, Single, Adult Male" is one sermon title I stumbled across recently, outdone, perhaps, by a Christmas address with the title, "A Teenage, Unwanted, Single-Parent, At Risk Pregnancy." No thoughtful pastor will dispute that the conditions of life represented by these titles need to be addressed. The question is whether they are best addressed by the kind of atomistic reading of texts that ends up robbing Jesus of all the attributes and functions rightly his that make him uniquely qualified to address all human needs.

or not, assert that every manifestation of "Christ" lies *within* the culture; Christians assert that every culture is in some sense *under* Christ's Lordship. In both ways of looking at the matter, there is an urgent need to probe what the expression "Christ and culture" means when the two controlling terms are not in every respect antithetical. Otherwise put, the two terms "Christ" and "culture" cannot be set absolutely over against each other, not only because Christians constitute part of the culture, but also because all authority is given to Christ in heaven and on earth, so all culture is subsumed under his reign.

Yet a distinction must be made. Only in the redeemed community do we find human beings who have cheerfully submitted themselves in principle to the reign of Christ, who confess the Lordship of Jesus Christ, who desire to live in line with his Word. It is a tragedy and a wickedness of immeasurable proportions that we who call ourselves Christians and have pledged allegiance to King Jesus often find ourselves in rebellion against his authority — and thus in sin. Even so, this subset of the entire culture is distinguishable from the rest of culture. So while we assert that in one sense culture itself is under Christ's authority — indeed, all cultures, embracing the incalculable range of language, symbolism, religions, philosophies, worldviews, customs, and artifacts passed on from one generation to another — in another sense, genuine Christians constitute an identifiable part of any particular culture. This tension is bound up with the different ways the New Testament speaks of God's reign. Christ reigns over all, including things Christian, non-Christian, and anti-Christian. When we contemplate Christ's reign in this sweeping sense, we are focusing on the mystery of providence, rather than his rule over people who have submitted themselves to his reign, since much of culture contests his authority and does not submit to his revelation. Much of culture claims it is free from his voice, or, at the very least, enjoys freedom to choose or reject what it wills from his voice. Nevertheless, from a biblical perspective Christ must reign, with all authority, until he has put the last enemy under his feet, death itself. Whether contested or even denied, this authority operates to bring about God's plans.

Created by God, this world cannot ever lose all the glory that God has built into it (Psalm 8), and God himself continues to do good and to bestow good gifts. For a start, he sends his sun and his rain upon the just and the unjust; he orders governments to reduce the dangers of anarchy in a world of malignity; he demonstrates his patience in holding out for repentance. All of the potential of the so-called "natural" world was called into being by God and operates under the authority of the resurrected Christ: all of art, music, administrative gifts, colorful diversity, creative genius. And yet everything is corrupted by sin. Our creative genius may build weapons of destruction, our administrative gifts may become exercises in personal power and self-promotion, our art may become wretchedly ugly and celebrate all that is disjointed, our nationalism easily identifies our own race or vision with the will of God, our democracy is in danger of claiming *vox populi, vox Dei*,[33] and our liberalism is tempted to confuse the pursuit of liberty with the pursuit of God — a vision of liberty that, in tragic irony, enslaves us in a new idolatry. Thus the word "culture" in "Christ and culture" may refer to that subset of culture that refuses Christ's authority, even if it cannot escape it. In such usage, culture frequently ignores Christ and Christians; sometimes culture explicitly contradicts Christ and Christians; sometimes culture persecutes Christ and Christians; on occasion culture very selectively approves and disapproves Christ and Christians. And the responses of Christians correspondingly adapt (sometimes wisely, sometimes unwisely) to such varying cultural stances.

The unease we feel at such tension will not be resolved until the last day. We await the return of Jesus Christ, the arrival of the new heaven and the new earth, the dawning of the resurrection, the glory of perfection, the beauty of holiness. Until that day, we are a people in tension. On the one hand, we belong to the broader culture in which we find ourselves; on the other, we belong to the culture of the consummated kingdom of God, which has dawned among us. Our true city is the new Jerusalem, even while we still belong to Paris or Budapest or New York. And while we await the consummation, we gratefully and joyfully confess that the God of all is our God, and that we have been called to give him glory, acknowledge his reign, and bear witness to his salvation. By the proclamation of the gospel, we anticipate the conversion of men and women from every language and peo-

33. "The voice of the people is the voice of God."

ple and nation. And as redeemed human beings we "seek the peace and prosperity of the city" in which we find ourselves (Jeremiah 29:7), until the new Jerusalem comes down from heaven. It is written: "The nations will walk by its light, and the kings of the earth will bring their splendor into it" (Revelation 21:24).

(4) I have repeatedly hinted that which aspect should be emphasized of the many things that the Bible says about the relations between Christ and culture depends, at least in part, on the concrete historical circumstances in which Christians find themselves. Are they being persecuted? Why or why not? Do they live in a democracy? If so, what kind? Is democracy necessarily a good thing, or may it be a bad thing? What kind of virtue is "freedom," so much touted in the West? Is secularism a necessary product of democracy? Is there any warrant, besides perhaps the purest pragmatism, for a "state church"? We shall discover that we cannot proceed much farther in our reflection on the relations between Christ and culture until we venture some tentative explorations of such matters as these.

THREE

Refining Culture and Redefining Postmodernism

I have argued that the great turning points in salvation history, *taken together,* constitute a bundle of non-negotiables as we try to navigate our way toward a stable grasp of how Christians should think about the relations between Christ and culture.

To advance the discussion, in this chapter I circle around to reflect at greater length on two terms, "culture" and "postmodernism." We have already seen that under the influence of Niebuhr's scheme the meaning of "culture" is not consistent throughout his five patterns. After a while, this inconsistency begins to hinder the discussion. At the end of the preceding chapter, I briefly indicated the direction in which the discussion should go — but this needs fuller exposition. In line with the title of this chapter, I would very much like to refine culture, but in fact my aim is much more modest: I seek to refine not culture but "culture" — that is, I am attempting to refine the term, not the reality. As for "postmodernism," although (as we have seen) the expression means quite different things in different parts of the world, so many are clamoring to take this movement into account in the assessment of culture (especially in America) that something further must be ventured. In this case I actually have a proposal to make.

Refining Culture

Virtually all serious consideration of the nature of culture today abandons the "high culture" approach that dominated discussion more than fifty years ago. By and large, Niebuhr was part of that change. Nevertheless, the more sophisticated and less elitist definitions of culture currently in vogue tend to raise several important questions pertinent to our theme. I have hinted at one or two of them, but perhaps it will be useful to put four of them out in the open by asking four questions.

(1) Doesn't the specificity of "cultures," each with its odd assembly of bric-a-brac, suggest that sweeping questions about "culture" (in the abstract singular) are too theoretical? Is it not the case that the bric-a-brac of one culture overlap with or sometimes contradict the bric-a-brac of another culture? In reality, how many people belong to one culture is surely indeterminable. After all, individuals assemble their bric-a-brac in individual ways. These individuals might be quite like one set of people in some ways, quite like another set of people in other ways, quite like a third set in still other ways — or quite like all of them in some ways, and quite like none of them in other ways. What, then, does "culture" (in some abstract or theoretical sense) mean?

To put the matter another way, Georges Devereux has argued that almost all cultural values develop and sustain themselves in conflict, in reaction to certain pressures — a sort of cultural form of Newton's third law of motion, that for every action there is an equal and opposite reaction.[1] Since all of us face different mixes of pressures (i.e., of "actions"), all of us emerge with different "cultures."

Henri Blocher suggests an analogy.[2] We often say that language is an element of culture. But since the time of Ferdinand de Saussure, linguists have distinguished between *langue* and *parole.* This is roughly the distinction between competence and performance. A parrot may be said to be speaking French; it would be misleading to say

1. Georges Devereux, *From Anxiety to Method in the Behavioral Sciences,* Studies in the Behavioral Sciences 3 (New York: Humanities Press; The Hague: Mouton, 1967), 210. Cf. also pp. 212-15, 224-25.

2. He advanced this at the colloquium in Vaux-sur-Seine where some of the material in this book was first presented. His material has now appeared in print, in his "Discerner au sein de la culture," *Théologie Évangélique* 4/2 (2005): 50-52.

that a parrot is a French speaker. A person learns, say, English, and thus is said to be an English speaker *(langue),* but the English he or she speaks is not English in the abstract, or the totality of all that goes by "English." The language spoken by an individual may be said to be English *(langue),* but what is actually spoken is the performance of that individual *(parole).* One of the things that has long interested linguists is the relation between *langue* and *parole.* Now insofar as language is an element of culture, what might it mean to say, under the rubric "Christ against culture," that Christ is against language? To say that Christ is against *langue* is as silly as saying that Christ is against English (or French, or Arabic). For the fact remains that as language constitutes an element of culture, it is to be thought of not only as *langue,* but as *parole:* that is, not only the language as a whole, but all the words, speeches, speech-acts, printed utterances, and so forth, of all the highly diverse people in that culture, all their individual expressions of *parole.* In some instances Christ might well be against specific *paroles* — hateful speech, for instance, or racist speech, or words inciting idolatry. But in that case, we have returned to the challenge of specificity. Is it any more coherent to think of "Christ against culture" than of "Christ against *langue*"? Isn't the construction too abstract? We can meaningfully speak of "Christ against culture" only when we bring culture, or *parole* as one essential element of culture, down to the level of the constituent elements.

Several facets of this critique of culture rather miss the mark. All of the definitions supplied in the first chapter ruled out the applicability of "culture" to the beliefs of a single individual. Recall Redfield's "shared understandings made manifest in act and artifact,"[3] for instance, or the definitions that speak of intergenerational transmission of culture, such as the one provided by Geertz: "an historically transmitted pattern of meanings embodied in symbols, a system of inherited conceptions expressed in symbolic form by means of which men communicate, perpetuate, and develop their knowledge about life and attitudes towards life."[4] Of course, how big the circle of a

3. Cited by Richard A. Shweder, *Why Do Men Barbecue? Recipes for Cultural Psychology* (Cambridge: Harvard University Press, 2003), 10.
4. Geertz, *The Interpretation of Cultures* (New York: Basic Books, 1973), 89.

shared culture is can vary considerably: one can speak of French culture, but one can also speak of Parisian culture, or the culture of the French Riviera, or the culture of a prominent French clan. One can speak of American culture and distinguish it from French culture, but one can also speak of Western culture over against, say, Chinese culture, and somehow include France and America under one umbrella. Within America, one can easily speak of the culture of New York City, of the Midwest, of the Louisiana bayou, of the Kennedys. We cheerfully admit that these various cultures may overlap in many interesting ways. In this sense, any culture can be thought of as filled with odd bric-a-brac, I suppose, and these bric-a-brac will inevitably be like and unlike the bric-a-brac of another culture — though the term "bric-a-brac" is a bit condescending. What we cannot do, if we are to remain with the definitions already established in these chapters, is reduce "culture" to the level of the isolated individual. Culture, as developed in almost all contemporary discussion, is essentially communal, even though the size of the community is highly variable.

The linguistic analogy is partly helpful, partly misleading. It is helpful in that the distinction between *langue* and *parole* reminds us that our consideration of culture in the abstract (analogous to the definition of language as *langue*) must soon descend to particular cultures (analogous to the definition of language as *parole*). If one wishes to evaluate what "Christ against culture" might mean, it is helpful to think beyond "culture" in the abstract to, say, the culture of Stalin's Russia, or the culture of Nazism, or the culture of Zen Buddhism, or the culture of the corporate West. But the linguistic analogy is misleading in that, at the level of *parole,* linguists are usually thinking of the language performance of the *individual,* and that is too narrow a focus when we think of culture. Still, performance is important. Québec French is distinguishable from the French of France. Even so, the French of the thirteenth *arrondissement* of Paris is also distinguishable from the French of Toulouse, just as the French spoken by lecturers at the Université de Montréal is distinguishable from what is spoken in the Gaspé. Linguists, as I've said, may keep narrowing the field down to the individual; those who study culture will not. If one tries to think through what "Christ against culture" might mean, it makes no sense to read this as "Christ against the particular culture of Joe Bloggs."

On the positive side, these questions about the significance of the *specificity* of particular cultures remind us that at least one of the reasons why Niebuhr identified no fewer than five distinguishable patterns of the relationship between Christ and culture stems from the fact that "culture" is never experienced in the abstract. Our experience of culture is invariably highly specific. If we extrapolate from our own experience — say, in a violent culture that persecutes Christians, where "Christ against culture" seems like an appropriate category — to the experience of others whose assumptions of "culture" are very different, we will be hard pressed to defend the priority of our choice of model. At least some of the differences in the New Testament in the approach of the earliest Christians to "Caesar" stem from radically different experiences of Caesar. So if we are going to uncover a broad, theoretical understanding of the relationship between Christ and culture, it is going to have to be complex, subtle, and flexible enough to embrace the specificity of cultures.

(2) Does the diversity of cultures around the world permit us to make any evaluation whatsoever as to the superiority or inferiority of any specific culture?

The question is interesting in its own right, of course, but insofar as we are allowing for the possibility that "Christ against culture" might be the best category in some cases, and not in others, doesn't that imply that some cultures are worse than others (and concomitantly that other ones are better)? To put it baldly: can we not agree that it is better to greet one's neighbors than to eat them?

Reacting against the condescension intrinsic to the colonial past, cultural anthropologists have for decades attempted to describe cultures in entirely neutral, purely descriptive, terms. Sometimes this passion for neutrality, for objective description without moral judgment, becomes, itself, a moral judgment: the only "good" cultural anthropology is the sort that refuses to make any moral judgments. The child sacrifice of the Incas gets a pass: the system was significant to those who lived under it, so who are we to condemn it? Even the Holocaust must be thought of from various perspectives: it was an unimaginable obscenity to those who were being gassed, but for the Aryan supremacists its chief failure was that it was halted before its task was complete. It all depends on one's point of view.

When I gave some of this material in lecture form, the first Q&A session found an international student, from a former French colony, asking whether I thought that any culture was superior to any other culture. It was a good question, of course, and stacked with layers of assumptions and tensions, granted the West's imperialism in Africa. In much of French West Africa, the mid-twentieth century witnessed a powerful movement called *la négritude,* in which young French West African intellectuals challenged the alleged superiority of French European culture. In their attempt to make space for West African culture, it was found useful to relativize *all* cultures.[5] This, of course, is very much in line with many of the assumptions of current cultural anthropology. But if there are contexts in which I am prepared to speak of Christ being *against* culture, is Christ equally against *all* cultures, or is he rather more against some than others? Is our meditation on Niebuhrian categories opening a very large can of worms?

In private discussion after the public Q&A, I asked my African interlocutor if he thought that one could responsibly make any judgments as to the relative superiority or inferiority of the culture of the Nazis as compared with, at the same time in history, the culture of the Netherlands, whose citizens were among the most generous and risk-taking in their commitment to hide Jews. He thought for a moment and suggested that this was a distinction in ideology, not culture. But that distinction is exactly what our definitions of "culture" will not allow. Labeling anything we want to condemn or praise "ideology" and the rest "culture" is a cop-out, undertaken for no other reason than to preserve the indefensible mantra of many cultural anthropologists: no culture is superior or inferior to any other.[6] So strongly is this held, in some circles, that any culture which challenges this mantra, such as a culture

5. I am indebted here to a former student, Mabiala Justin-Robert Kenzo, "The Dialectics of Sedimentation and Innovation in Theology: A Study in the Philosophical Hermeneutics of Paul Ricoeur with Implications for an African Theological Discourse" (Ph.D. diss., Trinity Evangelical Divinity School, 1998).

6. See the important essay by Thomas Sowell, "History Versus Visions," in his *Black Rednecks and White Liberals* (San Francisco: Encounter Books, 2005), 247-91; e.g., p. 248: "The central doctrine of multiculturalism — the equality of cultures — cannot be sustained when that means equality of concrete achievements — educationally, economically, or otherwise."

with a strong missionary vision, is necessarily colonial and therefore inferior — all without any sense of the sad irony in the position.[7]

None of this suggests that *every* assertion of cultural inferiority or superiority is wise or penetrating or true. Far from it: indeed, many such assertions constitute the fulcrum on which the most barbaric forms of racism, colonialism, and unrestrained nationalism turn. Six observations may bring some clarity.

First, any evaluation of a culture depends on a set of values — even as that set of values is in turn shaped by the culture that informs the evaluation. This is as true of the philosophical materialism of some cultural anthropologists as it is of Marxism, as it is of Christian faith. The broader the coalition of people who agree on some point — say, that the Holocaust was an enormous, barely comprehensible, evil — the wider the consensus evaluation.

Second, from a Christian perspective, everything that is detached from the sheer centrality of God is an evil. It is horrifically God-defying. In that sense, from a Christian perspective every cultural stance that does not sing with joy and obedience, "Jesus is Lord!" falls under the same indictment. In this sense, all cultures this side of the fall are evil.

But *third,* equally from a Christian perspective, God in his "common grace" pours out countless good things on all people everywhere. Though they may not acknowledge him, people enjoy the gifts he gives them, and these gifts are themselves good (James 1:17).

And *fourth,* as Christian revelation certainly insists that there are degrees of punishment meted out by a good God, we must assume that some cultural stances are more reprehensible than others — whether in and of themselves, or because of the increased responsibility of privileged people, or for some other reason. We need not resort to Dante's images of descending circles of hell: Jesus himself insists on the reality of *relative* degrees of punishment (e.g., Matthew 11:20-24; Luke 12:47-48), which presuppose *relative* degrees of good and evil in different cultures.

---

7. See the thought-provoking essay of Robert J. Priest, "Missionary Positions: Christian, Modernist, Postmodernist," *Current Anthropology* 42 (2001): 29-68, and the discussion it provoked.

Fifth, many of the distinctions among Niebuhr's five patterns turn, at the end of the day, on one's assessment of how evil any culture is. In other words, differentiation among the possible stances of Christ to culture turn, at least in part, on one's assessment of the values of each culture. I doubt that *any* probing analysis of the possible relations between God and culture can ignore such differentiated assessments about the moral value of a particular culture, however difficult or tentative such assessments must be.

Sixth, we human beings have a dismal propensity to corrupt good things, all good things. Consider one example. Springing from Steiner's provocative reflections in *After Babel,*[8] Henri Blocher raises the question whether the imposition of languages at Babel was a good thing or a bad thing.[9] If a bad thing, then presumably the unity of language before Babel was a good thing — yet it was this unity that enabled the people to attempt the massive rebellion symbolized by Babel. If that unity was so bad, then perhaps the diversity is itself a good thing. At the very least, even though the imposition of the diversity of languages was a rebuke and a restraint, it is not transparently clear whether the multiplicity of languages *in itself* was a good or bad thing. It was good in that it broke up this cabal of rebellion; it was bad in that it led to disjunctive groups (tribes? nations? races?) that were often at enmity with one another. In other words, we human beings can corrupt the unity and turn it into rebellion, and we can corrupt the diversity and turn it into war. One cannot fail to remark, however, that at Pentecost God did not give the gift of one language, a kind of restoration of the pre-Babel situation; rather, he gave the gift of many languages, so that the one message could be heard in all the relevant languages, thus preserving the diversity. Though it is true that the Apocalypse can picture many languages among the loci of ongoing rebellion (e.g., Revelation 10:11), it also pictures the great host of the redeemed made up of every tribe, people, nation, *and language* (e.g., Revelation 5:9; 7:9). There is no reason to think that the glorious unity

8. George Steiner, *After Babel: Aspects of Language and Translation* (Oxford: Oxford University Press, 1975), esp. 57ff.

9. Blocher adduced this example in his formal response at the conference in Vaux, to which reference has already been made. See his "Discerner au sein de la culture," 52.

we will enjoy in the new heaven and the new earth does not embrace the equally glorious diversity of race and nation *and language*.[10] (Perhaps no one will be offended if it takes some of us a few thousand years to get Mandarin under our belts!) Until then, we persist in our ability to corrupt unity and to prostitute diversity, the same unity and diversity often portrayed as "good" things.[11]

In short, from a Christian perspective, one must say that culture, like every other facet of the creation, stands under the judgment of God.

(3) But Christians themselves inevitably constitute part of culture. Is it not grossly misleading to try to sort out the relationship between "Christ" and "culture" if there are not two entities, but only one?

We have sidled up to this question before. Now we must push a little farther. The challenge is not simply that the Bible and Christianity are no longer, in the West, as culture-shaping as they once were,[12] but that Christians themselves, and thus the Christ they claim to represent, are unavoidably part of the culture.[13] Doesn't this mean that it is unrealistic to talk of "Christ" and "culture" as if they were two entities?

Yes and no. They are distinguishable entities, but not mutually exclusive entities, in the same way that the Hispanic-American culture is distinguishable from the broader American culture yet an integral part of it. The broader American culture influences the Hispanic-American culture, and vice versa. Similarly Christ and culture: Christians (representing "Christ" in the "Christ and culture" formula) are simultaneously distinguishable from the larger culture and part of it; Christians influence the culture, and vice versa.

---

10. Some have argued that Zephaniah 3:9 anticipates a time when all will speak one language. More likely it anticipates a time when all will use pure speech.

11. Of course, that is why "unity" is not an *invariable* good in Scripture: it may be nothing more than the fruit of some wretched compromise or other. For a thoughtful survey of the Bible's varying assessments of unity, see John Woodhouse, "When to Unite and When to Divide," *The Briefing* 279 (December 2001): 13-17.

12. Many, of course, have commented on this development. For an interesting recent discussion, see D. Spriggs, "The Bible: Cultural Treasure or Cultural Obstacle?" *Anvil* 19 (2002): 119-30.

13. The same point was powerfully made a quarter of a century ago, with somewhat different purpose, by Andrew F. Walls, "The Gospel as the Prisoner and Liberator of Culture," *Faith and Thought* 108 (1981): 39-52.

This is the sort of model advocated by Colin Greene. Greene criticizes "Niebuhr's typology" for its "tendency to put Christ and culture over against each other as 'two complex realities', whereas [he says] we wish to argue for the inevitable interaction and interdependence of both realities within a more comprehensive and hermeneutically intellectual framework."[14] Greene proposes instead a "critical interaction of Christ and culture" — similar to, but critically different from, Niebuhr's "Christ the transformer of culture." "This new model includes the postmodern experience of fragmentation and multiculturalism, which Niebuhr's study could not address."[15]

Greene's book is full of insight, yet his discussion of models, including his own "new model," is more than a little confusing. We have already seen, in chapter 1, that Niebuhr himself was fully aware that Christians are unavoidably bound up with the larger culture in which they are embedded — though doubtless he could be criticized for not developing that insight more fully. But to say that Greene's "new model," which focuses on "critical interaction of Christ and culture," is akin to Niebuhr's "Christ transforming culture," is scarcely obvious: if there is "critical interaction," one might have thought that one could just as readily speak of "culture transforming Christ" as of "Christ transforming culture." Of course, it is true that fragmentation and multiculturalism constitute part of the cultural mix today, and neither term dominated discussion when Niebuhr was penning his work. Yet it is hard to see why either fragmentation or multiculturalism threatens Niebuhr's typology, which spans twenty centuries of cultural phenomena and is certainly flexible enough to incorporate fragmentation and multiculturalism in the

14. Colin Greene, *Christology in Cultural Perspective: Marking Out the Horizons* (Grand Rapids: Eerdmans, 2004), 26. In n. 78 on the same page, Greene suggests that Niebuhr's fivefold typology can be reduced to three: (a) the "apostolic model," more or less the same as Niebuhr's "Christ against culture"; (b) the "Christendom model," which approximates Niebuhr's option, identifying Christ with the culture; and (c) the "pluralist model," which "unfortunately" entails "the capitulation of Christ to culture." Not only is this threefold typology less nuanced and therefore less comprehensive than what Niebuhr offers, but it is misleading on more than one front. For instance, to assert that the "apostolic" witness uniformly supports "Christ against culture" is terribly reductionistic.

15. Greene, *Christology in Cultural Perspective*, 26.

twenty-first century. Exactly *how* both developments should be incorporated will depend at least in part on what is meant by each term. For instance, "multiculturalism" may simply refer to the cultural and perhaps ethnic pluralism that is evident in many large cities today. For Christians accustomed to anticipating a new heaven and a new earth with "members of every tribe and language and people and nation" (Revelation 5:9), multiculturalism may be perceived to be something wonderful developing in the culture that biblically faithful Christianity can latch on to. On the other hand, where "multiculturalism" is a sloganeering word associated with left-wing social agendas that relativize all cultural values and all religious claims, except for the dogmatic claim that all such values are to be relativized, the word may bespeak a culture diametrically opposed to the exclusiveness of Christian claims — and in that case Christians will gravitate toward a "Christ against culture" paradigm. One could engage in similar musings with respect to fragmentation. But it is difficult to see why either fragmentation or multiculturalism, however understood, threatens Niebuhr's analysis.

Every culture keeps changing. Changes can be brought about by an almost infinite array of factors: fresh immigration, international events, economic trends, educational trends, the popularity of various political and economic ideas, developments in the media, pop entertainment, whether the people of that culture live their lives in a time of peace or a time of war, and much more. Inevitably, some groups within the broader culture will react to such changes in different ways. Some, for instance, may be delighted by the influx of new immigrants; others may resent them in some ways but lust for the cheap labor they represent; still others, driven perhaps by xenophobia, ascribe all fresh ills to the newcomers. New patterns, relationships, and symbolisms are called into being by such diverse responses, which are then passed on to the next generation. *How* people within the culture respond to the new immigrants, then, depends on complex commitments and ideologies that differ from group to group — commitments and ideologies that serve as the discriminating authorities in the minds of the various groups responding in different ways. Similar things could be said about how different groups respond to every other cultural change.

Transparently, Christians who constitute part of the broader culture are never immune from such cultural changes. How they think about the dominant emphases in this culture of which they are a part, and how they think about changes that take place within the culture, will largely be determined by *their* commitments and ideologies. Insofar as these commitments and ideologies are substantially shaped by the Christian Bible, Christians' "filters" and evaluative mechanisms and responses will differ, in smaller or larger ways, from those whose commitments and ideologies are substantially shaped by, say, the Qur'an, or by philosophical materialism, or by hedonism.

Clearly, then, it is useful to be able to speak of, say, the reactions of the Muslim community in France to some development or other in the broader French culture. Such discourse recognizes that not all Muslims in France will have the same reaction; equally, it recognizes that not everyone in the broader French culture will approve or even participate in some development or other. Moreover, all will agree that one may usefully describe these Muslim responses (generalizations though they may be) in two different ways: one might speak of them as the responses of the Muslim community *within* the one broad French culture, understanding that Muslims constitute an important part of the French culture. Alternatively, one might speak of them as the responses of the French Muslim *culture* to the broader (yet implicitly non-Muslim) French *culture* — that is, a clash of two cultures within the broader culture of France that embraces them both. Similarly, one may speak of how Christians in, say, America, understand cultural developments within the broad American culture. We may speak in this way even while we recognize that not all Christians will view things the same way, that the so-called developments within the culture may not impact every part of the culture the same way, that American Christians are in any case unavoidably part of this broader culture, and that American Christians themselves can be divided into an array of subcultures. It is not inappropriate, in another usage, to speak of the American Christian (sub)culture, over against the broader (non-Christian) American culture, once we understand that further divisions and alignments are possible. Once again, all the appropriate caveats need to be understood, but clearly such discourse is not incoherent or useless.[16] Equally clearly, it would be tedious to keep entering these caveats on every page.

The diversity of cultural commitments, then, within broader French or American (or any other) culture have different values, different ideas of the good, different voices of authority, and therefore different goals. That is what makes it possible to talk about "Christ and culture." Far from implying that the Christians who are aligned with the "Christ" half of this pairing somehow transcend culture or are perfectly uniform in their views, the "Christ and culture" formula is simply an easy way to summarize the possible relationships between Christians and non-Christians, not at the personal level or at the narrowly ideological level, but at the comprehensive level of "culture" as developed in this essay.

(4) But aren't there so many different "Christian" views on so many cultural issues that it is futile to speak of "Christ and culture"?

But that is just the point. It is this diversity that Niebuhr (and others who have indulged in similar analyses) try to categorize into a number of patterns. Like all such social categorizations, they are in

---

16. I therefore reject the approach to discussion of culture exemplified in, for instance, the influential book by Kathryn Tanner, *Theories of Culture: A New Agenda for Theology,* Guides to Theological Inquiry (Minneapolis: Fortress, 1997). Tanner surveys how "culture" is used in many recent works, especially those of cultural anthropologists, climaxing in the postmodern "cultural turn" (the expression has become influential owing to the work of Dale R. Martin and Patricia Cox Miller, eds., *The Cultural Turn in Late Ancient Studies* [Durham: Duke University Press, 2005]). Tanner sketches what theology might look like from the perspective of a postmodern view of culture with its attendant values of diversity, tolerance, freedom, and equality. This vision goes beyond what is proposed by the Yale School, that is, the postliberal theology represented by such figures as Hans Frei and George Lindbeck. The latter assume that local cultures enjoy a certain homogeneity, which leaves space for Lindbeck's proposal that theology be treated as a cultural-linguistic construction, each construction reflecting a particular local culture. By contrast, the postmodern "cultural turn" insists that diversity is far more radical: the diversity pulsates *within* local cultures, thereby destroying any notion of homogeneity on which Lindbeck's cultural-linguistic theology is based. This feels a bit like peeling the onion. One can always take off another layer, but my point is that there are invariably cultural parameters that bring subcultures together into recognizable identities, even if those parameters change from time to time. For this chapter, my purpose in spelling these things out is to make clear how it is coherent to talk about Christ and culture, despite the more extreme postmodern views of culture.

some ways idealized and simplified. But they are all trying to isolate the dominant patterns of justifiable relationships between Christ and culture.

Consider an easy contrast. The American Amish view of the relationship between Christ and culture is very different from any of the dominant Calvinistic views. Both are claiming to be Christian, yet one is advocating a very substantial withdrawal from (the rest of) American culture, and the other is advocating a very substantial transformation of culture. Unless we opt for the postmodern stance that refuses to privilege either position and thinks they are both "right" or "true" for their respective adherents (on which more below), we must ask how we can even begin to favor one ostensible Christian position over against another ostensible Christian position.

Although in setting up this contrast I have chosen the admittedly extreme form of withdrawal advocated by the Amish, there are milder (and more rigorously argued) forms of cultural withdrawal, still within the Anabaptist tradition, such as those advocated by a biblical scholar such as John H. Yoder and a systematician such as Stanley Hauerwas.[17] By "withdrawal," I am not suggesting that the Amish, or any others in the Anabaptist tradition, are withdrawing *from culture:* such withdrawal is of course impossible. By their own lights, those in the Anabaptist tradition are establishing communities with an *alternative* culture, a radically *Christian* culture.[18] Yet in their diverse theories of how to go about it, the Anabaptists are "withdrawing" from the broader culture in the sense that, at some level or other, they are convinced that active participation in that culture inevitably compromises Christian claims. The only way to be faithful to Christian commitments is some form or other of "withdrawal" in order to constitute a superior Christian culture.

Of course, one finds similar diversity among Calvinistic views of culture. One thinks, for instance, of the sharp differences between

17. For example, John H. Yoder, *The Politics of Jesus,* 2d ed. (Grand Rapids: Eerdmans, 1993); Stanley Hauerwas, *With the Grain of the Universe: The Church's Witness and Natural Theology* (Grand Rapids: Brazos, 2000); and Hauerwas, *Christian Existence Today: Essays on the Church, World, and Living in Between* (Grand Rapids: Brazos, 2001).

18. See, for instance, Duane K. Friesen, *Artists, Citizens, Philosophers — Seeking the Peace of the City: An Anabaptist Theology of Culture* (Scottdale: Herald, 2000).

Abraham Kuyper and Klaas Schilder.[19] But common to the thought of all of these thinkers is the view that the Lordship of Christ over all of culture demands that Christians, even while they pursue evangelism and disciple-making, must earnestly seek to establish Christ's claims within the broader culture in which they live, not by withdrawing and setting up counter-models, but by engaging and transforming the culture. I shall return to these questions in the last two chapters.

Three kinds of issues must be addressed here; the broader challenge of postmodernism I will take up again in a few pages.

First, that stance is most likely to be deeply Christian which attempts to integrate all the major biblically determined turning points in the history of redemption: creation, fall, the call of Abraham, the exodus and the giving of the law, the rise of the monarchy and the rise of the prophets, the exile, the incarnation, the ministry and death and resurrection of Jesus Christ, the onset of the kingdom of God, the coming of the Spirit and the consequent ongoing eschatological tension between the "already" and the "not yet," the return of Christ and the prospect of a new heaven and a new earth. One might expand or contract this list a bit, but the point itself must not be ignored.

We have already seen that at least one of Niebuhr's patterns should really be discounted, largely because it is so "liberal" that it discounts more than one of these turning points. But it is easy to see how downplaying these turning points can introduce other massive distortions into one's understanding of cultures and therefore of how to interact with them. For example, if creation is ignored, it becomes easy to develop a quasi-gnostic view of salvation and much more difficult to grasp that human responsibility is fundamentally grounded in the fact that we *owe* everything to our Creator. What is lost is a sense of indebt-

---

19. Most of the voluminous writings of Kuyper have not been translated from the Dutch into English. For an English introduction to his thought, see *Abraham Kuyper: A Centennial Reader,* ed. James D. Bratt (Grand Rapids: Eerdmans, 1998). The one important contribution of Schilder has been published in English as *Christ and Culture* (Winnipeg: Premier Printing, 1977). Henry R. Van Til (*The Calvinistic Concept of Culture* [Grand Rapids: Baker, 1959]) attempts a *via media* between the two, while Brian J. Walsh and J. Richard Middleton (*The Transforming Vision: Shaping a Christian World View* [Downers Grove: InterVarsity Press, 1984]) try to show what is involved in putting such a vision into effect.

edness. Equally sad, people might be tempted to a purely non-corporeal vision of "salvation," with devilish consequences in the physical world. Or again, if the fall is minimized, including the way that it is developed across the canon, sin is diminished. Worse, the fundamental nature of idolatry — the de-godding of God, the desperate failure to love God with heart and soul and mind and strength — fades into a ghostly image of itself, and this in turn dissolves one of the most central and controlling aspects of salvation described in the Bible, namely, being reconciled to God on God's terms. It has long been recognized that a weak understanding of what the Bible says about sin is inevitably tied to a weak understanding of what the Bible says is achieved by the cross — in particular, that dimension of the cross that is sometimes labeled "penal substitution." Such steps make it much easier to adopt Niebuhr's second category, "the Christ of culture," or, alternatively, his third, "Christ above culture" in the "synthesist" sense.

Failure to integrate, say, the exodus and the giving of the law robs us of the great Old Testament paradigm of liberation, of God-revealed norms, of a notion of holiness tied simultaneously to God and to the maintenance of what God has prescribed and proscribed, of the tension between being saved from something and being saved for something, of a people peculiarly belonging to God, of an entire covenantal structure that turns on a tabernacle/temple, a priesthood, a sacrificial system — all of which are taken up and modified in various ways in the New Testament. It is not difficult to imagine how these elements, rightly understood and integrated into contemporary Christian believers' self-understanding and outlook, contribute crucially both to their view of their *Christian* culture (i.e., the culture of the subgroup with which they most strongly identify) and of their place in, and relations with, the broader culture (of their country, region, ethnicity, etc.).

It would be easy to go through other turning points in the biblical history of redemption in order to observe how the omission or dilution of one or more of them easily generates a truncated or distorted vision of Christianity, and therefore of the relations between Christ and culture. Indeed, much of the rest of this book can be read as a meditation on how a robust biblical theology tends to safeguard Christians against the most egregious reductionisms. Not for a moment should this be taken as a claim that a full-blooded biblical theology can, by the expenditure of a little energy, be read off the text with universal assent. My claim is more modest: that stance is most likely to be deeply Christian which attempts to integrate all the major biblically determined turning points in the history of redemption.

One cannot forget that "offbeat" interpretations have been and are being advanced regarding *every* major Christian teaching, *every* major turning point in biblical theology — and, correspondingly, complex rebuttals have been offered. The problem is that in the contemporary climate, these offbeat interpretations convince some observers that all doctrinal matters are "open," and therefore that rigorous biblical theology is impossible, and therefore that biblically based worldview formation is also impossible, so much so that where it is attempted, the result is merely parochial. In part, this objection anticipates discussion in the second section of this chapter. Nevertheless, Christians committed to the attempt to synthesize biblical theology, however humbly advanced and however corrigible the result, must not be intimidated by the mere existence of an endless parade of offbeat interpretations.

For example, in support of his "straight line" extending from the creation to the consummation, Wolfhart Pannenberg interprets the fall (Genesis 3) as an element of the unfolding of creation, rather than as a catastrophic failure or as the onset of heinous rebellion. The "real point" of Genesis 3 is to provide an explanation of death's origins, of the difficulties intrinsic to birth and work — and this, not as a function of "real" rebellion, but in the context of his own critical assessment of how etiological tales arise.[20] Pannenberg's approach to Genesis 3 is compounded when he links "uncompleted" and "unredeemed," when he treats evil primarily as "risk" entailed by human independence, which is the "condition of [God's] purpose for the creature," and when his theodicy is entirely eschatological.[21] Because he is a systematician, at least Pannenberg is trying to paint a coherent picture, even if it is one that is rather farther removed from the context of the Pentateuch, not to say from Paul (see especially Romans 5:12-21; 1 Corinthians 15:21-22, 45-49), than he thinks.

20. *Systematic Theology*, 3 vols. (Grand Rapids: Eerdmans, 1991-98), 2:263.
21. Cf. 2:59-275, esp. 2:127, 2:132-36, 2:166-69.

A further problem is introduced by Walter Brueggemann,[22] who not only adopts a fairly "soft" reading of Genesis 3 but then argues that Old and New Testament writers present fundamentally conflicting visions of the passage and of God's response to human rebellion.

I mention these examples as mere illustrations of tendencies that run in the wrong direction. By contrast, I am arguing that that stance is most likely to be deeply Christian which attempts to integrate all the major biblically determined turning points in redemption — including creation, fall, the call of Abraham, and so forth.

Second, that stance is most likely to be deeply Christian which attempts to balance the various turning points in the history of redemption. In other words, it is not merely a matter of including all the turning points, but of how they hang together. Eastern Orthodoxy assigns a higher place to the incarnation than does the West; correspondingly, it diminishes, relative to the West, the place of the cross. Various cultural self-understandings flow from these commitments. As some Christians put their Bibles together, they place dominant emphasis on evangelism, with social improvement a more distant mission; others reverse these priorities. Transparently, these commitments will shape one's understanding of the "proper" relationship between Christ and (the broader) culture.

Third, unavoidably the location of contemporary Christians within their corners of the world will have a shaping influence on which elements of the Bible's story line they wish to emphasize. Christians facing overt persecution in southern Sudan or in northern Nigeria will necessarily develop a different outlook than their brothers and sisters in Geneva, Switzerland, in Vancouver, Canada, and in Tulsa, Oklahoma (respectively, a thoroughly international city, a highly secularized Pacific-rim city, and a Bible-belt city in which it is sometimes difficult to find someone who will admit to *not* being a Christian). Christians pondering how best to interact with the broader culture, and bear witness to it, in Oslo or Helsinki, will necessarily have a somewhat different set of priorities than Christians in, say, Haiti, with its endemic poverty, or in Johannesburg, with its devastating AIDS statis-

22. For instance, *An Introduction to the Old Testament: The Canon and Christian Imagination* (Louisville: Westminster John Knox Press, 2003), 32, 37-39.

tics and staggering numbers of orphans. But wherever they live, those who are best informed should not be insisting that theirs is the only way to think responsibly about the relations between Christ and (the broader) culture. Rather, they should be striving simultaneously to grapple with *all* the turning points in redemptive history, even while they recognize that their *own* cultural location demands that certain biblical emphases must have a higher priority than others. This way of putting it allows for three things: (a) a greater cross-cultural Christian consensus on what Scripture *says,* (b) a flexible accommodation to the demands of particular enveloping cultures, and (c) an implicit understanding that when the broader culture changes — when, say, persecution stops, when a Constantinian revolution takes place, when the church is in greater danger of being seduced by power than by being pummeled by brutality — the comprehensiveness of Scripture's story line and the multiplicity of its interlocking emphases still allow it to exercise a reforming, shaping, correcting function in the way Christians should think of themselves in the world. It follows that that stance is most likely to be deeply Christian which not only recognizes the comprehensive turning points in redemptive history but reads its own times well and ponders deeply how best to respond and take initiative within that (broader) cultural setting.

To sum up: Recall, once more, the definition of culture provided by Geertz: it is "an historically transmitted pattern of meanings embodied in symbols, a system of inherited conceptions expressed in symbolic form by means of which men communicate, perpetuate, and develop their knowledge about life and attitudes towards life."[23] Culture is not the idiosyncratic possession of the individual, even though an individual may well embody a particular culture. Transparently, the locus of a particular culture is variable and may overlap with other cultures, but this does not mean that one culture cannot be usefully compared and contrasted with another culture.[24] Because Christians self-consciously look to Scripture (not least as interpreted in the

23. See Geertz, *The Interpretation of Cultures,* 89.
24. This point is recognized by the use of the word "culture" found in many titles of books and articles that simply assume the point I have been making — e.g., Joseph Bottum, "When the Swallows Come Back to Capistrano: Catholic Culture in America," *First Things* 166 (October 2006): 27-40.

"transmitted pattern of meanings" understood in their Christian group), even while some of the "transmitted pattern of meanings" in their group may have more to do with the fact that they are the citizens of Burkina Faso or Pago Pago, they will inevitably find themselves in continuity with, and in discontinuity with, their fellow citizens who do not share their Christian heritage and commitments. Equally, they will find themselves in continuity with, and in discontinuity with, Christians living in other parts of the world who are embedded in quite different cultures. For this reason we can usefully speak of the relations between (a particular form of) Christianity and (other) cultures — or, so as not to drown in caveats, we may simply say we can think about Christ and culture, with the caveats understood from here on in this book.

Moreover, the Christian heritage of meanings and values turns on disclosure from God that makes us look at everything differently.[25] In the much-quoted words of C. S. Lewis, "I believe in Christianity as I believe that the Sun has risen, not only because I see it, but because by it I see everything else."[26] That is why consideration of Christ and culture promises to be fruitful and revealing: it is a consideration of a dif-

---

25. One recalls the words of Günther Dehn, *Man and Revelation* (London: Hodder & Stoughton, 1936), 7-8: "Theology is not promoted by culture but by the belief in God's revelation as an event beyond all human history, to which Scripture bears witness and which finds confirmation in the Confessions of our Church. Only a theology that clings inexorably to these most essential presuppositions can help build up a Church that really stands unshaken amidst all the attacks of the spirit of the age. And such a Church alone will be the salt of the earth and the light of the world; any other church will perish along with the world." One may quibble with his use of certain terms: for example, "culture" for Dehn is in this context naturalistic, but he does not mean to deny that the fundamental revelation took place outside of or apart from all human culture, that is, outside all lived human experience — any more than by the expression "beyond all human history" he means to say that the revelation of Christ is *not* historical. It is his way of underscoring the supernatural *origin* of the revelation, rather than a denial of the locus of its self-disclosure.

26. C. S. Lewis, *The Weight of Glory: And Other Essays* (1949; San Francisco: HarperCollins, 2001), 140. Lewis may be thinking along similar lines in one of his allegorical novels. In *Out of the Silent Planet* (New York: Macmillan, 1946), 101, he writes, "We do not truly see light, we only see slower things lit by it, so that for us light is on the edge — the last thing we may know before things become too swift for us." I am indebted to Michael Thate for making this connection for me.

ferent way of seeing, of a different vision, even when we are looking at the same thing.

Redefining Postmodernism

The discussion so far still leaves open whether each ostensibly Christian culture can legitimately claim to be as Christian as any other ostensibly Christian culture. If not, then the best that a discussion of Christ and culture can do is talk about the options — which is, of course, what Niebuhr does. But where Christians agree that Scripture is the "norming norm" (to resurrect a beloved Reformation expression), then we ought to be attempting a more comprehensive synthesis — not only a description of what the relation between Christ and culture *is* in particular times and places, but a probing of what the relationship *ought* to be in the light of Scripture. Such an effort must result in a synthesis that is flexible enough to account for the diversity *within Scripture itself;* it must also be unified enough to hold the diverse strands together. Otherwise there is little hope of Scripture correcting us on these matters; there is little hope of Scripture functioning as the norming norm.

One of the impediments to this quest, however, at least in the English-speaking world, is the widespread perception that such grand syntheses are impossible. Postmodernism has rendered them obsolete. It is worth mentioning again that while "postmodernism" is virulently healthy in North America, where it enjoys many complementary and sometimes competing definitions, as a category in France it is largely dead. This springs in part from the fact that in France, postmodernism was tightly connected with certain literary and critical readings of texts, which readings are no longer in vogue, but never gained control of the philosophical schools: the analytic tradition of philosophy, regnant in much of Europe, never succumbed to postmodernism's reductionisms. Further, the influence of François Lyotard, who taught his readers to be deeply suspicious of all "big pictures" or "metanarratives," made it inconsistent to speak of post-modern*ism,* any more than of any other "ism." A very recent French work, written by an able philosopher, can speak of "postmodernity" as a phenomenon,[27] but certainly not of "postmodern*ism*." By contrast, postmodernism in America has become a sloganeering word that touches almost every human domain. Still, it must be said that some strands of European thought are profoundly anti-metaphysical — a stance that, in America, would be labeled postmodern, even if the label does not quite work in France. More important yet, owing to the power of global communications, highly diverse forms of "postmodernism" appear as outcroppings in places as diverse as French West Africa and Taipei, Taiwan, where I have been asked to speak on "ministry in postmodern churches."

Even within the evangelical community, the diversity of voices regarding the place and even the meaning of postmodernism continues to rise.[28] More broadly, the number and range of really unyielding and sometimes virulently shrill sirens show no sign of diminishing. The recent work by Gianni Vattimo, Richard Rorty, and Santiago Zabala on *The Future of Religion*,[29] a combined European and American project, is profoundly anti-metaphysical. Religion in general and Christianity in particular, they say, is moving to the place where it must abandon "onto-theology," "realism," and "objectivism," and as a result it is losing any capacity it once had to order the public square. Its function is merely to provide private comfort, and in that capacity it performs a civic duty, it displays civic virtue. The authors disagree on how Christianity arrived at this point — Rorty thinks Christianity is capsizing owing to progressive Enlightenment pressure, while Vattimo thinks that the change springs from Christianity's own message: the "actual message" of Christianity has nothing to do with metaphysics but only with love understood in ways congruent with postmodern nihilism — but they agree on the central thesis. And if they are right, then it is entirely inappropriate to enter into a discussion of the relationship between Christ and culture.

Others happily adopt the postmodern turn, but, noting post-

27. See Luc Ferry, *Apprendre à vivre: Traité de philosophie à l'usage des jeunes générations* (Paris: Plon, 2006), chap. 5, pp. 169-227.

28. See, for instance, Myron B. Penner, ed., *Christianity and the Postmodern Turn: Six Views* (Grand Rapids: Brazos, 2005).

29. *The Future of Religion* (New York: Columbia University Press, 2006).

modernism's reluctance to speak about the true reality of God and equally suspicious of metaphysics, they argue that the only way forward is a return to the process thought of Whitehead, Hartshorne, and Ogden.[30] Certainly when there is so much suspicion that all constructs say much more about the human knowers than about what is ostensibly known, it is terribly easy to take the next step and infer that we ourselves establish reality — nicely captured in Rifkin's biting summary:

> We no longer feel ourselves to be guests in someone else's home and therefore obliged to make our behavior conform with a set of preexisting cosmic rules. It is our creation now. We make the rules. We establish the parameters of reality. We create the world, and because we do, we no longer feel beholden to outside forces. We no longer have to justify our behavior, for we are now the architects of the universe. We are responsible to nothing outside ourselves, for we are the kingdom, the power, and the glory for ever and ever.[31]

Even in the slightly more subdued prose of a broadly Christian writer such as Franke,[32] the problems are acute. Constantly they place much emphasis on our finiteness, on our cultural location, and on the context-specificity of each knower, and very little emphasis on the content of the divine revelation (however much that content is disclosed within and to human cultural contexts). The result is predictable: the authority of the divine revelation is progressively domesticated, while scarcely a word is heard about how this divine revelation is able to *critique* culture.

Inevitably, this stance is eliciting strong rebuttal. Franke's latest book was strenuously taken apart by Paul Helm,[33] and that review has

30. So, for instance, John W. Riggs, *Postmodern Christianity: Doing Theology in the Contemporary World* (Harrisburg: Trinity Press International, 2003).

31. Jeremy Rifkin, *Algen: A New Word — A New World* (New York: Viking, 1983), 244.

32. Most recently, see John Franke, *The Character of Theology* (Grand Rapids: Baker, 2005).

33. It was published in the online journal, *reformation21:* see http://reformation21.org/Shelf_Life/Shelf_Life/113/?vobId=1184&pm=247.

set off a flurry of exchanges.[34] Others have joined in sometimes scathing denunciation of the strongest postmodern voices, intent on preserving a place for "objective truth" and for the possibility of knowing it.[35] On the face of it, we seem set, at least in America, for an unyielding confrontation between modernism and postmodernism, between foundationalism and postfoundationalism — a "take no prisoners" war in which there can be only winners and losers.

But there is another way. A chastened modernism and a "soft" postmodernism might actually discover that they are saying rather similar things. A chastened or modest modernism pursues the truth but recognizes how much we humans do not know, how often we change our minds, and some of the factors that go into our claims to knowledge. A chastened postmodernism heartily recognizes that we cannot avoid seeing things from a certain perspective (we are all perspectivalists, even if perspectivalists can be divided into those who admit it and those who don't) but acknowledges that there is a reality out there that we human beings can know, even if we cannot know it exhaustively or perfectly, but only from our own perspective. We tend to sidle up to the truth, to approach it asymptotically — but it remains self-refuting to claim to know truly that we cannot know

---

34. See further: http://www.generousorthodoxy.net/thinktank/2005/11/response_to_hel.html; http://reformation21.org/Front_Desk/Helm_s_Response/121/; http://reformation21.com/Front_Desk/Postmodern_Blues/133/; http://sacradoctrina.blogspot.com/2005/11/character-of-theology-john-frankes.html.

35. The literature is now voluminous. From the perspective of Christians, see, most recently, the essays in Millard J. Erickson, Paul Kjoss Helseth, and Justin Taylor, eds., *Reclaiming the Center: Confronting Evangelical Accommodation in Postmodern Times* (Wheaton: Crossway, 2004); Andreas Köstenberger, ed., *Whatever Happened to Truth?* (Wheaton: Crossway, 2005); and many of the essays of J. P. Moreland, e.g., "Truth, Contemporary Philosophy, and the Postmodern Turn," *Journal of the Evangelical Theological Society* 48 (2005): 77-88. Sometimes these voices speak from the perspective of a deep commitment to natural theology: e.g., see J. Budziszewski, *What We Can't Not Know* (Dallas: Spence, 2004), and Budziszewski, *The Revenge of Conscience* (Dallas: Spence, 2004). There are also blistering (and very funny) attacks from scientists committed to philosophical materialism (see especially Paul R. Gross and Norman Levitt, *Higher Superstition: The Academic Left and Its Quarrels with Science* [Baltimore: Johns Hopkins University Press, 1994]) and from literary critics (e.g., John M. Ellis, *Against Deconstruction* [Princeton: Princeton University Press, 1989]; and Ellis, *Literature Lost: Social Agendas and the Corruption of the Humanities* [New Haven: Yale University Press, 1997]).

the truth.[36] To set such a modest modernism and such a chastened postmodernism side-by-side is to see how much alike they are. They merely put emphases in different places.

In fact, though they do not always recognize it themselves, there are writers who think of themselves as moderate foundationalists and others who think of themselves as cautious postfoundationalists who are approaching this center from opposite sides. One of the striking elements of the book by Grenz and Franke, *Beyond Foundationalism,*[37] is that they refer to none of this moderate foundationalism, the "soft" postmodern literature, still less interact with it.[38] Foundationalism, as they caricaturize it, becomes for them a mere whipping boy — and this is pretty common among some postmodern writers. It is almost as if they cannot defend their own position unless they can demonize modernism and its attendant foundationalism, usually cast in its most extreme form. But as there are chastened foundationalists, so also there are modest or "soft" postfoundationalists. For all that Alvin Plantinga sets out to disown foundationalism, his careful insistence that belief in God may be properly basic suggests that postfoundationalism may be more flexible than some think possible[39] — indeed, in this instance, D. Z. Phillips goes so far as to argue that Plantinga's

---

36. I have tried to spell these matters out in *The Gagging of God* (Grand Rapids: Zondervan, 1996) and *Becoming Conversant with the Emerging Church* (Grand Rapids: Zondervan, 2005).

37. Stanley J. Grenz and John R. Franke, *Beyond Foundationalism: Shaping Theology in a Postmodern Context* (Louisville: Westminster John Knox Press, 2000).

38. The point is well made by Millard J. Erickson, "On Flying in Theological Fog," in *Reclaiming the Center,* 330-31. The moderate foundationalists to whom Erickson points are William Alston, "Two Types of Foundationalism," *Journal of Philosophy* 73 (1976): 165-85; Timm Triplett, "Recent Work on Foundationalism," *American Philosophical Quarterly* 27 (1990): 93; Robert Audi, *The Structure of Justification* (Cambridge: Cambridge University Press, 1993); and Audi, *A Contemporary Introduction to the Theory of Knowledge* (London: Routledge, 1998). Others who belong to the list are former anti-foundationalists who now mount a strenuous defense of chastened foundationalism, none more important than Laurence Bonjour et al., *In Defense of Pure Reason: A Rationalist Account of A Priori Justification,* Cambridge Studies in Philosophy (Cambridge: Cambridge University Press, 1997). See the penetrating essay by J. Andrew Kirk, "The Confusion of Epistemology in the West and Christian Mission," *Tyndale Bulletin* 55 (2004): 131-56.

39. Of Plantinga's many books, see especially his *Warranted Christian Belief* (New York: Oxford University Press, 2000).

critique of foundationalism never quite escapes the grip of what he sets out to deny.[40] Kevin Vanhoozer is fully aware of the strengths of the assorted forms of postmodernism but finds ways to preserve a place for meaning and truth conveyed through texts.[41] Science has learned to speak of "deflationary" or "minimal and piecemeal realism."[42]

More broadly, Christian Smith adopts a "perspectivalist realism": "Things are not of human construction and interpretation all the way down; there does exist an ordered reality objective of human consciousness of it, which provides materials which humans then interpret to construct what for them is reality."[43] A recent book by Esther Meek[44] offers thoughtful criticism of both merely rationalist approaches to knowledge, and of the postmodern drift toward skepticism, but ends up with a complex epistemology that is full of hope and joyful knowing. On the one hand, she critiques the common Western stance in which "people think that knowledge has to be something you are sure of, that can't be wrong, or it isn't knowledge,"[45] which finally makes the verb "to know" and its cognates "a success word: when we use it we imply that we were successful at getting the truth right."[46] The quest for truth rapidly becomes a quest for infallibility and absolute certainty. The result, as Talbot puts it in his useful review of Meek, is this: "Classical and modern philosophy both cycle from an initial state of skepticism through some proposal for attaining certainty back to skepticism as the result of the proposal's

40. See especially Phillips's *Faith After Foundationalism: Plantinga-Rorty-Lindbeck-Berger — Critiques and Alternatives* (San Francisco: Westview, 1995), esp. 29, 45, passim.

41. Perhaps Vanhoozer's most important work for our purposes is *Is There a Meaning in This Text? The Bible, the Reader, and the Morality of Literary Knowledge* (Grand Rapids: Zondervan, 1998).

42. The expression belongs to Sergio Sismondo, *Science Without Myth* (Albany: SUNY, 1996).

43. Christian Smith, ed., *The Secular Revolution: Power, Interests, and Conflict in the Secularization of American Public Life* (Berkeley: University of California Press, 2003), xvi.

44. Esther Lightcap Meek, *Longing to Know: The Philosophy of Knowledge for Ordinary People* (Grand Rapids: Brazos, 2003).

45. Meek, *Longing to Know*, 32.

46. Meek, *Longing to Know*, 26.

failure to deliver."[47] In this light, postmodernism is merely the "newest capitulation to skepticism" when it claims there is "no absolute truth, no metanarrative, no single grand story, no single way-things-are."[48] But by adopting a more modest stance regarding what is required to speak of the human capacity to know, and by recognizing the plethora of faculties, sensibilities, integrations, and cultural realities that go into all human knowing, it remains entirely appropriate to speak of human knowing. Whether one follows Meek in all her arguments or not, at the very least one is made aware how outmoded, simplistic, and painfully reductionistic much of the debate between modernism and postmodernism really is. That the problem remains acute in many parts of North America is exemplified by a debate, recently held in Michigan, between a well-known "emerging church" leader and a more "traditional" Christian thinker. As part of the structure of the debate, each party was allowed to ask the other some questions. The more "traditional" Christian actually submitted his questions two months in advance. One of them was this: Can you list any beliefs that are *necessary* to genuine Christianity? If so, what are they? The "emerging church" leader hemmed and hawed and eventually provided a list of several things demanded by ortho*praxy* — but not one demanded truth or belief. This reluctance to speak of truth is notoriously distant from the biblical writers.[49]

47. Mark R. Talbot, "Can You Hear It? Esther Meek's *Longing to Know* as Skillful and Joyful Activity — A Review Essay," *Christian Scholar's Review* 34 (2005): 367.
48. Meek, *Longing to Know,* 31.
49. See, among others, chapter 7 of my *Becoming Conversant with the Emerging Church.* The failure to recognize — both at the popular level and in some serious scholarship — that postmodernism is frankly embarrassed to talk about "the truth" and "knowing the truth" and the like, is one of the reasons why it is sometimes difficult to interact with more moderate postmodern thinkers, who seem constantly driven to place the best possible construction on even the most unreconstructed and immoderate postmoderns. See, for instance, S. Joel Garver, "D. A. Carson on Postmodernism: A Critique and Explanation," http://www.joelgarver.com/writ/revi/carson/htm. Garver is certainly right to say that when the best postmodern theorists disown "objective truth" they do not wish to disown every theory of truth, but only that which buys into a strong form of the subject/object dichotomy. Nevertheless I still think he is far too soft in his reading of Derrida and others — and more importantly, he fails to recognize how widespread is the reading of Derrida and others that engenders suspicion of *any* truth claim in which "truth" conforms in some measure to reality, however much it is mediated

This is not the place to engage at length the ever-widening lists on postmodernism. For the purposes of this inquiry, it is sufficient to suggest that there is ample intellectual space to speak of human knowing, however finite and contingent human knowledge may be when measured by the limitless knowing of Omniscience. Moreover, to be able to talk about Christ and culture in the ways I am suggesting, it is necessary not only to be able to talk about particular truths that are essential to Christianity, but to be able to talk about the Bible's story line, the Bible's metanarrative, the big picture. To put the matter negatively, we must reject, in the strongest terms, the idea that there is no big picture. One of the most amusing yet penetrating brief treatments I have read on this subject is that of Ian Rose.[50] In the tradition of C. S. Lewis's *The Screwtape Letters,* Rose depicts the legions of hell being instructed on how to convince everyone today that There Is No Big Picture, precisely because that one Big Lie is sufficient to destroy Christianity. This lie is far less shocking than a crass "God is dead" or the like, so it is more believable, but no less destructive.

In short, a "soft" postmodernism is likely to win widescale assent that there are two kinds of perspectivalists in the world, two kinds of postmodernists: those who admit it and those who don't. Both our finitude and our fallenness drive us to this conclusion. We see through a glass darkly. Nevertheless, we do see. If an unchastened postmodernism extends its claims toward raw relativism and denies the possibility of knowing the big picture, it is not only idolatrous and anti-Christian but borders on the self-refuting and the silly.

---

through the cognitive processes of finite, culturally located human beings. David T. Koyzis (*Political Visions and Illusions: A Survey and Christian Critique of Contemporary Ideologies* (Downers Grove: InterVarsity Press, 2003]) rightly recognizes how strong is the modern denial of objective meaning, combined with the promotion of group identity and individual will. Alvin Plantinga thinks of perspectivalist epistemology as the product of a worldview he calls "creative anti-realism": that is, we the users of the language, we the knowers, are responsible for the fundamental lineaments of reality ("On Christian Scholarship," in *The Challenge and Promise of a Catholic University,* ed. Theodore Hesburgh [Notre Dame: University of Notre Dame Press, 1994], 276). See also the important book edited by Daphne Patai and Will H. Corral, *Theory's Empire: An Anthology of Dissent* (New York: Columbia University Press, 2004).

50. *The Briefing* 325 (October 2005): 13-14.

Concluding Reflections: Worrying over Worldviews

In recent years, a rising number of authors have pooh-poohed the notion of "worldview" in general and of "the Christian worldview" in particular. Some are suspicious of worldview reasoning on the grounds that no finite human being can ever capture a true view of the world. And if we cannot capture a true view of the world, then isn't our "worldview" nothing more than an idol we have set up to worship? And isn't that idolatry all the more transparent if we try to impose it on others, even other Christians, who live in other cultures? Sometimes the assault on the legitimacy of worldview thinking is more sophisticated than this,[51] but it never falls far from this set of objections.

A "worldview," after all, is nothing other than a view of the "world" — that is, of all reality. A worldview is comprehensive only in the sense that it tries to view the whole. But no one, to my knowledge, ever suggests that a worldview "captures a true view of the world" (!). This is the oft-repeated postmodern trick of erecting a straw man: either one captures a true view, or there is no such thing as a valid worldview.[52] The very notion of "capturing" a true view sounds demeaning and domesticating; worse, if "true view" smuggles in notions of perfection, that is, a view of all reality that accords perfectly with reality itself, then transparently a "worldview" in this sense is the prerogative of Omniscience alone. But the bar has been raised too high. There is a lesser but entirely coherent sense in which a human being may see the "whole" of reality — for this is, in fact, what the Bible's storyline provides. A worldview must be comprehensive enough to address the question of deity (If there is a God, what is he like?), the question of origins (Where do I come from?), the question of significance (Who am I?), the question of evil (Why is there so much suffering? If things are not the way they're supposed to be, why not?), the question of salvation (What is the problem, and how is it resolved?),

---

51. For example, Carl Raschke, *The Next Reformation: Why Evangelicals Must Embrace Postmodernity* (Grand Rapids: Baker, 2004), esp. chapter 4, "*Sola Fide:* Beyond Worldviews."

52. I have briefly described the penchant most postmodernists display for argument by absolute antithesis, in *The Gagging of God,* 106-17, and elsewhere.

the question of *telos* (Why am I here? What does the future hold?). It does not purport to identify all the subatomic quarks; it does not claim to say all that might be said about God. It merely claims to cast a broad enough vision to be able to see the shape of the whole. And that, I have argued, is precisely what the Bible provides.

I have not attempted to address the epistemological question, that is, to provide a detailed map as to how one comes to this biblically grounded worldview. Such reflection belongs to another project. Nevertheless it must be said that a Christian worldview, a Christian theological vision, is more than a system of beliefs (though it is never less): it also includes the volition that self-consciously thinks and acts in line with such beliefs. The biblical story line, which finally centers on the gospel of Jesus Christ, establishes the *summum bonum,* the highest good, the thing we actively cherish and pursue. That is why John can speak both of believing the truth and of doing it. But to argue, with Raschke, that in this postmodern age we need to go "beyond" worldviews into a stance in which we admit God is so Wholly Other that we can receive him only by faith, and that this response is entirely in line with the Reformation's insistence on *sola fide,*[53] is confused at several levels. In particular, once again it has distorted "worldview" into something unrecognizable by any side in the discussion. After all, the attempt to take the Bible's story line seriously leaves plenty of space for what is unknown about God: modernists, too, read Deuteronomy 29:29 ("The secret things belong to the LORD our God, but the things revealed belong to us and to our children forever"), the end of Romans 11 ("Oh, the depth of the riches of the wisdom and knowledge of God! How unsearchable his judgments, and his paths beyond tracing out!"), and many similar passages. Still more importantly, faith, according to the Bible, is often nurtured and strengthened *precisely by the bold articulation and defense of the truth.* Trust in God, fostered and nurtured by the power of the Spirit, is grounded not so much in what is unknown about him but in what he has disclosed of himself — not only in supernatural acts, the chief of which is the resurrection of Jesus, but in words of promise and instruction, which are to be believed and acted upon. Raschke's view of

53. Raschke, *The Next Reformation,* chapter 4.

faith has more in common with Bultmannian existentialism[54] than with the Reformation, let alone with the New Testament.

Perhaps this is the place to point out that the postmodern penchant for affirming the unknowability or the incomprehensibility of God, often with pious reference to Calvin's affirmation of the doctrine, habitually overlooks some fundamental distinctions. In particular, there is an enormous chasm between what Calvin means by "God is incomprehensible" and what Kant means by "God is incomprehensible." For Calvin, God extends immeasurably beyond what human beings may know, but that does not mean that human beings may not know any true things about him, the more so since this God has graciously chosen to reveal to his image bearers some true things about himself. Kantian distinctions between the noumenal world and the phenomenal world head in a very different direction and end up making our conception of God little more than the result of the ordering power of our minds, with only the most uncertain connection between our mental construals and the reality.[55] To adopt the Kantian view of God's unknowability and bless it with Calvin's name is somewhere between a historical blooper and a sleight of hand. Moreover, even though we regularly speak of God in analogical language, some elementary distinctions steer us around some avoidable pitfalls.[56] One can say true things by means of a metaphor.[57] Further, if Scripture necessarily deploys analogy to refer to much of what God has disclosed of himself in Scripture, it is useful to distinguish between univocal analogy and equivocal analogy. Thus a statement such as "God exists" is not, for Christians, a *metaphorical* statement (i.e., it is not a product of human creativity), but a *univocal analogical* assertion: the spiritual being "God" can be said to "exist" in many of the same

54. Recall Bultmann's unwillingness to include no more than a bare "das" as the content or object of Christian faith.

55. For an example of the failure to observe this distinction, see, for instance, John R. Franke, *The Character of Theology: An Introduction to Its Nature, Task, and Purpose* (Grand Rapids: Baker, 2005), 13-15.

56. See, among others, Donald Bloesch, *The Battle for the Trinity: The Debate Over Inclusive God-Language* (Portland: Wipf & Stock, 2001), esp. 13-27, 61-64, 101-4, and the bibliography at 108-9 n. 2.

57. See the elegant work of Janet Martin Soskice, *Metaphor and Religious Language* (Oxford: Oxford University Press, 1985).

ways that we say that we ourselves "exist." The statement "God is our heavenly Father" is, by contrast, an *equivocal analogical* statement: that is, although God is not univocally what we mean by "father," yet *mutatis mutandis* ("equivocally") God is the "heavenly Father" to those who are his children.[58]

In sum: I have been arguing in this chapter that neither current discussion on culture nor current dependence on certain strands of postmodern thought may be permitted to dissuade us from reflecting on Christ and culture. Inevitably, any Christian belongs to and embodies, in some sense, the broader culture of his or her tribe or language or nation or group. Nevertheless, by virtue of adhering to, with greater or lesser fidelity, the vision of reality set out by the Bible, and structured by the Bible's story line, such a Christian enjoys a world-view — a view of the world — that necessarily conflicts with the assorted worldviews of surrounding people who do not adopt that vision of reality and the trust and obedience it elicits. Discussion would become unbearably tedious if I were to reiterate constantly the limitations and essential corrigibility of all worldviews, the kinds and degrees of overlap with other worldviews, and the like. I cannot continually say that by "Christ and culture" I really mean "a Christian culture and its relation to its surrounding culture, understanding that every Christian culture is necessarily shaped by its surrounding culture even while it forms part of it, and even while it has strong ties to Christian cultures in other parts of the world by virtue of shared allegiance to the Bible and its story line, to which all Christian cultures lay claim, which authoritative text has, for Christians, a norming authority that enables them in substantial measure to withstand the pull in the direction of other elements in the broader culture," and so forth. We will usually take such caveats as the "givens" and speak, more economically, of Christ and culture, but do so in such a way that these broader considerations are not ignored.

At this juncture it may be helpful to reflect on several large visions that compete with the Bible and the gospel it trumpets for the allegiance of men and women. Such competition demonstrates why it is worth thinking hard about Christ and culture. In each case I shall try to

---

58. I am indebted to Robert Yarbrough for some discussion on these matters.

delineate some of the ways in which these visions of the good interact with and compete with a Christian vision grounded in the Bible's story line. Insofar as these different visions of the good shape different cultural groups, we are discussing competing cultures — more precisely, in our case, Christ and culture. That is the purpose of the next chapter. For those who are addicted to matters epistemological in the current debates surrounding postmodernism, however, the following few pages will either cure their addiction or feed it.

One (Epistemological) Step Further

Debates on these matters have become, in North America, so steeped in subtlety that it may not be misguided to probe the intricacies a little further. Readers who are uninterested in current debates entangled in epistemology, postmodernism, and faith may safely skip these few pages without loss.

I shall proceed by interacting with a recent book by James K. A. Smith, *Who's Afraid of Postmodernism? Taking Derrida, Lyotard, and Foucault to Church.*[59] Smith reads the contributions of the seminal thinkers Jacques Derrida, François Lyotard, and Michel Foucault in such a way that they become helpful to Christians rather than ogres or demons.

Begin with Derrida. Derrida's unpacking of deconstruction is in some ways summarized in his much-repeated slogan "there is nothing outside the text" *(il n'y a pas de hors-texte).* But Derrida is not a linguistic idealist, holding that there is literally nothing outside text or that all the world is somehow nothing but massive text. Rather, he is insisting that there is no access to uninterpreted text, to uninterpreted reality. As Smith puts it, "[E]verything must be interpreted in order to be experienced. . . . [Derrida] is what we might call — for lack of a better term — a comprehensive hermeneuticist who asserts the ubiquity of interpretation: all our experience is always al-

---

59. Smith, *Who's Afraid of Postmodernism? Taking Derrida, Lyotard, and Foucault to Church* (Grand Rapids: Baker, 2006). Hereafter, page references to this book will be given parenthetically in the text.

ready an interpretation" (39). In fact, this stance "can be considered a radical translation of the Reformation principle *sola scriptura*. In particular, Derrida's insight should push us to recover two key emphases of the church: (a) the centrality of Scripture for mediating our understanding of the world as a whole and (b) the role of community in the interpretation of Scripture" (23). Of course, Smith knows that some might well respond that if we have only interpretations, including interpretations of the gospel, we cannot know that the gospel itself is true. In fact, he charges me with maintaining "a version of this criticism" (43).

> Carson is clearly worried that because folks like Stanley Grenz, Brian McLaren, and other "hard postmodernists" (as he calls them) reject modern notions of absolute or "objective" truth, they are giving up on truth altogether. But in his criticisms, it becomes clear that Carson simply conflates truth with objectivity: for Carson, one can only [*sic*] be said to know "truly" if one knows "objectively."[60] While Carson rightly notes that human knowledge can never pretend to omniscience, this doesn't mean we can't claim to know in a finite but real manner. But his affirmation of finite knowledge always elides into an affirmation of objective knowledge. Although he does not define objectivity (quite an oversight, given his project), Carson clearly means this to carry some connotation of self-evident givenness: if a truth is objective, then it is not a matter of interpretation. (43)

Smith has so completely misrepresented me that I scarcely know where to begin. Perhaps a few observations will suffice.

(a) Absolutely nowhere have I affirmed "if a truth is objective, then it is not a matter of interpretation." I spent scores of pages in *The Gagging of God* denying this point, and even in the more popular *Becoming Conversant with the Emerging Church* I repeated, in various ways, that there are only two kinds of perspectivalists: those who admit it and those who don't. We cannot escape our finitude; indeed, Christians have an even more profound analysis of our limitations

60. Here he cites my book *Becoming Conversant with the Emerging Church*, 105, 130-31, 143 n. 46.

than do the most radical postmoderns, because we confess not only our finitude but our fallenness.[61]

(b) I cheerfully admit that "objective" and "objectively" are slippery words, and in *Becoming Conversant* I did not take as much time as in *The Gagging of God* to make some necessary distinctions. Nevertheless I would have thought that an alert reader would get the point that I repeatedly made in the larger work: human beings may know objective truth *in the sense that they may know what actually conforms to reality,* but they cannot know it objectively, that is, they cannot escape their finitude and (this side of the consummation) their fallenness, and therefore the limitations of perspectivalism, and thus they cannot know anything completely or from a neutral stance. What is this but another way of saying that all of our knowledge is necessarily interpreted knowledge? That is why I developed at some length the long-discussed nature of the hermeneutical spiral, of asymptotic approaches to knowledge, of distanciation and the fusion of horizons. We may know some things truly, that is, our knowledge of them may conform to reality, not because we have omniscient knowledge of them (that standard belongs to God alone), but because the knowledge we have of them, however partial, however mediated, is predicated on the revealing words and acts of God: human knowledge is still knowledge *of the truth.* To put it another way, all interpretations are not equal. If they were, then the strongest criticisms leveled against "hard" postmodernism necessarily return. Two interpretations may, of course, be equally valid renderings of what actually is the ("objective") truth, even if we cannot know it "objectively," because they are looking at the same reality from different perspectives; but some interpretations actually distort the truth, or betray the truth, and thus are false interpretations.

(c) That is why the Bible so constantly emphasizes the importance and reliability of *truth.* What we proclaim is the *truth* of the gospel. Of course, it is possible, one more time, to insert all the footnotes and readily acknowledge that apart from grace and the work of the Spirit we would not have come to discern this truth and bow to it, that our interpretations are necessarily partial and potentially flawed, and

---

61. See especially chapters 2 and 3 of *The Gagging of God.*

all the rest. But if we spend all our time in such footnotes, then we betray the massive biblical emphasis on truth and on proclaiming the truth and bearing witness to the truth.

(d) Many of the leaders of the emerging church movement — though certainly not all, as I have frequently insisted — have begun with the *true* insistence (now there's irony for you) that all our knowledge is interpreted and have drifted toward very substantial relativizing of all interpretations. I do not see how that point can be disputed. The example I gave in *Becoming Conversant* of the college student who as a result of reading their material had become embarrassed by all that the Bible actually says about truth was merely one painful example. All of the biblical verses on truth that I included at the end of the book were offered in answer to his dilemma.[62] That is becoming a pastoral challenge of very considerable proportions.

So now we turn to Lyotard. Many postmoderns identify with his "incredulity toward metanarratives," what he calls the *grands récits,* the "big stories." Smith argues that metanarratives have a peculiar meaning for Lyotard. They are "a distinctly modern phenomenon: they are stories that not only tell a grand story (since even premodern and tribal stories do this) but also claim to be able to legitimate or prove the story's claim by an appeal to universal reason" (65). Thus what he ends up opposing is one variety or another of the "big story" behind the modern science of modernism — whether the grand narrative is Hegel's dialectics of Spirit, or Kant's emancipation of the rational, or whatever. These grand narratives are meant to be legitimating; they constitute the basis on which other knowledge claims are built. Nevertheless, Lyotard contends, these grand stories have no independent status; they are themselves the product of certain people and cultures. "Lyotard very specifically defines metanarratives as universal discourses of legitimation that mask their own particularity;

---

62. Smith, *Who's Afraid of Postmodernism?* 43 n. 10, fails to wrestle with this pastoral dilemma when he refers to my "concordance of passages," charging me yet again with an "unwarranted conflation" of truth and "objectivity." But I have repeatedly distinguished "objectivity" in epistemology (which I have consistently denied that we have) and our (necessarily interpreted) knowledge accurately reflecting what is "objectively" out there, even if we cannot know it exhaustively, immediately, or noninterpretatively.

that is, metanarratives deny their narrative ground even as they proceed on it as a basis. . . . [T]he problem with metanarratives is that they do not own up to their own mythic ground. Postmodernism is not incredulity toward narrative or myth; on the contrary, it unveils that all knowledge is grounded in such" (69). Postmodernism wishes to overthrow the universalizing pretensions of modernism.

All of this, Smith contends, is a very good thing for the gospel. It is reminiscent of Francis Schaeffer and Cornelius Van Til. Lyotard was not trying to overturn Christianity; he was trying to overturn modernism, and Christians should be grateful for his effort.

This is both correct and naive. It is correct insofar as Smith rightly summarizes Lyotard's thought. Yet it is naive. Smith thinks that he has defined metanarrative so tightly that what we thought to be the biblical metanarrative turns out to be something else. But most Christian thinkers have seen in Lyotard's "incredulity toward metanarrative" a destructive threat to the sweeping authority of the Bible's controlling story line. In fact, Smith acknowledges that Christian thinkers such as Middleton and Walsh, Grenz, Ingraffia, and others detect in Lyotard a very considerable danger for Christian claims. But Smith judges that these thinkers are worrying about nothing, because "the biblical narrative is not properly a metanarrative" (69). Frankly, I doubt that, were the question put to him, Lyotard would agree. Certainly popular writers like McLaren are now so suspicious of metanarrative in some comprehensive sense that they refuse to present Christ's claims as grounded in the sweeping story line of Scripture. Not once do they come out and say that this story line is *true*.

Smith goes on to excoriate the many Christians who, he says, "have bought into the modernist valorization of scientific facts and end up reducing Christianity to just another collection of propositions. . . . Knowledge is reduced to biblical information that can be encapsulated and encoded" (74). He then returns to my list of texts that use "true" or "truth," a list that seems to irritate him: "The chapter is a collection of lists of proof texts that are supposed to have the self-evident force of criticizing 'hard postmodernism' just by documenting the texts — a sort of miniconcordance of Bible verses that use the words 'true' or 'truth.' Carson's critique of McLaren on this score, particularly on questions of narrative ([Carson], 163-66), is an epic adventure in missing the point" (74 n. 17). He then asks, "But isn't it curious that God's revelation to humanity is given not as a collection of propositions or facts but rather within a narrative — a grand, sweeping story from Genesis to Revelation?" (74). Frankly, I do not find it curious at all; it is glorious, and I have emphasized the importance of the narrative, this big story, this — yes, let's call it that — *metanarrative,* in the strongest terms.[63] Not once do I pit propositions against the biblical narrative. All I have done is insist that the sweeping narrative includes propositions that cannot be ignored by appealing to the narrative. When truth is mentioned, McLaren is inclined to say that Jesus is the truth, and thus the truth is personal and relational. Well, yes, that is *one* use of truth in *one* New Testament writer. That same writer nevertheless uses "truth" and related terms to refer as well, and more commonly, to *propositions.* My list of references was not provided to construct a list of propositions that together constitute the sum of Christian belief, over against biblical narrative. Few have insisted on the non-negotiable importance of the biblical narrative more than I have. I provided the list to show the extent to which biblical writers are happy to talk about truth in propositional terms (although those are not the only terms), propositions that accord with reality (i.e., propositions that are "objectively" true, even though we cannot claim to know them objectively). I confess I am sorely tempted to characterize Smith's response as an epic adventure in missing the point.

And so, at last, to Michel Foucault. Smith nicely traces Foucault's publications from his earliest efforts. Foucault's studies of institutions of power — prisons, schools, hospitals, and factories — taught him that "power is knowledge." At the heart of all such institutions, and no less at the heart of sexual and financial relationships, are networks of power. Much in line with Nietzsche, Foucault insists that only one drama is ever played out, "the endlessly repeated play of dominations."[64] Foucault seems to have become less Nietzschean with time, almost (it appears) returning to a classic liberal or Enlightenment position, and Smith carefully draws attention to the debate

---

63. For a start, see chapters 5 and 6 of *The Gagging of God.*

64. Smith, *Who's Afraid of Postmodernism?* 87, citing Michel Foucault, "Nietzsche, Genealogy, History," in *Language, Counter-Memory, Practice,* ed. Donald F. Bouchard (Ithaca: Cornell University Press, 1977), 150.

among Foucauldian scholars as to who the real Foucault is.[65] Still, Smith's concern is to identify the ways in which Foucault may be a positive influence for what Smith calls "a postmodern church." Preserving Foucault's usefulness among postmodern Christians requires us to "stand him on his head a bit" (Smith's expression, 103). We must see the evils that Foucault sees — Smith himself primarily applies Foucault to capitalism — and yet reject Foucault's warnings against all forms of "disciplinary society." Rather, precisely because God *does* exercise authority, God's people must form disciplinary societies that are able to stand up and pull away from the seductive and destructive attractions of, say, MTV. Certainly the need for godly discipline, empowered by the Spirit of God, is very great. But of course, Foucault himself makes no exceptions for God. Elsewhere Foucault explicitly ties everything that he finds wrong with the exercise of power to what he understands of Christian institutions. In other words, despite the fact that Smith wants postmodern Christians to learn something valuable from Foucault, even he has to admit that Christians must go directly counter to Foucault when it comes to Christian discipline and the exercise of power intrinsic to it. I suppose it is not entirely misleading to think of this as "standing Foucault on his head a bit," though it seems a bit of an understatement.

Smith's own proposal is that the emerging church align itself with the movement known as Radical Orthodoxy (109-46).[66] Postmodern thinkers such as Derrida, Lyotard, and Foucault have rightly taught us to be deeply suspicious of traditions that anchor truth, claim authority, or exercise coercive power. Smith writes, "We must appreciate the sense in which many advocates of postmodern theology or religion are deeply critical of particular, determinate formulations of religious confession" (117-18). The entire Cartesian project is over, they insist, a failed dream. They reject "the Cartesian equation of knowledge and certainty" (118) and follow instead the wisdom of

---

65. The same point was recently made in a useful article by Richard Wolin, "Foucault the Neohumanist?" *The Chronicle of Higher Education,* 1 September 2006, B12-B14.

66. Smith himself has written a helpful introduction to the movement that discusses the major players: see James K. A. Smith, *Introducing Radical Orthodoxy: Mapping a Post-secular Theology* (Grand Rapids: Baker, 2004).

Derrida, who once wrote, "I don't *know;* I must *believe.*"[67] Smith describes their position as follows:

> In other words, the postmodern theologian says, "We can't *know* that God was in Christ reconciling the world to himself. The best we can do is *believe.*" Why? Because to know would mean being certain. We know that such certainty is an impossible dream; therefore, we actually lack knowledge. We don't know; we can only believe, and such faith will always be mysterious and ambiguous. But this isn't a bad thing; quite to the contrary, it is liberating and just. It is precisely when we think we know something about God that we start erecting boundaries and instituting discipline. (119)

Smith does not quite buy into this postmodern analysis, yet he is sympathetic to broad swaths of it. "Much in this critique," he writes, "has been rightly affirmed by many who have tried to think through the shape of the emerging church in postmodernity" (119). There is, he says, a similar "refusal of the Cartesian paradigm that characterizes Radical Orthodoxy" (120). This is the direction in which he wants to steer postmodern theologians. Human beings cannot finally live and make sense of anything without being grounded in some tradition — and that is the concern of Radical Orthodoxy. In fact, there is some kind of connection between Derrida's "I don't know; I must believe," and the famous adage of Augustine: "I believe, therefore I understand." In that sense, postmodern Christians are properly "dogmatic": they are rich in the doctrinal *beliefs* of earlier generations of Christians, even while rejecting Cartesian certainties. In this way of looking at things, Smith asserts, ancient Christians of the patristic period were perennial postmoderns. Of course, even this much "dogmatism" is offensive to most emerging church leaders, but at this juncture Smith tries to correct those leaders and nudge them in the direction of Radical Orthodoxy:

> This is not to advocate a return to an uncritical fundamentalism or the triumphalist stance of the Religious Right. Rather, it is to af-

67. Smith, *Who's Afraid of Postmodernism?* 118, citing Jacques Derrida, *Memoirs of the Blind,* trans. Pascale-Anne Brault and Michel Naas (Chicago: University of Chicago Press, 1993), 155.

firm that our confession and practice must proceed unapologetically from the particularities of Christian confession as given in God's historical revelation in Christ and as unfolded in the history of the church's response to that revelation. To be dogmatic, then, is to be unapologetically confessional, which requires being unapologetic about the determinate character of our confession, contra the Cartesian anxiety exhibited by much postmodern theology. This should translate into a robust appropriation of the church's language as the paradigm for both thought and practice. (123)

To all this, seven things must be said.

(1) Smith has described the classic weakness of all "hard"[68] postmodernists, but he does not refute it; he comes very close to adopting it. "We can't *know* that God was in Christ reconciling the world to himself," the postmodern theologian says. "The best we can do is *believe*."[69] And why is that? "Because to know would mean being certain." And then this theologian adds, without a trace of embarrassment, "We know [*sic!*] that such certainty is an impossible dream." The harder the postmodernism, the more absolute the claim, and the more internally illogical it is. If the postmodern theologian *knows* that such certainty is impossible, he or she must know it *certainly*. But that means certain knowledge is not impossible after all. On the other hand, if the postmodern theologian merely misspoke, and merely *believes* that such certainty is impossible, then perhaps he or she is mistaken. I have seen many "hard" postmoderns fall into this trap of internal incoherence, but rarely so unambiguously and in the space of two adjacent sentences. There is no reason to think that Smith himself wants to follow this line of reasoning without caveat, even though he says that much in this postmodern stance "has been rightly affirmed." Yet he has bought into it enough that he can write, "It is pre-

---

68. By "hard" in this context, I have in mind those postmoderns who set the modern/postmodern polarity in sharpest antithesis, insisting that moderns seek certainty and that the only viable alternative, postmodernism, eschews it. See the earlier discussion.

69. All of the ensuing quotations are from the two block quotes above, so I will not repeat all the references here.

cisely this refusal of the Cartesian paradigm that characterizes Radical Orthodoxy" — and this becomes his warrant for siding with Augustine (whom, it appears, he misunderstands: see below). In other words, if Smith had exposed the internal incoherence of the archetypal postmodern theologian he is discussing, instead of adopting this rejection of "the Cartesian paradigm," he would have found it far more difficult to make his next moves toward Radical Orthodoxy.

(2) The notion that all Cartesians think that knowledge is tied to certainty is so easily falsifiable that it is a little tiresome to see it trotted out again. In fact, a substantial number of "soft" postmoderns avoid this pitfall the way they would an E. coli infection. But once we acknowledge that many moderns seek "certainty" in relative terms only and distance themselves dramatically from implicit claims to omniscience, then the polarity that drives Smith's argument breaks down. I have already discussed the ways in which "soft" postmoderns and chastened moderns can listen to each other more sympathetically, and need not repeat the argument here.

(3) Once again it is important to return to the actual language of Scripture. Biblical writers are not embarrassed to talk about truth, including propositional truth; equally, they are not at all hesitant to speak about knowing people, knowing God — and knowing things and knowing truths. When Luke introduces his Gospel, he tells Theophilus that he is writing "that you may *know* the *certainty* of *the things you have been taught*" (Luke 1:4, emphasis added). After his resurrection, Jesus "presented himself to [his disciples] and gave *many convincing proofs* that he was alive" (Acts 1:3). Of course, many biblical writers also stress the crucial importance of faith. My point is that they can talk about faith *and* truth, about believing *and* knowing. Clearly this knowing is not the knowledge of omniscience; the "certainty" that Luke wants Theophilus to enjoy is not the certainty that belongs to God alone. But this is the language of Scripture, and it is entirely appropriate to the modes and extent of knowing of which human beings are capable.

(4) That brings us to Augustine, "I believe, therefore I understand." Since Smith does not tell us what he thinks the noun "faith" or the verb "to believe" mean, I am not quite certain that I have understood him aright. But in common with other theologians in the Radical Orthodoxy movement, I think he has slightly skewed the meaning

of these words from the semantic range found in the New Testament and in Augustine.

Begin with Paul's statement in his letter to the Corinthians of what the gospel is (1 Corinthians 15:1-11). One of the non-negotiable components of the gospel, Paul asserts, is the resurrection of Jesus Christ. As part of his argument, Paul dares to ask what the implications would be if Jesus had *not* been raised from the dead (15:12-19). He lists several: (a) The eyewitnesses who claimed to have seen the resurrected Jesus turn out to be liars. Note: the issue is *truth*-telling, that is, witnesses giving reports that conform to reality. Obviously, neither the witnesses nor the Corinthians claim an omniscient grasp of the resurrection: the witness is necessarily perspectival. But Paul insists that it must be a true witness, that is, that the report must conform to reality, or else the witnesses are liars. The truth of Jesus' resurrection, then, is "objective" in the sense that it takes place *out there,* in space/time history, in the real world, even if human beings can never claim epistemological objectivity of the sort that belongs only to Omniscience. (b) If Jesus has not risen from the dead, then people are still lost. The assumption, of course, is that other realities the Bible talks about remain *true,* including the fact that we are lost in our trespasses and sins *unless* Jesus died and rose again on our behalf. (c) The faith of the Corinthian believers is futile. In other words, part of what validates faith, in Paul's understanding of faith, is that faith's object must be true. If the Corinthians believe that Jesus rose from the dead, but in fact he did not rise from the dead, their faith is invalidated by the fact that faith's object is false. Of course, faith is more than recognition that something is true. In the Bible, faith characteristically involves trust in God and his Word, trust in God's Son. In Hebrews, faith includes the element of perseverance (see how strong that element is in Hebrews 11, for instance). But without exception, faith is invalidated if its object is untrustworthy, or, where ostensible facts are concerned, if the object of faith is not true. The Bible *never* encourages us to put our faith in what may or may not be true. (d) It follows that if we believe something that is *not* true, "we are to be pitied more than all others" (15:19). In other words, Paul does not think faith is virtuous because those who exercise the faith are sincere or devout. Faith without a true object, Paul asserts, is pitiful.

In much of the Western world, however, faith is not at all tied to the truthfulness or reliability of its object. Faith is little more than personal, subjective, religious preference. Many people think that faith is utterly nonfalsifiable, and therefore competing faiths cannot usefully or realistically be discussed. Mercifully, Smith does not go so far. Yet for him, "faith will always be mysterious and ambiguous." Well, yes and no: faith is mysterious in that where it is *true* faith (in the Pauline sense) it is not only something that we exercise but also a gift from God (e.g., Ephesians 2:8-10). I suppose we might say that there are ambiguous elements in faith in that we trust God and his Word even where we cannot clearly see the way ahead. But the point to observe is that in the Bible it is *right* to trust this God with the future, not because of what we do not see or know, but because of what we *have* come to know of this God — including such *truth* as the *fact* that God raised his own dear Son from the dead for our justification. Faith enables us to have confidence in God where we do *not* see, because it is grounded in the immutable character of God that we *have* come by grace to perceive as utterly reliable. Smith does not work this out, for he is too busy trying to distinguish faith from knowing, introducing a polarity utterly unknown in Scripture.

When Augustine writes, "I believe, therefore I understand," he thinks of faith in a *biblical* sense, not in Smith's slightly woolly sense, still less in the street sense of much Western subjectivism. Over against modernism's autonomous human thinker, Augustine knows full well that we Christians are finite, dependent, created, redeemed beings. The beginning of all understanding is faith in the God who has made us and redeemed us in Christ. Neither in Augustine nor in the New Testament does this mean that we should abandon offering "many convincing proofs" in Luke's sense (Acts 1:3), or "reason for the hope you have" in Peter's sense (1 Peter 3:15). We still follow Paul when we say, "Since, then, we know what it is to fear the Lord, we try to persuade people" (2 Corinthians 5:11). At the same time, we recognize that if anyone is in fact persuaded and comes to understand these things, it is because of the gracious work of the Spirit of God in their lives (1 Corinthians 2:14). And always we insist that what we are urging people to believe is the truth, not because we claim to have gained access to this truth from an epistemologically neutral vantage point, but because it conforms to what God has given, whether people acknowledge it or not. Augustine's "I believe, therefore I understand," is therefore a world away from Derrida's "I don't know; I must believe." Augustine, like Paul (e.g., Galatians 2:15-18; Romans 3:27-31), emphasizes the epistemic necessity of faith; but, like Paul, he insists that what he is talking about is "the truth of the gospel" (Galatians 2:14), which is precisely what Derrida could *not* affirm.

(5) Where Smith carefully distances himself from his imaginary interlocutor, from the "postmodern theologian," it is over the former's commitment to confessional orthodoxy. At one level, this is immensely reassuring. On what basis, then, does Smith espouse this confessional orthodoxy and commend it to his postmodern contemporaries? I must take up again the second block quote cited above, and this time highlight one repeated word:

> This is not to advocate a return to an uncritical fundamentalism or the triumphalist stance of the Religious Right. Rather, it is to affirm that our *confession* and practice must proceed unapologetically from the particularities of Christian *confession* as given in God's historical revelation in Christ and as unfolded in the history of the church's response to that revelation. To be dogmatic, then, is to be unapologetically *confessional,* which requires being unapologetic about the determinate character of our *confession,* contra the Cartesian anxiety exhibited by much postmodern theology. This should translate into a robust appropriation of the church's language as the paradigm for both thought and practice.

So near, and yet so far. This is typical of Radical Orthodoxy: it simply isn't very "radical," for it fails to get to the *radix,* the root, of anything. It rightly applauds Christian belief structures and Christian conduct, in line with historic orthodoxy and orthopraxy. For this we are grateful. Yet it cannot give a reason for this move other than saying that we affirm that our *confession* proceeds from the particularities of Christian *confession* — unapologetically, even! Well, yes, that is not exactly false: Christian confessionalism ought to be in line with historic Christian confessionalism. But is the content of historic Christian confessionalism *true?* Do we believe this merely because earlier Christians have believed it? I do not think that Smith would want to be so minimalistic. This confession, he writes, is "given in God's historical revelation in Christ and [is] unfolded in the history of the church's response to that revelation." Great. Is the revelation *true,* or do we confess the revelation simply because others have confessed it? Both the New Testament writers and Augustine unambiguously affirm the *truthfulness* of this revelation and are prepared to give reasons for holding to it, even while they insist that faith is necessary to come to terms with it — not faith in some subjective sense, nor merely in some confessional sense that is divorced from truth claims, but faith in the robust epistemic sense that has objects proclaimed to be *true.*[70]

(6) Smith's last sentence in that block quote, "This should translate into a robust appropriation of the church's language as the paradigm for both thought and practice," is his way of tipping his hat in the direction of the postliberal theology characteristic of the Yale school. Once again there is much to be thankful for in this appeal. Christians *ought* to be familiar with the cultural-linguistic language of Scripture, using it comfortably such that it shapes our thoughts and conduct. But if that is *all* that is said, it simply does not go far enough. In fact, it is a disturbingly intellectualist approach: let us align our cultural-linguistic expressions with those of Scripture, and we will think in line with Christian confessionalism and all be better people for it. Yet the biblical cultural-linguistic matrix is not an end in itself. We are not saved and transformed by linguistic expressions that talk *about* God and Christ and the gospel. Rather, we are saved and transformed by God, by Christ, by the good news of Christ crucified and risen, and all that flows from this triumph of grace. *Of course* we should be steeped in the cultural-linguistic matrix of the biblical reve-

70. Implicit in Smith's position is another obscurity typical of Radical Orthodoxy: it masks distinctions that must be made between the authority of Scripture and the authority of later tradition. This is not to give in to the sort of "Bible alone" approach that is willfully ignorant of how Christians across the ages have wrestled with the "givenness" of Scripture or that acts as if contemporary interpreters of Scripture somehow stand outside cultural location. None of the Reformers who robustly espoused *sola Scriptura* aligned themselves with such ignorance. Yet the Reformers were right to locate final authority in the God who has given Scripture, not in the people who articulate their confession.

lation, hiding Scripture in our hearts, reflecting on and delighting in God's words and ways. But we ought to do so because what this biblical revelation tells us of God and his ways is *true*. We proclaim it because it is *the truth*. We are not saved by words about the cross (no matter how biblical), but by the cross. Of course, we do not have access to the cross apart from words: in that sense, Derrida is right. But the words themselves insist that we trust the God and his actions to which the words point. Failure to see and emphasize the extratextual reality is merely an intellectualist idolatry. We proclaim the God who is there (as Schaeffer taught us to say), the incarnated Word, the death and resurrection of God's Son, the historic bestowal of the Spirit — even as we cheerfully acknowledge that we cannot make such proclamation *apart* from words. Like Radical Orthodoxy, postliberalism typically stops one crucial step too soon.

(7) *Who's Afraid of Postmodernism?* Smith's title asks. Well, not I, though I confess I am getting a bit bored with it. Surely thoughtful Christians should avoid too close an alignment with either modernism or postmodernism, for both are far too heavily dependent on the "I" or the "we" of Cartesian thought. Yet there are things to learn from both modernism and postmodernism (though Smith wants to learn only from the latter). It does no good to camp out with those moderns who demonize postmodernism, for in fact, whether we like it or not, we are all perspectivalists; equally, it does no good to camp out with those postmoderns who demonize modernism, for in fact, within the limitations of what it means to be a finite creature touched by grace, we can know and proclaim the truth.

FOUR

Secularism, Democracy, Freedom, and Power

—⁓⁓—

The attempt to refine what we mean by "culture" and how to think about postmodernism sets the stage for this chapter. The empirical realities of the larger culture are enormously diverse. Inevitably, the kinds of pressures they generate push Christians, and everybody else, in many different directions. In the Western world, these various directions are frequently responses to four huge cultural forces: the seduction of secularization, the mystique of democracy, the worship of freedom, and the lust for power. These are not the only important cultural forces, whether in the West or elsewhere; I am not even insisting that these are the most important ones. But their power to shape cultures in many parts of the world, not least in the West, provides an opportunity to compare the shaping of culture by such forces as these with the shaping of culture effected by allegiance to the Bible and its story line, culminating in Jesus Christ and his gospel.

The Lure of Secularization

Part of the challenge is definition. On the lips of many, not all of them secularists, "secular" is a word with positive overtones. It calls to mind Jesus' insistence that Caesar, as well as God, is to be given his due. It forces us to recall the theory of Gelasius: there are two swords of legitimate power. Even "secularization," which customarily refers to the process, sometimes has a positive ring. One remembers Peter Berger's description of the de-divinization of nature,[1] which left in place God's order over nature, with enough space to live without fear of the demonic and to begin genuinely scientific exploration. But "secular*ism*" is usually understood to be the social reality that fosters nonreligious or even anti-religious consciousness.

In more popular parlance, however, all three words — "secular," "secularization," and "secularism" — have to do with the squeezing of the religious to the periphery of life. More precisely, secularization is the process that progressively removes religion from the public arena and reduces it to the private realm; secularism is the stance that endorses and promotes such a process.[2] Religion may be ever so important to the individual, and few secular persons will object. But if religion makes any claims regarding policy in the public arena, it is viewed as a threat, and intolerant as well.

In reality, the social pressures of secularization are far more unrelenting than this simple distinction between private religion and public religion suggests. To preserve Christian faith even in one's private life is viewed by many as a mark of weakness. If "God" has any place at all, it is not outside human consciousness. Religion in general and Christianity in particular may have some instrumental value, but not much; religion may have some mythological value as that which represents the best and noblest in the human spirit, but to reify the myth is to depreciate humanism.[3] Nowhere is this pressure more powerful than in our universities.[4] Christian faith must not only be private in the sense that it is not permitted to have a voice in direction, priorities, literary theory, science, or anything else, but

1. Peter L. Berger, *The Sacred Canopy: Elements of a Sociological Theory of Religion* (Garden City: Doubleday, 1969). (The British title is *The Social Reality of Religion*.)

2. That is the usage, for instance, in the important book edited by Christian Smith, *The Secular Revolution: Power, Interests, and Conflict in the Secularization of American Public Life* (Berkeley: University of California Press, 2003).

3. That, essentially, is the view of David Boulton, *The Trouble with God: Building the Republic of Heaven* (New Alresford: John Hunt Publishing, 2002).

4. See especially George M. Marsden and B. J. Longfield, eds., *The Secularization of the Academy* (New York: Oxford University Press, 1992); George M. Marsden, *The Soul of the American University: From Protestant Establishment to Established Nonbelief* (New York: Oxford University Press, 1994).

it must also be so private that it becomes invisible: Christians become nervous about talking of their faith and thus become unpracticed in witness.

Where secularism becomes as vehement as that, it is, *de facto,* a "religion": it strongly advocates its own view of the ultimate good, it articulates its own belief system, it establishes its own code of ethics. For instance, the Anti-Defamation League, a strong voice for secularism — David Klinghoffer amusingly comments that the group "is Jewish only in the sense that bagels are Jewish"[5] — provides a recommended reading list for school children that ostensibly fosters "anti-bias education" but inevitably advances secular teaching on, say, homosexuality: for example, *Gloria Goes to Gay Pride,* according to the group's website, is summarized this way: "A young girl participates in the Gay Pride Day parade."

Apart from the obvious attractions of secularism's appeal, there are more seductive subtleties that need to be challenged. I mention three.

(1) A considerable literature argues — or, worse, presupposes — that the processes of secularization, as understood here, are historically inevitable. Secularization thus becomes tied, in popular outlook, to the effluent from the Enlightenment, to material prosperity, and above all to the idea of progress. Today there is a small but growing and important riposte that questions these connections.[6]

(2) More subtle yet is the pressure to drift toward what Avery Cardinal Dulles calls "the Deist minimum."[7] Deism — whether in the form espoused by Thomas Jefferson, which judged Christianity, as he (mis)understood it, to be the highest form of religion, or in the French form espoused by Thomas Paine, following the *encyclopédistes,* who were profoundly opposed to Christianity — has produced, in the West, "a favorable climate in which the various forms of biblical reli-

---

5. "Speaking Out: That Other Church," *Christianity Today* 49/1 (January 2005): 62.

6. See the survey by Richard John Neuhaus, "Secularization Doesn't Just Happen," *First Things* 151 (March 2005): 58-61. In particular, see Christian Smith, *The Secular Revolution;* and Christopher Lasch, *The True and Only Heaven: Progress and Its Critics* (New York: Norton, 1991).

7. "The Deist Minimum," *First Things* 149 (January 2005): 25-30.

gion could and did thrive."[8] The heritage of this Deism left various forms of civil religion that believed in one God, in God-sanctioned moral law, in some loose form of providence, and in some kind of rewards and punishments after death (with much greater emphasis on the rewards than on the punishments!).

Unfortunately, however, naive Christians often think that these signs of residual civil religion and the Deism on which they are based constitute solid evidence of Christian commitments. Conversely, they see the erosion of civil religion, and the Deism on which it is based, as an erosion of genuinely Christian commitments. Neither assessment is realistic. Worse yet, some Christians, more knowledgeable but not necessarily wiser, are tempted to speak to public issues solely in the categories of Deism, hoping thus to gain wider exposure and establish a broader consensus. At a certain level of public policy, they may on occasion be right. But arguing for morality from the assumption of Deism is a far cry from upholding Christianity. Deism has no power to check the advances of secularization, for it is religion without either robust intellectual defense or genuine power. Deism is not a halfway house between secularism and Christianity; it is in fact a form of secularism.

At the popular level, this instinctive lust to accommodate contemporary cultural predilections produces the self-help bromides of a Joel Osteen, which are easily detached from Scripture for the very good reason that they are not, despite superficial appearances, grounded in Scripture.[9] Equally, it produces various strands of "liberal" Christianity that take their cues from contemporary cultural agendas much more readily than from the Bible. Most of these latter strands are in serious decline: "To the degree that this form of Christianity has assimilated itself to the dominant ethos, reasons for anyone joining it are harder to come by."[10]

8. Dulles, "The Deist Minimum," 29.

9. Joel Osteen, *Your Best Life Now: Seven Steps to Living at Your Full Potential* (New York: Warner Faith, 2004). His seven steps to "living at your full potential" are: (1) enlarge your vision; (2) develop a healthy self-image; (3) discover the power of your thoughts and words; (4) let go of the past; (5) find strength through adversity; (6) live to give; (7) choose to be happy.

10. Luke Timothy Johnson, *The Misguided Quest for the Historical Jesus and the Truth of the Traditional Gospels* (New York: Harper Collins, 1996), 64.

(3) As Western culture becomes more polarized, the barriers to meaningful interaction between, on the one hand, Christians who are trying to be faithful to the Bible, and, on the other, people who are committed to one form or another of secularism, become more acute. At one level, of course, this is scarcely a new problem, even if the nature of the polarity varies over time. It can be argued, for instance, that what the eighteenth-century philosopher David Hume so strenuously set himself against was not historic confessional Christianity but a form of christianized British natural theology.[11] Yet most observers hold that in recent decades the polarization of positions has become both more extreme and considerably more hardened. But I shall return to this observation in the next section.

At this point we must reflect briefly on the culture of those who thoughtfully espouse secularism and the culture of those who thoughtfully espouse biblically informed Christianity. At the risk of repetition, I must again underscore the fact that these two groups may embrace many shared cultural values. Even within the orbit of things discussed here, both groups may warmly espouse a shared commitment to some form or other of the separation of church and state — even though the reasons each group advances for supporting the separation of church and state may be quite different. To secularists, God, if he exists, is not the sort of personal being whose mandates extend beyond personal religious experience and perhaps general moral tenets; to Christians, their own Master has taught them that some sort of distinction between Christ and Caesar must be maintained, with each receiving his due. I shall return to this subject in the next chapter. But after all such caveats have been entered, *the way one views the world* is quite different in the two groups: in short, their *worldviews* are different, and so the cultures they espouse and reflect are decidedly different.[12] To the one, the processes of secularization spell liberation from (false views of) God and the maturation of what it means to be human; to the other, the very basis of what it means to be human is established by God himself, and all attempts to

11. That is the perceptive suggestion of Kirsten Birkett, "A Treatise of Hume's Nature," *Case* 7 (2005): 7-12.

12. See Pope Benedict XVI, *Christianity and the Crisis of Cultures* (San Francisco: Ignatius, 2006). (The European title is *The Europe of Benedict: In the Crisis of Cultures*.)

liberate oneself from God are nothing more than further instances of idolatry. To the one, ethics is finally grounded in the will of legislatures, or in international law, or in contemporary political agendas that promise liberation of various kinds; to the other, ethics must finally be grounded in God's gracious revelation, or it proves not only unstable but massively destructive.[13]

Christians whose worldview — whose way of looking at the world[14] — is decisively shaped by the Bible's story line cannot forget that we human beings have been made in the image of God; that our first obligation is to recognize our creatureliness, and thus our joyful obligation to our Creator; that sin is nothing other than de-godding God; that our dignity as God's image bearers is horribly marred by our rebellion; that the entire race, and all of human history, is rushing toward final accountability before this God who is no less our Judge than our Maker; that there is a new heaven and a new earth to gain and a hell to fear; that our sole hope of reconciliation with this God is by the means he himself has provided in his Son; that the people of God are made up of human beings from every language and tribe and nation, and, empowered by God's Spirit, are growing in personal and corporate obedience and love, rejoicing to come under the reign of God in anticipation of the consummation of that reign. Meanwhile, we are enjoined to do good to all, especially — but certainly not exclusively! — those of the household of faith. In other words, Christianity does not claim to convey merely religious truth, but truth about all reality.[15] However complicated the issues may be, however disputed the way ahead may be, this vision of reality is radically different from a secularist vision that wants Christianity to scuttle into the corner of

13. One contemplates with horror the dimensions of evil reflected in the tragic reality that, during the twentieth century, about 170 million human beings were murdered by their own governments, quite apart from the losses in wars. See the website "Freedom, Democracy, Peace; Power, Democide, and War," at www.hawaii.edu/powerkills/welcome.html (last accessed 18 February 2006).

14. I will not here again take up the challenge of those who deny there is such a thing as a "worldview." By worldview I mean, as I explained in chapter 3, a reasonably comprehensive interpretation of reality (whether thought through or not) that affects all we do. Everyone has one.

15. That is the central thesis of Nancy R. Pearcey and Phillip E. Johnson, *Total Truth: Liberating Christianity from Its Cultural Captivity* (Wheaton: Crossway, 2004).

the hearth by the coal shovel, conveniently out of the way of anything but private religious concerns. Christians informed by the sweep of the Bible's story line will not be intimidated, for instance, by academic sneering. As Paul in Athens was distressed by the idolatry he witnessed in that highly sophisticated and learned city (Acts 17:16), so Christians today will learn to ask the question, "What does Jesus Christ think of the university?"[16] Not to ask the question is already to sell the pass. Conflict between two cultures, both of which are making sweeping but mutually conflicting claims, is inevitable.

In much common usage, "authenticity" refers to something narrowly personal. It means something like "being sincere." An "authentic" person is someone who is not a hypocrite. But how is authenticity to be measured, unless there is a standard by which to assess the integrity or the hypocrisy? "Authentic Christians" are not those who are merely very sincere and who call themselves Christians. If "authenticity" is to retain any utility in this discussion, the "authentic Christian" is the one who is most shaped in thought, word, and deed by Christianity's foundational documents, by Christianity's Lord, by Christianity's creeds.[17] That is one of the reasons why reading and rereading the Bible, and knowing and reciting the creeds, are part and parcel of what gives us the categories and labels by which we think. Of course, it is possible to enjoy a merely professional knowledge of such

16. That is precisely the point made by Charles Malik, *A Christian Critique of the University* (Waterloo, ON: North Waterloo Academic Press, 1987), 24-25. The same point is picked up by Duane Litfin, *Conceiving the Christian College* (Grand Rapids: Eerdmans, 2004), 79. According to Litfin, Malik "does not presume the validity of the *secular* [emphasis mine] academic world and then ask what that world thinks of Jesus Christ; he starts with the most profound truth the race has known, the Lordship of Jesus Christ, and then asks in its light what we are to make of the university." Indeed, it has long been noted that the idea of a *uni*versity, as opposed to a *multi*versity, presupposes a unity of truth best safeguarded in the glad confession that all truth is God's truth: cf. D. A. Carson, "Can There Be a Christian University?" *Southern Baptist Journal of Theology* 1/3 (1998): 20-38, and the literature cited there.

17. This is one of the valid emphases of Radical Orthodoxy — though admittedly its adherents tend to lay rather more stress on the ancient creeds than on the Scriptures themselves. But the commitment of the project to reconstruct the way we talk about reality is highly salutary. For a competent introduction to the movement and its chief proponents, see James K. A. Smith, *Introducing Radical Orthodoxy: Mapping a Post-Secular Theology* (Grand Rapids: Baker; Bletchley: Paternoster, 2004).

sources. Authentic Christianity demands more: a love for the God who has thereby disclosed himself, a response to him in obedience and faith. But it is futile to speak of loving and trusting and obeying this God if his words do not delight us and terrify us and instruct us and shape us. When they do, our worldview is progressively transformed, and the culture of which we are a part, and which we pass on to others, cannot help but diverge from the culture of those who embrace the processes of secularization. In such instances, Christ and culture are heading in different directions.

The Mystique of Democracy

Most people in the West would say, unhesitatingly, that democracy is a good thing. Certainly in America, the notion that democracy ushers in peace and is therefore the right of all human beings has influenced government foreign policy for almost a century — since Woodrow Wilson's Fourteen Points. Undeniably, the establishment of democracy has brought about magnificent transformations. Out of the rubble of World War II, out of the failed totalitarian régimes of the Land of the Rising Sun and the Thousand Year Reich, emerged two strong democracies. Democracy kept on rolling through Western Europe: Italy, Greece, Spain. It proved a remarkable triumph in South Korea. It was one of the grand ideas that contributed to the overthrow of the Soviet empire, most of whose former satellites are moving, at various rates, toward less totalitarian and more democratic ideals. Part of the impetus behind the current military conflicts in Afghanistan and Iraq is the hope that well-established democracies in those countries will not only overcome their respective internal divisions but also become attractive magnets throughout the Middle East, drawing other Muslim countries toward the benefits of democratic government, free markets, relative freedoms, and fewer outbursts of fanatical aggression. No one brought up under a democratic form of government can remain ignorant of its many inconsistencies, of course — its fumblings, inefficiencies, and corruptions; none can be unaware of how thin may be the line between democracy and demagoguery. Even so, one has to be extraordinarily ignorant of history not to sympathize with the oft-repeated assessment of Winston Churchill: democracy is the worst form of government, except for all the other kinds.

Before we reflect on the ways in which democracy helps to establish a culture that is rather adjacent to, and sometimes in conflict with, the demands of Christ, it is worth remembering that democracy is a complex phenomenon. The complexity extends from form to underlying ideology to degree of maturity. The relatively direct but certainly restrictive democracy of ancient Athens is rather different from the complex levels of voting in the United States, where even the president is voted in through the mediating institution of the electoral college. Different countries call up competing mythologies. The United Kingdom harks back to 1215 and the *Magna Carta* and proudly remembers that Westminster is the "mother of all parliaments" — though its history since the thirteenth century has included various civil wars, one regicide, the institution and abolition of slavery, and the rise and fall of the British Empire. The French dwell fondly on the Revolution of 1789, the overthrow of clericalism, and the elevation of *liberté, égalité, fraternité* — but of course the French Revolution led directly to Robespierre's Reign of Terror and to the Napoleonic Wars, while the exigencies of history have, since 1789, driven France through two empires, two monarchies, two dictatorships, and, the last time I counted, five republics. America is justly proud of its Constitution and attendant Bill of Rights, of a form of government with well-defined divisions of power, but this form of democracy did not prevent the Civil War (proportionately the bloodiest war, by far, in its history), its long struggles over slavery and racism, miscellaneous assassinations and attempted assassinations of its presidents, and of course the usual assortment of injustices, inequities, instances of manipulative populism, and embarrassing mistakes in foreign policy.

One of the strengths of Ketcham's recent book[18] is its careful delineation of the quite different roots of democracy in, say, North America, Europe, and Asia. For instance, the Confucian ideological contributions to many Asian forms of democracy have steered democracy toward hierarchical and communal ideals rather removed from

---

18. Ralph Ketcham, *The Idea of Democracy in the Modern Era* (Lawrence: University Press of Kansas, 2004).

most Western forms of democracy. One might also ponder how democracies evolve. The changes may be so slow that it is not impertinent to ask the question, "When did the United Kingdom become a democracy?" — and recognize that no simple answer will prove convincing. Or consider how strongly most of the framers of the U.S. Constitution saw democracy not so much as a form of government in which wisdom is found in majority opinion, but as a form of government in which accountability to the people is established, with mechanisms for turfing out the "rulers" every few years before their individual power, not to say the power of government itself, becomes both unresponsive and corrupt.[19] By contrast, today's politicians of all stripes are inclined to appeal to "the wisdom of the American [substitute "French," "British," "Canadian," etc.] people."

More challenging yet are the "democracies" that preserve almost none of the freedoms and values that most in the West traditionally associate with "democracy." Many a ruler in sub-Saharan black Africa has been elected with reasonable fairness, and begins with the genuine support of the majority of the people, only to turn into a tyrant who is ousted only by a coup. The democratically elected governments recently put into place in Iraq and Afghanistan are still very fragile (especially the former), and neither is anywhere near as supportive of "freedom of religion" as are the democracies of the West — but in all fairness, "freedom of religion" does not look like quite the same issue when 99 percent of the people of Afghanistan are Muslim. The reasons voters put in some government or other are so complex that what is mandated by the vote is not always easy to discern. Many have argued, for instance, and with some justification, that the recent Palestinian vote (2006) that put Hamas into power sprang less from a majority resolution of the Palestinian people to wipe out Israel than from being fed up with the obscene corruption of Arafat and his cronies — a more sensational version of the vote in Québec that brought

19. Nowhere is this clearer than in *The Federalist Papers,* of course. But it is also well worth perusing the collection edited by Bernard Bailyn, *The Debate on the Constitution: Federalist and Antifederalist Speeches, Articles, and Letters During the Struggle over Ratification,* 2 vols. (New York: The Library of America, 1993), which includes not only much of the work of James Madison and Alexander Hamilton but also that of many others, including their opponents.

the *Parti Québecois* into power, not because there was a clear majority commitment to secede from the rest of Canada (as the subsequent referendum demonstrated), but because a majority of voters was fed up with the squabbling, parochialism, and corruption of the more traditional parties. In a word, democracy is messy.

Many serious commentators have noted that to have a reasonably stable democracy in the Western sense, various conditions must prevail. At the very least, there must be an independent judiciary, a free press, some system of equality before the law (usually with an enshrined constitution and a disciplined police force), structures to ensure that the military is under civilian control, and a system of changing who is in charge without bloodshed (usually a stable two-party or multi-party system). One can add other *desiderata,* such as a reasonable level of education in the populace, but the idea is pretty clear: what most Westerners mean by "democracy" might well be labeled "liberal democracy," over against the "illiberal democracies" that have sprung up in many parts of the world. The latter expression, "illiberal democracies," is Zakaria's, whose penetrating book argues that superficial democratic forms of government, without real measures of assured liberty already in place, readily give rise to totalitarianism — demonstrated in the rise of fascism in the twentieth century.[20] In other words, a democratic vote or two doesn't establish very much. Ideally, it will be the first step toward something more substantial,[21] but an illiberal democracy may pass a vote, even a reasonably clean vote, merely to justify a tyrant, a butcher, or an ideologue (religious or otherwise). There is no evidence of which I am aware that the recent vote in Iran was substantially corrupt, but the new president, President Mahmoud Ahmadinejad, belongs to that remarkable subset of human beings who deny that the Holocaust took place. He still vows to wipe Israel off the map. As he tightens the imposition of Muslim *shari'a* at home, Christians in that country are feeling the pressure from fresh rounds of violent persecution. It appears, then, that in

20. Fareed Zakaria, *The Future of Freedom: Illiberal Democracy at Home and Abroad* (New York: Norton, 2004).

21. That is, of course, the assumption in a book with the moral clarity of Natan Sharansky, *The Case for Democracy: The Power of Freedom to Overcome Tyranny and Terror* (New York: Public Affairs, 2004).

Iran, Christ and culture are bound to clash, in substantial measure, for years to come. Yet this government was democratically elected. Obviously, then, thoughtful Christians cannot happily espouse every appeal to democracy.

But let us restrict ourselves now to Western democracies, democracies that have enjoyed a sustained history of the freedoms we largely take for granted. From the Western perspective, the only democracy worthy of the name is surrounded by assorted liberties and safeguards; it is what Zakaria calls a liberal democracy. What about such democracy? How will Christians think of it?

Some years ago, I talked with a pastor in Slovakia. He said that when the Berlin wall came down, almost immediately new freedoms were introduced into his country. A mere three weeks later, for the very first time in his life he had seen pornography sold on the streets of Bratislava. That is not a development Christians will applaud — but neither is a complete subjugation of the press by the government. In short, freedom brings with it many good things, but precisely because we human beings are capable of corrupting any system whatsoever, inevitably it has the potential for bringing with it many evil things, too. Experts tell us that the income from the sale of porn in North America now outstrips income from the sale of alcohol, illegal drugs, and cigarettes *combined*.

The issue is much more complicated than what is suggested by the story related by the Slovak pastor. Majority rule means there is also a minority. There is no particular reason to think that the majority will always, or even often, sympathize with Christian ideals. With the rapid self-distancing of most Western countries from their Judeo-Christian heritage, the polarities between the views of the democratic majority and the view of the Christian minority — and similarly, of course, from other minorities — loom larger. In theory, democracy tries to protect the rights of minorities; in reality, that is a very tricky thing. Sometimes legislators and judges have been so concerned to protect the minority that the views of the majority are ignored.[22] But where the views of the minority are shaped by religious commit-

22. See, for instance, Richard John Neuhaus, "The Tyranny of the Minority," *First Things* 154 (June/July 2005): 63-64.

ments, especially Christian commitments, there the Jeffersonian "wall of separation between church and state" has for some time demanded the privatization of religion — which brings us back to the challenge of secularization, described in the first section of this chapter. If Christians weigh in on, say, abortion, homosexuality, or stem cell research, they are inevitably charged with smuggling Christianity into the public arena, where it does not belong. If they weigh in, as Christians, on, say, the homeless, the poor, public welfare, and consumerism, then they are widely (if sometimes condescendingly) thought to have prophetic voices.

There is an array of issues here that must be probed a little more deeply. The nature of freedom has been inserted into the argument, and I shall briefly reflect on that subject in the next section. The relation between church and state is clearly a broader issue than the appeal to democracy itself, and I must return to the larger issue in the next chapter, for Christians have given quite disparate accounts of what "the" Christian view of the state should be. For now it is enough to underline the fact that even these preliminary reflections demonstrate that Christians cannot possibly view democracy as "the cure" for the world's ills. For many pragmatic and moral reasons, we may concur that, granted attendant structures and liberties, it is the form of government least unaccountable to the people and least likely to brutalize its citizens without some eventual accounting. It is a form of government most likely to foster personal freedoms, including, usually, freedoms for Christians to practice and propagate their faith. But it has also proved proficient at throwing off a sense of obligation to God the Creator, let alone the God and Father of our Lord Jesus Christ, which is another way of saying that it is proficient at fostering idolatry. Its freedoms, so many of which are enormously praiseworthy for political, religious, personal, and artistic reasons, include the freedom to be hedonists, to pursue a life revolving around entertainment, to become inured against responsible family life, communal interaction, and self-denying service in the endless worship of massive egos, passing fads, and this-worldly glitter. Laying up treasures in heaven does not seem to be on the radar screen of many Christians. Christians with a firm grasp of the Bible's story line from creation to consummation, even while they offer thanks for the freedoms that democracy provides, will not overlook the fact that democracy, rule by the people, what we might call the kingdominion of the people, cannot compete for righteousness with the kingdominion of God. History coughs up many examples where democracy cannot be counted on to do the right thing: one need go no further than Weimar Germany. Taking into account what the Bible says about the moral accountability of people and nations alike, we may sometimes wonder how long it will be before God calls to account some of the major democracies of the West, as he has done by war and plague in the past, as he has done with respect to every civilization in the past. For this remains God's world, a world in which righteousness exalts a nation, while sin condemns any people (Proverbs 14:34). Even while Christians are being tugged, by Scripture itself, to being good citizens, not least within a democracy, their ultimate citizenship, and thus their ultimate loyalty, lies elsewhere (Hebrews 13:14). Tensions between Christ and culture are unavoidable because tensions between democracy and religion are unavoidable.[23]

The Worship of Freedom

By now readers of this chapter will have detected that the four sections that make it up are not independent but intertwined. We have already seen how the lure of secularization is inescapably tied to the mystique of (especially Western) democracy. Democracy is also irrefragably tied to notions of freedom. Yet freedom is far more than a political category. One may be "free" from the constraints of the state, but one may also be "free" from traditions, free from God, free from morality, free from inhibitions, free from oppressive parents, free from wise parents, free from assignments of various kinds, free from sin, and much more. Americans like to think of themselves as inhabiting "the land of the free," and thus are inclined to assign freedom or liberty to the very highest rank among the virtues. "Live free or die," one state slogan puts it. It is hard to imagine any state with the slogan,

23. See the many thoughtful essays in the Spring 2004 anniversary issue of *Public Interest.*

"Be holy or die" — so once again, without for a moment disavowing the many ways in which Christians want to embrace freedom, it is easy to uncover ways in which the worship of freedom may actually displace the worship of God. Christ and culture may at some points share common perspectives, but it is not hard to see how they are likely to clash.

We must probe a little more deeply into the nature of freedom from state coercion. In America, while the right bemoans the power of the left in some sectors — in particular, the media, the courts, and the universities — the left bewails the power of the right in the executive and legislative branches of government during much of the last twenty-five years. Some of the most fascinating purple prose was written after the 2004 elections. "[W]hat troubled me yesterday," Tom Friedman wrote in *The New York Times,* "was my feeling that this election was tipped because of an outpouring of support for George Bush by people who don't just favor different policies than I do — they favor a whole different kind of America. . . . Mr. Bush's base is pushing so hard to legislate social issues and extend the boundaries of religion that it felt as if we were rewriting the Constitution, not electing a president."[24] Garry Wills made a more desperate connection:

> The secular states of modern Europe do not understand the fundamentalism of the American electorate. . . . [W]e now resemble those nations less than we do our putative enemies. Where else do we find fundamentalist zeal, a rage at secularity, religious intolerance, fear of and hatred for modernity? Not in France or Britain or Germany or Italy or Spain. We find it in the Muslim world, in Al Qaeda, in Saddam Hussein's Sunni loyalists. Americans wonder that the rest of the world thinks us so dangerous, so single-minded, so impervious to international appeals. They fear jihad, no matter whose zeal is being expressed.[25]

24. "Two Nations Under God," *The New York Times,* 4 November 2004, Editorials/Op-Ed: http://www.nytimes.com/2004/11/04/opinion/04friedman.html?ei=5090&en=141d38656c8&oref=slogin.

25. "The Day the Enlightenment Went Out," *The New York Times,* 4 November 2004: http://www.commondreams.org/cgi-bin/print.cgi?file=/views04/1104-25.htm.

In a similar vein, Robert Kuttner said that the Democrats "neither warned the mainstream voters of the danger of a theocratic president whose base rejects modernity nor articulated a compelling moral language of their own."[26] And Maureen Dowd, never to be outdone, wrote, "W. ran a jihad in America so he can fight one in Iraq — drawing a devoted flock of evangelicals, or 'values voters,' as they call themselves, to the polls by opposing abortion, suffocating stem cell research and supporting a constitutional amendment against gay marriage. . . . Only Dick Cheney can make 'to serve and to guard' sound like 'to rape and to pillage.'"[27]

What is remarkable about these opinions is not only the extraordinarily intemperate language but also the drumming insistence that Bush and those who vote for him are taking away democracy and returning to theocracy. In a very shrewd essay, Ramesh Ponnuru, who quotes some of these same sources (and others), imagines, for the sake of argument, that the social conservatives have their way: what would America look like?[28] He suggests that "the wish-list of Christian-conservative organizations involved in politics" would prohibit abortion, and perhaps also the research that destroys human embryos. They would restrict pornography and try to ensure that the government not recognize homosexual relationships as marriages. Probably they would try to get more prayer in the schools and less evolution. They would replace sex education with abstinence education. They would insist that the tax laws promote marital stability. Most of them think that "religious groups should be able to participate in federal programs without compromising their beliefs." The very conservative among them might try to ban sodomy and contraception and a few other things that almost everyone recognizes as unattainable. After going through this list, Ponnuru comments:

> It is not my purpose here to argue that this agenda, or even the relatively restrained version of it, is one we should wish to see en-

26. "An Uncertain Trumpet," *The American Prospect* (Online Edition), 12 December 2004: http://www.prospect.org/web/printfriendly-view.ww?id=8870.

27. "The Red Zone," *The New York Times,* 4 November 2004, Section A, p. 25.

28. "Secularism and Its Discontents," *National Review* 56/24 (27 December 2004): 32-35; much of the summary in the following lines is from p. 33.

acted (or even allowed by the Supreme Court). My point, rather, is to note that introducing nearly every one of these policies — and all of the most conservative ones — would merely turn the clock back to the late 1950s. That may be a very bad idea, but the America of the 1950s was not a theocracy.[29]

In other words, when voters choose something other than what these liberal writers want, these writers cannot conceive of it as the outworking of democracy; rather, they see it as the sacrifice of democracy. This judgment is grounded in the assumption that theological considerations cannot be admitted into the reasonings of any voters: in other words, religion is private, the values of secularism are unquestioned, and those who challenge this stance are not democrats at all. Worse, in the mind of leaders of the left, what is being destroyed is their freedoms, and thus their vision of America.

This stance is not universal on the left, of course, but it is surprisingly common. Consider Amy Gutmann's recent book.[30] At first, Gutmann appears to understand the problem: she criticizes liberals for demanding too much freedom and for allowing too little for those who disagree with them. Under the banner of equal freedom for all ways of life in a democracy, she says, liberals typically end up wanting to curtail the freedom of those whose vision of the good demands more structure. The liberal-egalitarian ethos ends up wanting nothing to prosper but the liberal-egalitarian ethos — so inevitably when it seeks to shut down options that seem to be "narrower," it appears to others as nothing more than a mean-spirited agenda-driven mess of contradictions. To her credit, Gutmann recognizes the problem. She wants a form of liberalism, she says, in which liberals do not defend mere atomistic individualism but understand full well that individuals usually flourish in the context of private associations, "identity groups" (hence the title of her book), including churches. Moreover,

---

29. Ponnuru, "Secularism and Its Discontents," 33. Similarly, one recalls the address of John F. Kennedy to the Greater Houston Ministerial Association on 12 September 1960: see Ithiel deSolaPool, *Candidates, Issues, and Strategies: A Computer Simulation of the 1960 and 1964 Presidential Elections,* 2nd ed. (Cambridge: MIT, 1965), esp. 107-10. I am grateful to Michael Thate for this latter reference.

30. *Identity in Democracy* (Princeton: Princeton University Press, 2004).

liberals should not merely put up with these identity groups in some concessive fashion: they must heartily endorse freedom of association. So far so good.

But Gutmann treats all associations — churches, drama groups, NAACP, even groups identified by such words as "geek, jock, bimbo, and hottie," as nothing more than the result of *individual* choices. These identity groups are fluid and changing, little more than the contexts of individual freedom of choice. Thus the primacy of individual freedom of choice is front-loaded into the discussion. Gutmann says virtually nothing about obligations and responsibilities — whether to family, country, church, or God — obligations and responsibilities that may well exist *whether we have chosen them or not.* For our purposes, the responsibilities and obligations of Christians are finally mandated by God himself, even as the joys and privileges of Christians are grounded in God himself. But none of this is taken into account by Gutmann. Because in her view "free people" join and leave many different associations and thus have multiple and changing identities, group identity must not be allowed to stifle individual freedom of choice: that is, the individual can mix and match identities as he or she desires, and governments must protect such freedom. If gays insist on their right to membership in the Boy Scouts, or feminists insist that they have equal rights of participation in the leadership of Orthodox Jewish life, then government has both the right and the obligation to force these groups to comply. If many members of these groups feel that *their* rights and freedoms are thereby being trampled into the mud of the liberal-egalitarian vision, that's their problem: their views cannot be allowed to supersede "democratic justice" and "civic equality."

It is deeply troubling to discover that Gutmann does not even see the problem. If the Boy Scouts are allowed to exclude gays, she says, then they themselves must not be allowed to meet on any public property, as such permission would signal government support for the inferiority of gays. Gutmann never considers that by *excluding* the Boy Scouts from meeting on public property, the government is signaling the inferiority of the Boy Scouts, for no other reason than that they disagree with the liberal-egalitarian assumptions on this subject. Gutmann goes so far as to say that religious groups should not be treated with special consideration, but she does not tease out what this means. Might it mean, for instance, that Catholics must progressively be pressured by the government toward the ordination of women? of homosexuals? What is that saying about freedom? about religious freedom? Gutmann simply does not see that while she is trying to define all of democracy, she herself belongs to an identity group, a rather narrow-minded tribe more eager to impose their ideological views on everyone else than are most of the members of other identity groups she is still committed to marginalizing.[31]

The point of these observations is neither to demonize the left nor to imagine that only those on the left are trying to promote their position within Western democracies. Quite the opposite: every position on every spectrum tries to promote its viewpoint and elect its representatives, save for those who prefer to remain aloof from the system out of either lethargy (e.g., everyone who does not bother to vote) or an ideology of separateness (e.g., the Amish). Obviously there are voices on the right who try to convince the electorate that they constitute "the moral majority" (that terminology is American, of course, but the idea is certainly not uniquely American). Thus every position that is angling for a greater say in the democratic mix is in some sense trying to "impose" its will on others, in the sense that it is trying to build a majority voice, a consensus. But at the moment, the voices that not only push their own position (which is certainly a democratic thing to do) but also insist that their opponents are neither truly democratic nor truly supportive of freedom are almost all on the left.[32]

---

31. Although I have used Gutmann as my foil in this discussion, her approach is far from unique. See, for instance, Alan Race and Ingrid Shafer, eds., *Religions in Dialogue: From Theocracy to Democracy* (Aldershot: Ashgate, 2002), which brings together spokespersons from the three major monotheistic religions to push the thesis implicit in the title. But why are these worthy spokespersons all more deeply committed to the same view of democracy than they are to their ostensible religions? Note that I specified "the same view of democracy": my point is that there are other ways of conceiving of democracy than that of Gutmann, which in fact in the name of freedom is merely trying to impose on "democracy" a certain tribal perspective.

32. This is not the same thing as saying that all the voices from the left adopt that stance: see, for instance, the more careful work of Jeff Spinner-Halev, *Surviving Diversity: Religion and Democratic Life* (Baltimore: The Johns Hopkins University Press, 2000), whose aim is "to defend the choice that people make to live an illiberal life" and

Even if we get by these initial debates over the nature of freedom in a democracy, several other areas demand a few comments:

(1) Because assumptions about the existence of "natural law" or "nature's God" were much stronger in America at the time of the founding of the nation than they are now,[33] what was meant by "rights" was also rather different from the contemporary conception. "Rights" were bestowed by "nature" or by God; government was therefore morally obligated to defend these rights *by not intruding upon them.* Freedom was thus tied to God-given (or nature-given) freedoms that must not be breached by government. By contrast, very often today "rights" have to do with entitlements, which are "granted" by government — and, inevitably, must be paid for by every bigger government, which makes "positive" law out of the democratic will, without reference to some higher law, natural law, or God's law. Notions of "freedom" have undergone a huge shift.

(2) The problem of the tension between majority rule and the obligation to preserve the freedoms of the minority are easily exemplified in an issue like pornography. Suppose the majority say that pornography is bad and ban it: at what point does this jeopardize the freedom of those who think pornography is harmless and perhaps that the ban even threatens the freedom of the press? Suppose, in-

---

to consider how such cultural and religious groups may protect their "identities" within the context of a liberal democracy (pp. 5-6). Nevertheless, sometimes one wonders, in cynical mood, if some of the intemperance of the press, in particular, is grounded in rising frustration that they are being listened to less and less. Between 1900 and 2000, daily newspaper readership in the United States fell from 52.6 percent of the adult population to 37.5 percent. For those in the 18-34 age bracket, the figure was down to 19 percent. Add to this the not-so-subtle shift from attempts at evenhanded reporting to the kind of "investigative journalism" that always assumes that those in power are corrupt, and one begins to understand the dynamics. Ordinary readers are constantly being told that all those whom we elect to office are thieves and thugs, morons and megalomaniacs. Certainly some of them are. Nevertheless, when the aim of the press is not so much to report the news as evenhandedly as possible but to uncover the evil that really *must* be there in elected officials, the virtue of balancing powers begins to slide over into the vice of suspicion, divisiveness, one-upmanship, and self-righteous triumphalism.

33. See Jon Meacham, *American Gospel: God, the Founding Fathers, and the Making of a Nation* (New York: Random House, 2006); David L. Holmes, *The Faith of the Founding Fathers* (Oxford: Oxford University, 2006).

stead, the majority say that pornography is harmless and protect it: at what point does this jeopardize the freedom of people who are convinced that it is demeaning to women and dangerous to children? Or again: an individual here and there who abuses narcotics and doses himself up with hallucinogenic drugs is scarcely a threat to public order and the common good; but when such practices become an epidemic, the common good is threatened in many ways, and the state has an interest in intervening, even though individual liberties are thereby being curtailed. Usually legislatures and judiciaries try to adjudicate such differences in perspective by trying to determine what is in the public interest, or by trying to be sensitive to what a mythical "average community" judges to be obscene, or the like. But such devices merely expose the chasms that divide contemporary opinion,[34] some of which are generated by debates over the preceding point — that is, whether there is such a thing as transcendent morality.

Or consider the outpourings of wrath in the worldwide Muslim community over offensive cartoons of the prophet Muhammad published in the Danish press. Christians, of course, have put up with that sort of thing for centuries. Countercultural "exhibits" like *Piss Christ* and the Dung Madonna may arouse protests, letters to the editor, and attempts at legislation but no massed marches resulting in the deaths of scores of people in country after country. Decent people, of course, try not to give unnecessary offense to others, whether to Christians or to Muslims or to any other group. Nevertheless, it is possible to sympathize with Muslim protests only on the assumption that Islam is true and the freedoms inherent in democracy are wicked. After all, where people are free to disagree, to disagree strongly, some forms of satire are bound to erupt. Must they all be suppressed by force? That

---

34. This is also why some opinions can swing back and forth. Gambling in America was astonishingly prevalent in the last third of the nineteenth century, but it was progressively banned on moral grounds over the following decades as the social damage, cost to government, and transparent corruption all became more and more obvious. For the last two or three decades, the drift has been in the opposite direction, under the twin banners of freedom to choose one's pleasures and the hope for windfall taxes to boost government incomes — without, of course, weighing what such action will cost the government down the road as it seeks to address problems of addiction, lost jobs, corruption, broken homes, and the like. Where is the freedom?

means that it is always the party in power that cannot be satirized — an extraordinarily dangerous proposition. One begins to understand why Ibn Warraq's *Why I Am Not a Muslim* is not permitted wide circulation in Muslim countries, but *The Protocols of the Elders of Zion* is readily available. Respect for Islam does not convert into respect for Judaism or Christianity. By contrast, in a democracy one may protest if government funds are used to desecrate certain religions, but one does not issue a *fatwa* against someone who draws an offensive cartoon. Moreover, the worldwide protest in Islam occurred many months after the publication of the cartoons, and only after many of the protestors had an ample supply of Danish flags to burn in all the protests: after all, how many Danish flags would have been available for burning in Palestine or Karachi or Cairo unless there had been considerable planning?

One understands when the government decides to intervene in the interest of public safety, as when American Nazis threatened to march through the largely Jewish town of Skokie three decades ago. But by and large, religious people, not least Christians, know that they do not have to listen to or read the propaganda of those who despise them and are happy to celebrate and honor the freedom that allows them to worship in peace, knowing full well that if they crush those who disagree with them today, the crushing may be in the opposite direction tomorrow. There is something to be said for seeing freedom as a political expression of the dignity of human beings made in the image of God, even if that freedom is sadly abused. Equally, there is a great deal to be said for the view that a liberal democracy allows for, and even encourages, what Carter calls "the dissent of the governed,"[35] without that dissent turning to bloodshed. Yet while Christians, knowing that this is a fallen and broken world, not only concede such freedom but applaud it, they also know that in the consummation of the kingdom there will be no dissent of the governed: we will have minds and hearts perfectly attuned to the will and pleasure of our Maker and Redeemer. Our *ultimate* hope, therefore, can never rest in the freedoms that democracy seeks to institutionalize. Such free-

---

35. Stephen L. Carter, *The Dissent of the Governed: A Meditation on Law, Religion, and Loyalty* (Cambridge: Harvard University Press, repr. 1999).

doms are at best stopgap measures to mitigate evil in a rebellious world. As such, they deserve the support and nurture of Christians and non-Christians alike. But that is a far cry from giving them the sort of ultimacy often assigned them.

(3) Many observers have rightly concluded that unless a democratic state is made up of citizens who are largely in agreement over what is "the good," that state will tend to fly apart, forcing the government itself to become more and more powerful and intrusive in order to hold things together. In the words of David Hart,

> [T]he gradual erosion — throughout the history of modernity — of any concept of society as a moral and spiritual association governed by useful ethical prejudices, immemorial reverences, and subsidiary structures of authority (church, community, family) has led inevitably to a constant expansion of the power of the state. . . . We call upon the state to shield us from vice or to set our vices free, because we do not have a culture devoted to the good, or dedicated to virtue, or capable of creating a civil society that is hospitable to any freedom more substantial than that of subjective will. This is simply what it is to be modern.[36]

The irony, then, is that as citizens espouse increasingly diverse visions of what it means to be free, governments (including the courts) step in to resolve the divergences and end up making people less free.

(4) The optimism expressed by some thinkers regarding the attractiveness of freedom from coercive control (as we in the West view coercive control) strikes some of us as naively optimistic. The recent book by Michael Novak, for instance, thinks that the "clash of civilizations" is far from inevitable, because the universal desire for freedom will damp down the most controlling forms of government and religion.[37] Novak is not expecting the Muslim world to become secularized (he does not think that the future lies with the successors to

36. David B. Hart, "The New Pornography Culture," *The New Atlantis* 6 (Summer 2004): http://www.thenewatlantis.com/archive/6/hart.htm.
37. *The Universal Hunger for Liberty: Why the Clash of Civilizations Is Not Inevitable* (New York: Basic Books, 2004).

Ataturk); rather, he hopes — indeed, expects — forms of Islam to arise that will accommodate the modern world, including democracy and market economy, in much the same way that Catholicism made similar adjustments. Well, maybe, but I wouldn't hold my breath. The book has the feel of utopianism: give them time, and they'll all be nice democrats like us, even if they get there by a different route. It is always possible that serious clashes will be averted for a time: one certainly hopes so. But both Scripture and history testify that power blocs of various kinds keep forming, for sin will out: there will be wars and rumors of wars, even if the end is still to come (Matthew 24:6).

By now it should be clear why democracy, as valuable a form of government as it can be, must never be confused with the Christian vision of the good, and why a democratic culture cannot be aligned isomorphically with a Christian culture. Christians will cheer on democracy, believing that, by and large, it benefits the greatest number of people, provides mechanisms for limiting human power (and for ensuring that power can change hands without bloodshed), and usually provides more freedoms than other forms of government. These freedoms inevitably allow many things to foster (I almost wrote "fester") that Christians will dislike, but the same freedoms protect freedom of worship, freedom to bear witness, freedom to change one's faith without government reprisals, and much more. Nevertheless, all notions of freedom invoke, implicitly or explicitly, subsidiary notions of *freedom from* and *freedom to* or *for*.[38]

The democratic tradition in the West has fostered a great deal of *freedom from* Scripture, God, tradition, and assorted moral constraints; it encourages *freedom toward* doing your own thing, hedonism, self-centeredness, and consumerism. By contrast, the Bible encourages *freedom from* self-centeredness, idolatry, greed, and all sin and *freedom toward* living our lives as those who bear God's image and who have been transformed by his grace, such that our greatest joy becomes doing his will. Even if that direction ("freedom *toward*") will

---

38. This is one of the major planks of the book by Richard Bauckham, *God and the Crisis of Freedom: Biblical and Contemporary Perspectives* (Louisville: Westminster John Knox Press, 2002).

not be perfected until the new heaven and the new earth, already the Christian is beginning to glimpse the glory of the words, "I tell you the truth, everyone who sins is a slave to sin. . . . So if the Son sets you free, you will be free indeed" (John 8:34-36). The grand paradox inherent in such commitments falls right out of the Bible's story line: that means our greatest freedom is to become slaves to Christ.[39] "The hardness of God is kinder than the softness of men, and his compulsion is our liberation."[40] That produces a culture that may overlap with one or more of the notions of freedom in the cultures of our age, but it is certainly different from all of them and will in substantial measure be incoherent or even repulsive to most of them. David Hart is right: very often decisions handed down by the Supreme Court "should serve to remind us that between the biblical and the liberal democratic traditions there must always be some element of tension. What either understands as freedom the other must view as a form of bondage."[41]

The Lust for Power

In the three previous sections, we have noted ways in which the topics of those sections — secularization, democracy, and freedom, respectively — cannot properly be labeled either "good" or "evil." They can be either, depending on the context of their operation; indeed, because of multiple contexts, they are regularly both.

So also for power.[42] Despite the opinion of some deconstructionists and other sentimentalists, the exercise of power is not always a bad thing. Within the family, a complete want of discipline, an utter power vacuum, regularly results in disoriented and anarchic children. When violence erupts in the streets, when a bank is being

39. See especially Murray J. Harris, *Slave of Christ: A New Testament Metaphor for Total Devotion to Christ,* New Studies in Biblical Theology 8 (Leicester: Apollos, 1999).

40. C. S. Lewis, *Surprised by Joy: The Shape of My Early Life* (London: Geoffrey Bles, 1955), 215.

41. Hart, "The New Pornography Culture."

42. In this section I use "power" very loosely to include the exercise of authority in its various forms, including personal physical force, legal coercion, moral suasion, demagoguery, and force of arms.

robbed, when drug-fuelled gangs go wild, when a young woman is being raped, most of us are pretty glad if the police show up in strength and exercise a little power. Even at the international level, some evils have to be opposed by force. Doubtless war should never be more than the last resort (though it often is), but not many of us would argue that it was morally wrong to stop Hitler or to put an end to the genocide perpetrated by Serbia. Indeed, when the conditions of "just war" are actually met, all but pacifists will be driven to the conclusion that it is a moral failure *not* to go to war, since it betrays lack of love for neighbor, an unwillingness to sacrifice for the sake of others. Journalists who love to criticize those who are "in power" are of course exercising their own form of power as they do so. Much as we sometimes dislike the way the power of the media is dispensed, most of us who have lived the better part of our lives in countries with a free press would hate to see that freedom taken away, for the reduction of the power of the fourth estate sooner or later results in unchecked power in the state itself.

Yet every form of power can be abused. Where a family dynamic is nothing more than the expression of raw power and various reactions to it, the potential damage is incalculable. The police whose task is to serve and protect can become corrupt and exercise their power for personal gain, or simply because the exercise of power becomes intoxicating behavior. Even "just wars" invariably include incidents or patterns, let alone individual decisions, that are morally inexcusable, generated by too much power and too little conscience. As necessary as the media are to preserve a relatively free society, the lust for power — spelled out in money, influence, exposure, high-profile jobs — is so intense that it frequently blinds those who hold these jobs as to the nature of their calling and thus to the importance of truth and integrity.

Of course, both good and bad motives may also characterize those who exercise power in the name of Christ. The lust to be "first," to be Number One, did not die out with Diotrephes (3 John 9). Having rejected the authority of the pope, many a Protestant pastor exercises papal-like authority in his much smaller fiefdom. One is not long in the ministry before one observes some curates, assistant ministers — whatever a particular denomination labels them — subtly trying to undermine their seniors, wickedly trying to assume power, covering the operation with a gauze of pious verbiage and a veneer of humility. Yet it is no answer to imagine that ministers of the gospel should have no authority, no power, at all: one need only read the Pastorals to be reminded of the authority of the Word itself, the authority of moral suasion, the power inherent in good example, to say nothing of the power of the Spirit at work through the gospel and through believers. Moreover, not every minister of the gospel is hungry for power in some improper sense. The example of Christ is a constant constraint on those with sensitive consciences: the Master was the perfect suffering Servant, but he was also the one who cleared the temple precincts by overturning the tables of the money changers and driving out their animals with a whip. As Richard John Neuhaus never tires of telling us, one does not have to choose between being a thug or a wimp. However falteringly, we try to learn when it is right to suffer abuse and love those who persecute us, very much like the Master himself, and when it is right to clear the temple, very much like the Master himself. Thus the very nature of the gospel message, centered as it is in the obscenity of the cross, has a curtailing effect on the lust for power, as long as the gospel itself is prized above all things.

Even here, we are still picking at the edges of things. The lust for power is so subtle and absorbing that it is inadequate to say nothing more than "Sometimes power is good, sometimes it is bad" — as true as that may be. The fact that every exercise of power has at the very least the potential to corrupt demonstrates how deeply flawed we human beings are. The lust for power very often reflects our desire to control others. Even when we think this is for their good — and sometimes it is, though not nearly as often as we'd like to think — this desire to control people is very difficult to distinguish from lack of love of neighbor; it is almost impossible to disentangle from our desire to play God, which is a breach of the first commandment.

Here, too, of course, the attractiveness of power is linked in subtle ways to the other siren voices described in this chapter: freedom, democracy, and secularism. (1) The more power we exercise over others, and the less power others have over us, the more we judge ourselves to be "free." In this light, even rampant consumerism can be seen as a subset of the lust for power: the shiny toys make us as good

141

as, or, preferably, better than, our neighbors; the more we possess, the "freer" we are to order our lives as we will and to handle the vicissitudes that come our way with independence and aplomb: better medical care, another holiday abroad, vast sums spent on psychotherapy. If consumerism doesn't trip us up, its opposite might. For oddly, even that seductive form of superiority that apes humility, such that we find ourselves boasting of our self-denial and asceticism, easily succumbs to the same lust for power. All it needs to do is pander to our desire to lord it over others, even in our own minds. (2) We have already seen that the practice of democracy is very much bound up with balancing the powers of different branches of government and of extra-governmental institutions, including the media. Christopher Lasch was not wrong when he insisted that, in contemporary America, democracy is linked in the popular mind with a sense of hope that is itself grounded in notions of progress, individualism, secularism, and wealth[43] — all of them linked with power. (3) Insofar as secularism deludes us into thinking that God is dead or, equally damning, snookers us into thinking that God exists to bless our personally designed and self-defined mode of spirituality, while remaining accommodatingly irrelevant to how we live, it enhances our sense of personal power.

None of this exonerates religionists from similar pursuits of power. Under the guise of submission to God, we may simply be invoking the word "God" to enhance our authority and bolster our opinions. Lust for power is not restricted to those who make no profession of religion. Even the desire to be "useful" or to "extend the kingdom" may in part (so treacherous are our motives) be a mask for an unquenched hunger for power. Moreover, I have briefly described

43. Christopher Lasch, *The True and Only Heaven: Progress and Its Critics* (New York: Norton, 1991), and *The Revolt of the Elites and the Betrayal of Democracy* (New York: Norton, 1996). Lasch himself wants hope to be linked with memory (personal and corporate), virtue, humility, limits, and the spiritual discipline of religion. Lasch argues that when hope is uncoupled from its proper theological context, it is simultaneously uncoupled from humility and from any understanding of limits. Democracy, he argues, must be based on a conception of human equality that is itself grounded in a shared sense of human frailty. See the penetrating discussion of Patrick J. Deneen, *Democratic Faith* (Princeton: Princeton University Press, 2005).

manifestations of power in the context of the West, especially in America, but it would be an easy exercise to describe manifestations of power under very different cultures and regimes, from China to Liechtenstein, from Saudi Arabia to India.

But Christians who are committed to thinking through the doctrinal and ethical implications of "the whole counsel of God" necessarily face some curbs on this universal lust for power. The doctrine of God reminds us that we are not ultimate: God is. The doctrine of creation tells us we are not our own: we are responsible to the One who made us. Any "power" we exercise is derived, and we will be held accountable for what we do with it. The doctrine of sin will challenge us not to indulge in the creative stances that endlessly excuse our idolatry. The entire plotline of the Bible tells us, again and again, "Be reconciled to God." The death of Christ removes the huge load of guilt we otherwise bear, while his resurrection enables us to anticipate the new heaven and the new earth, the home of righteousness — even while his example calls us to renounce self-promotion, for we are called to suffer with him and only then to reign with him.

*   *   *

These biblical realities make for a worldview that is sharply distinguishable from the worldviews around us, even where there are overlapping values. We cannot embrace unrestrained secularism; democracy is not God; freedom can be another word for rebellion; the lust for power, as universal as it is, must be viewed with more than a little suspicion. This means that Christian communities honestly seeking to live under the Word of God will inevitably generate cultures that, to say the least, will in some sense counter or confront the values of the dominant culture. But to say the least is not enough. Christians thus shaped by Scripture envision a church that not only counters alternative cultures but also seeks sacrificially to serve the good of others — the city, the nation, common humanity, not least the poor. Salt does not confront; it enhances. Believers must be the best possible citizens (cf. Jeremiah 29:7; cf. also 1 Peter 1:1; James 1:1), and that means that Christians, who are taking their cue (and thus their worldview) from outside the dominant culture, not only shape and form a Christian culture recognizably different from that in which it is embedded but also become deeply committed to enhancing the whole.

Yet there are pitfalls everywhere, and in the remaining two chapters I want to outline two of them, not so much to adopt a contrarian stance as to foster expectations that are themselves shaped by Scripture.

FIVE

Church and State

—⟨∽∽∽⟩—

This chapter makes no attempt to lay out a comprehensive, still less a utopian, theory of the ideal relationship between church and state. Yet in some sense debates about church and state are subsets of more comprehensive debates about Christ and culture. Indeed, in some countries debates about church and state are the *only* form of the Christ-and-culture debates that receive much attention. My aim is to clarify this discussion a little and to demonstrate through this optic, one more time, that choosing one of Niebuhr's models is an exercise in reductionism.

Clarifying Reflections on Crucial Expressions

In much of the Western world, the word "religion" has primarily negative overtones, in contrast with, say, "spirituality." If one were to say "religion and politics," then for most people this paired expression would call up instant comment on the separation of church and state. More precisely, the theme of the separation of church and state would enter the discussion, but not necessarily that expression: the expression itself is used in several countries, but some Western democracies frequently deploy other expressions to wrestle with similar catalogs of concerns.

In fact, we have now stumbled into a host of terms that are used so variably, not to say sloppily, that accurate thought is becoming difficult — the more so if we are trying to take our cues from the New Testament, where some of these words are not found, and the rest are used in ways rather far removed from their dominant usage today. The list of troubling expressions includes "religion," "church," "state," "nation," "faith," "society," and several others I have already probed somewhat in this book, including the words "faith" and "culture." So a little unpacking seems to be in order.

Religion

Today we commonly think of religion as a particular system of ultimate values in which the pursuit of the ideal life is embodied. The assumption of such a quest necessarily challenges the *status quo*. This assumption arises most clearly in Christianity and in substance in the Judaism out of which Christianity sprang. But such a quest was very much at odds with surrounding "religions" in the first century, which focused on sacred rites and cultic observance, on preservation and conservation of ancient traditions. The influence of Christianity and the rise of multiculturalism have together encouraged other "religions" to become quests. Where countries have become deeply Christianized, Christianity itself becomes far less questing and far more conserving: in other words, it begins to think of itself as a "religion" in the older, obsolete, pagan sense. Sometimes renewal comes from within the Christianized community: that is, a subgroup restores this essential "questing" element, just as the remnant of God's people in the Old Testament challenged the degrading *status quo* into which their nation had fallen. Thus to speak of Christianity in the first century as one of many "religions" is more than a little misleading. To do so gives the impression either that Christianity was primarily cultic and conserving instead of questing and transforming, or that all the ancient pagan religions were, like Christianity, interested in the pursuit of the ideal life, eager for ethical and spiritual transformation, and living with eternity's values in view.[1]

1. In fact, during the first three centuries pagans sometimes thought of Chris-

146

Although many English translations of the New Testament use the word "religion" at some point or other, there is no Greek or Latin word in the first century that means exactly what "religion" means in the twenty-first century. The extraordinarily interesting article on *religion* in the *Oxford Latin Dictionary* provides ten categories of meaning for the word, two or three related to the earlier sense of "cultic observance" or the like, and many having nothing to do with "religion" at all. The RSV renders 1 Timothy 3:16 as "Great indeed, we confess, is the mystery of our religion (εὐσέβεια, *eusebeia*): He was manifested in the flesh...." But the Greek word properly means "godliness" (so ESV, NIV, TNIV) or, in French, *piété* (Segond, Colombe): this "mystery" regarding the person and work of Christ is the key to our "godliness" or "devotion" or "piety."[2] The Greek word often rendered "religion" in James 1:26-27 is θρησκεία *(thrēskeia)* and has more to do with reverence and worship than with "religion." We need not work through other Greek and Latin words: the general point — that the first century had no word for "religion" that meant exactly what "religion" commonly means today — is easily made.

To compound the problem of word meanings, many contemporary Christians, following the example of Western culture at large, increasingly use "religion" in an entirely pejorative sense. Whether "religion" is taken in its old cultic, conserving sense or in the sense of questing for the ideal life, they would say that both of these uses engender structures of thought in which *we* are the ones performing the "religious" acts, or *we* are the ones pursuing the ideal life. The danger of such language, they would say, is that the overtones swamp the biblical emphasis on grace, on God working in us both "to will and to act in order to fulfill his good purpose" (Philippians 2:13).

---

tianity as a "philosophy," reflecting a time when "philosophy" meant something like *worldview* — an entire frame of reference that established meaning, direction, values, theory of origins, and the like, such as the philosophy of Stoicism or the philosophy of Epicureanism. Contrast the more restricted contemporary sense of "philosophy," which refers to a fairly narrow academic discipline with assorted branches and, on the whole, with much more interest in critiquing worldviews than in establishing them.

2. Hence TNIV's "the mystery from which true godliness springs is great: He appeared in a body...."

One immediately begins to see the problem. Today we speak of the importance of "freedom of religion." But what do we mean by "religion"? If Christians busily distance their faith from religion, are we saying that we do not include Christianity among the religions that are supposed to be "free"? Are we saying that only cultic structures of pious observance are to be preserved in freedom, while quests for the ideal life are not similarly protected? Or are we saying that quests for the ideal life are protected, but cultic expressions of the same are not protected?

In fact, for thoughtful Christians who engage in diverse fields of discourse, the word "religion" commonly has slightly different meanings in different contexts. When we uphold freedom of religion as something to be desired, we include Christianity with all other religions, claiming the same sort of freedom; when we explain the distinctive elements of biblically faithful Christianity, we often distinguish Christianity from religion. When we decry the most virulent forms of secular humanism, we are tempted to argue that it is a form of "religion" (i.e., with its own absolutes, its own pursuit of the ideal life, its own "gods," and so forth), intimating, implicitly or explicitly, that secular humanists cannot fairly write us off as people of "religion" when they are people of "religion" as much as we — though a few minutes later, in another discourse, we decry "religion," or, in another conversation, defend religious people over against secularists. Small wonder that it is difficult to achieve accuracy of thought and expression on these matters. The reality is that all of us use "religion" in different ways, and we are best off acknowledging the point and allowing the context to guide the sympathetic reader.

Church

Historically this word has been used in highly diverse ways — and, transparently, we must sort out some of this discussion if we are to make progress in thinking through the relationships between "church" and "state." Those who think of bishops as constituting a third office, distinguishable from, on the one hand, deacons, and, on the other, pastors-elders, often appeal to the formula of Ignatius:

Where the bishop is, there is the church.[3] For many, the bishop not only defines the church but establishes its valid organic connection with the apostles: there must be traceable descent from the first century to contemporary bishops if a church is to think of itself as validly the church. Nevertheless, the arguments that try to connect this view of bishops to the New Testament documents are exceedingly flimsy. Moreover, the primary alternative explanation for what the church is enjoys a readier defense from those same documents: the church is the people of God called out by the gospel. This suggests that maintaining fidelity to the biblical gospel is of paramount importance for identifying the church. Certainly the apostle Paul makes that point when he asserts that if even an apostle or an angel from heaven (let alone a bishop!) deviates from that gospel, let him be *anathema* (Galatians 1:8-9). From such texts as these has sprung the view, surely right in its essentials, that the church is the people of God where the gospel is faithfully proclaimed, where the sacraments/ordinances are rightly observed, and where godly corporate discipline operates.

What differences might this polarization of opinion regarding the nature of the church make for our discussion of church and state? The differences are primarily pragmatic: a denomination with an episcopal structure is likely to have one or two or a handful of powerful voices to interact with government authorities, while local churches not attached to such authority structures are more likely to respond piecemeal. Of course, local churches without an episcopal structure may nevertheless group together in powerful associations[4] that can support public figures dealing with church/state relations.

3. It must be said, however, that Ignatius's formula is not as unambiguous a support for the threefold office and for definition of the church by appeal to episcopal office as some think. Ignatius himself was not concerned to focus on the office so much as to defend the truth. In Protestant confessionalism, the church is marked, at the very least, by the gospel, that is, by the truth, and by faithful observance of sacraments. This truth is what Ignatius was trying to uphold. It is anachronistic to read into Ignatius's formula an emphasis on the office *per se* at the expense of the primacy of gospel fidelity with which Ignatius himself was concerned.

4. "Associations" rather than "denominations": this is why an expression such as "the Baptist church" can refer to the local church that meets around the corner, but not to an ostensible denomination — unlike, say, "the Anglican church," which can have either local or denominational reference.

For our purposes, another debate over the meaning of "church" is more significant. For many, "church" is merely a collective noun for Christians. If we accept this linkage, discussion of the relations between church and state is tantamount to a discussion of the relations between Christians and the state. Those who hold this view arrive at it in various ways. Some few have a minimalist understanding of "church": where two or three are gathered in Jesus' name, they say, there is the church. They then observe how the church in the New Testament is tightly bound up with spreading the gospel and teaching the Word of God and, because they too equate "church" and "Christians," give the impression that spreading the gospel and teaching the Word of God are the only valuable things that Christians can do. Others drift toward a maximalist interpretation. Perhaps they have inherited the notion of a parish church made up of all the Christians living in a geographical area. But however achieved, this equation between church and any collective of Christians, such that "church" and "Christians" can be used interchangeably, skews discussion in a maximalist direction. John Stott is a fine example of a Christian leader who takes this approach. When he argues that *Christians* ought to be involved in various forms of social care, he means, equally, that *the church* ought to be involved in various forms of social care. In other words, when he asserts that part of *the Christian's* obligation is to be involved in some enterprise or other, this is, for him, virtually indistinguishable from asserting that *the church's* mission mandates such enterprise.[5]

But suppose that "church" in the New Testament cannot be reduced to a collective of Christians: immediately the possibilities are more subtle. When the church meets together in the New Testament,

5. For instance, of his many relevant writings see the easy way in which "church" and "Christians" can be swapped back and forth in *Issues Facing Christians Today: A Major Appraisal of Contemporary Social and Moral Questions* (London: Marshall, Morgan and Scott, 1984). More explicitly, see his *Christian Mission in the Modern World* (Downers Grove: InterVarsity, 1975), 24: "Now [Jesus] sends *us,* he says, as the Father had sent him. Therefore *our* mission, like his, is to be one of service. He emptied himself of status and took the form of a servant, and his humble mind is to be in *us* (Philippians 2.5-8). He supplies *us* with the perfect model of service, and sends his *church* into the world to be a servant *church*" (emphasis added). I am grateful to Mark Dever for the latter reference.

it comes with praise to him who sits on the throne and to the Lamb; it comes together for mutual encouragement (not least in psalms, hymns, and spiritual songs), for the kind of well-rounded admonition, instruction, and correction that the comprehensive teaching of Scripture entails (2 Timothy 3:16-17), and for the Lord's Supper (1 Corinthians 11:17-34). Its meetings may see the conviction and conversion of outsiders (1 Corinthians 14), and serious matters of discipline are weighed there (Matthew 18:15-18). Its distinctive leaders — pastors/elders/bishops[6] and deacons — have certain assigned responsibilities. The metaphor of the church as an organism — at least two distinctive uses of "body," for instance, not to mention pictures of the church *as a unit* being the bride of Christ — makes one wonder if one is doing full justice to the word "church" if it can be said to refer to two or three Christians who happen to meet at a bus stop and happily exchange a biblical verse or two. No doubt Christ is with them, but does this small collective of Christians *function* the way the *church* does in the New Testament?

There are important entailments for the topic of this book and this chapter. It is hard to ignore the many injunctions of Scripture to do good, to show mercy, to care for the poor, to be concerned with matters of justice. If all such responsibilities belong to the church *as a church,* to the church *as an institution,* then surely the leaders of the church — its pastors/elders/bishops and deacons — should take responsibility for them and direct them. But what we find in the New Testament is that the initial leaders, the apostles, were careful to carve out for themselves the primacy of teaching the Word of God and prayer (Acts 6:2). Even matters of justice *within the congregation* were in some measure handed over to other spirit-filled men (6:1-7). When the distinctive duties of pastors/elders/bishops are canvassed, the priority of the ministry of the Word and prayer is paramount. These ministers preach and teach and evangelize (the ministry of the Word extends beyond preaching). It is within the church that people are baptized and come together around the Lord's Table. Yet at the same time Christians are busy serving as salt in a corrupt world, as light in a dark world. Like the exiles in Jeremiah's day (Jeremiah 29:1-7), Chris-

---

6. I shall use "bishops" and "overseers" interchangeably.

tians learn to do good in the city where they live, knowing full well that the prosperity of their city is both for the city's good and for their good. This may not be *the church's* mission, under the direction of the church's leaders; it is certainly the obligation *of Christians.*

This discussion suggests that there are opposing dangers for thoughtful Christians. On the one side, some Christians apparently think that faithful evangelism and teaching the Bible are the only things about which they should be concerned. They need not get involved with, say, the indigent, or those who suffer from AIDS or who are abused. They need not concern themselves with the arts. More generally, they certainly do not need to get directly involved with the challenges of government. This stance is in danger of a docetic Christianity that overlooks the wholeness of the Bible's teaching, that skirts the perennial tension between the "already" and the "not yet," that simultaneously recognizes our heavenly citizenship and (with Paul) our citizenship in Rome (or France, or Australia, or Kenya). On the other side, some Christians become so engrossed in ministries of compassion and justice to the exclusion of evangelism and teaching the Bible, or so fascinated by the challenges of governing, that they delude themselves into thinking they are faithful when in reality they are overlooking what is central to any Christian's obligation to the risen Lord. They marginalize their responsibilities as members of *the church* of Jesus Christ, the church that lives and dies by the great commission.

Mercifully, there have often been better examples of how to hold these things together. I mention three. The Evangelical Awakening witnessed massive social change led by Christians converted under the ministries of Howell Harris, George Whitefield, John Wesley, and their contemporaries. These Christians were instrumental not only in getting slavery banned throughout the British Empire but also in passing laws outlawing child labor in the coal mines and in reforming the prison system. They began countless institutions to help the indigent, and they founded trade unions to tame the rapacity that sprang from the first flush of the Industrial Revolution (three of the first major union leaders were Methodist ministers who were transported to Australia for their pains). But what is remarkable about these leaders is that by and large they were first and foremost gospel Christians, deeply engaged in their local churches, extraordinarily disciplined in their own Bible reading and evangelism. The John Newton who could say that he knew two things, namely, "I am a great sinner, and Christ is a great Savior," was the same John Newton who encouraged Wilberforce to stay in politics and tackle both the slave trade and slavery itself.

Or consider Abraham Kuyper (1837-1920), about whom I shall say more in the final chapter. His approach to an early form of "sphere sovereignty" led him to start a Christian university, establish Christian unions, found a Christian political party, and much more of the same. But he insisted in the strongest terms that the church *as church* not run these movements or be responsible for them. He was a life-long churchman committed to the gospel; at the same time, he understood the value of wielding godly influence in the broader society. Yet he was adamantly careful not to tangle the church *as church* in the broader engagements that he vigorously pursued as a Christian. Inevitably this sort of distinction has an important bearing on what we think the relationship between church and state ought to be. When Americans speak of "the wall of separation" between church and state, do they really imagine a wall of separation between *the church as an institution* and the state, or between *Christians* and the state?

My third example is a couple of contemporary churches, both in major urban centers, belonging to two different denominations. Both churches are known for the excellence of their expository, Bible-teaching ministry; both have congregations that are growing rapidly, mostly by conversion, with an average age in the low 30s. Both insist on distinguishing between the forms of ministry and service in which the church *as a church* engages and the forms of ministry and service in which Christians belonging to those churches engage. At one church or the other — the patterns are not quite the same in the two congregations — Christians are involved in helping those suffering with AIDS, running programs for the poor, setting up nonprofit companies with various social ends in view, serving in senior branches of government, bringing Christian witness to bear both in assorted artistic enterprises and in legislative decisions, and much more. The senior minister at one of these churches tells me that a significant percentage of prayer times in his church find Christians beseeching God to help those involved in such endeavors; the senior minister of the other has helped raised funds, outside the church, to finance some of these service operations. Yet neither judges it appropriate for the church *as a church* to be running these operations.

In any case, in all these examples Christians have been heavily involved in activities widely perceived to be the responsibility of the state. Moreover, in all these examples the elementary distinction between what *Christians* do and what *the church as a church* does has obvious bearing on any discussion of the relationship between church and state.

Nation/State

The reason the terms "nation" and "state" need a little probing is that for the Christian, the New Testament documents touching on the relationships between church and state presuppose that the Roman Empire is the "state," whereas what we mean by "state" today has subtle differences — the more so as we move from state to state. Seven things must be said:

(1) It is worth reflecting a little on an argument advanced by Eric Werner in his book *Le système de trahison*.[7] Werner argues that if a state is neither nation nor empire, treason does not seem all that bad. For instance, for a Japanese citizen to engage in something treasonous is horribly shameful, for Japan is a tightly knit "nation," not a melting pot of peoples. Add to this a shame culture, and treason seems horribly vile. Again, in the heyday of the British Empire, it was particularly reprehensible to act in a way that would knowingly harm the Empire. By contrast, where a state delights in its rollicking diversity, treason itself becomes democratized.[8] There is no "big idea" by which everything must be tested. In America, prosecutors may zealously go after those who have engaged in treason, but the media are never outraged. Rather, they are intrigued, sometimes even vaguely admiring.

(2) The Roman Empire of the first century certainly falls into the

---

7. Lausanne: L'Age d'homme, 1986.
8. So, for that matter, does heresy — but that is another argument.

"empire" category of Werner's analysis, but it was nevertheless characterized by a number of polarities that are relevant to our discussion. (a) Rome established law and order, eschewing anarchy, rebellion, and corruption, but especially at the higher levels of government the grossest forms of debauchery and corruption grew exponentially until little more than a shell of discipline remained. (b) Rome's military might combined with a more-or-less acceptable legal system and excellent roads and communications — not surpassed in the Western world until the eighteenth century — to spread the cherished *pax Romana* throughout the Empire, and yet it succeeded in this regard by its own brutal use of force. (c) The Empire was astonishingly multiethnic and multicultural, while prizing all things Roman. In the religious realm, Rome, as we saw in the second chapter, arranged godswaps when it took over fresh territory: it insisted that the local people adopt some of the gods in the Roman pantheon while Rome itself adopted some of the local gods into its own pantheon. Orators like Cicero and Juvenal might despise and decry this invasion of foreign gods, but the emperors established the imperial policy. Yet these foreign deities were soon themselves Romanized and thus domesticated. Above all, these tendencies meant that Rome was (d) simultaneously tolerant and intolerant, syncretistic and exclusivistic.[9] Pluralism and tolerance triumphed as long as no religion claimed exclusive truth or threatened the imperial order. The gods were bound up with the social order; they were tied in complex webs of relationships with people, land, leaders, elites, and the emperor himself. Thus the foreign gods "were simply annexed"[10] to the pantheon of the Empire — and anything that threatened or was perceived to threaten the Empire called down violent suppression. Of course, the Roman Empire enjoyed a plethora of nongovernmental associations and clubs. Recent research has shown how popular these were — not, as has sometimes been argued, because people were trying to find so-

9. See especially Robert Turcan, *The Cults of the Roman Empire,* trans. Antonia Nevill (Oxford: Blackwell, 1996), 1-27. Cf. also D. Jeffrey Bailey, "Development and Diversity in Early Christianity," *Journal of the Evangelical Theological Society* 49 (2006): 45-66.

10. The expression is that of P. Garnsey, "Religious Toleration in Classical Antiquity," in *Persecution and Toleration,* ed. W. J. Sheils (Oxford: Blackwell, 1984), 6.

lace in the midst of a declining culture, but as part of public *pietas* and even civic loyalty.[11] But where Rome detected any possibility of disloyalty and thus perceived the threat of sedition, its response could be brutal.[12] This is the "state" that New Testament writers have in mind when they say various things about it.

(3) In the first century most "nations" were perceived to exist *within* the "state" of the Roman Empire. In Matthew's form of the great commission, believers are told to make disciples "of all nations" (Matthew 28:19) — and although that injunction could certainly extend to peoples outside the sway of the Empire (one thinks of the conversion of the Ethiopian eunuch in Acts 8), most evangelism and church-planting depicted in the New Testament takes place among the "nations" *within* the Empire. After the breakup of the Empire, whatever order existed was often established by feudal lords who were allied together in forms of government tied to ethnic self-awareness, an awareness fed by common language, culture, and geography. Thus the notion of "nation" enjoyed almost tribal/cultural associations for a long period of time. It enjoyed only loose overlap with the notion of "state."

(4) Toward the end of the eighteenth century, the rise of the nation-state in Europe (and ultimately elsewhere) transformed the political landscape. Before that time, many tribal/cultural groupings, more or less locally governed, clustered around larger political associations that occasionally realigned themselves in various ways. The change to the nation-state is nowhere better typified than in Bismarck and the founding of modern Germany. Nevertheless, the tension between "nation" and "state" within the "nation-state" runs forward into more recent centuries. Hitler's National Socialism played with the notion of the German *people,* the German *nation* — as easily *Volk* as *Nation* — who somehow needed and deserved to be governed by one leader and constitute one nation-state. Only a few weeks ago Canada's Parliament granted the category "nation" to Québec. The word "nation" is a little more ambiguous in French than it now is in En-

11. So, rightly, Philip A. Harland, *Associations, Synagogues, and Congregations: Claiming a Place in Ancient Mediterranean Society* (Minneapolis: Fortress, 2003).

12. Here Harland does not seem to read the sources rightly: see the telling critique of Wendy Cotter, *Catholic Biblical Quarterly* 68 (2006): 542-43.

glish, and it might in this context mean nothing more than the recognition of a culturally distinctive people. Certainly that is what Prime Minister Harper had in mind, for his final edit of the bill that recognized Québec as a "nation" added the words "within a united Canada." Not surprisingly, now that Québec may call itself a "nation," some of the *séparatistes* want more of the trappings of a "nation" in the political sense, including the ability to conduct their own foreign affairs. The fact of the matter, however, is that they have to look to Ottawa, the "national" capitol, to find such permission (which will not be readily granted). One immediately perceives how slippery and variegated the terminology can be as soon as one steps over the Canadian border into the "United *States.*" The dynamic tension between the legitimate authority of the individual states and the authority of the federal government in Washington perpetually undergoes subtle shifts. But no state in the United States has the authority to conduct its own independent foreign relations with other countries. To offer one more example of political developments that have confused the terminology: perhaps nowhere has the notion of the nation-state been more at odds with the tribal/cultural perceptions of its peoples than in Africa, where the last gasp of colonialism drew lines on a map and constituted "states" that rode roughshod over countless tribal/cultural (i.e., "national" in the older sense) sensibilities.

The rise of the nation-state placed more and more power in the hands of central government. Mediating institutions — including clubs, associations, unions, local government, education and social elites, even churches and other religious institutions — were increasingly authorized, inspected, held accountable, and in some measure bureaucratically controlled by the state, by the central government. Sometimes this has been done with a light touch; sometimes not. Sometimes the government has seen the church as an ally; sometimes not. As Germany became a nation-state, the idea gained momentum that "the state is not an end in itself but rather the exemplar, expression, and servant of national culture." Because the church was part of that culture, "Philosophers like Hegel and Fichte, poets like Heine, social scientists like Durkheim, and theologians from Schleiermacher to Troeltsch argued that religion (properly understood) supplies the cultural warmth, the moral inspiration for what Bismarck would call 'Practical Christianity.'"[13] Of course, one might well argue that such Christianity is a long way removed from what is mandated by Scripture. No less important for the sake of the present argument, however, is the implicit vision of the state as binding up in itself and finally expressing and nurturing national/cultural self-identity. In this context the suggestion of a separation between church and state would have seemed ludicrous. Nevertheless, it is the nation-state that is here quietly accumulating ultimate power.

(5) In most Western countries the rise in the authority of the nation-state over against all (other) mediating institutions has marched roughly in step with the rise of a secular outlook. Of course, how this pairing has taken place has varied enormously from country to country. Thus, roughly contemporaneous with the developments in Germany described in the last paragraph were quite different developments in France and America. The American Constitution, and still more the Bill of Rights, set its face against the "establishment" of any church. The French Revolution of 1789 generated a radical anti-clericalism that so removed ecclesiastical authority and mediation from public life that the separation of church and state (an expression used in France as early as 1905) "meant specifically transferring church temporalities to cultural associations supervised by a minister of cults."[14] But whether we think of Germany, France, or America, or even a country like the United Kingdom with its established church, it is difficult not to perceive a rising commitment to secularism on the part of the instruments of state — a point developed in chapter 4. Transparently, this reality has an enormous bearing on Christians trying to think clearly about appropriate relationships between church and state.

(6) While states have been accruing more power and now substantially regulate or even control all (other) mediating institutions, at least in the West but also in some other parts of the world, these states are democratic. That is a far cry removed from the experience of the apostle Paul. But if there is some sense in which Christians are ob-

13. Russell Hittinger, "The Churches of Earthly Power," *First Things* 164 (June/July 2006): 28.
14. Hittinger, "The Churches of Earthly Power," 28.

ligated to be good citizens, then within a democratic structure they have an obligation to try to change things in a way that was not open to first-century believers. Once again, then, our understanding of the relationship between church and state is going to be influenced in some measure by changing understandings of the state. Better put, how we appropriate the examples and instruction of the New Testament demands the most careful thought.[15]

(7) If we extend our reflections on the relations between church and state to countries that stand well outside the Western tradition that I have been briefly describing — nations such as China, Turkey, Saudi Arabia, Sudan, Malaysia, Kyrgyzstan, to mention only a few — then how we move from the Scriptures, from Christianity's foundational documents, to a faithful articulation of appropriate relationships between church and state becomes a daunting task.

But we must first remind ourselves of some of the biblical emphases.

A Survey of Biblical Priorities for the Relationships Between Church and State

As for biblical themes and passages, earlier chapters have sketched (a) some of the turning points in redemptive history, (b) some of the more important elements of Jesus' preaching of the coming kingdom of God, and (c) preliminary reflections on the remarkable significance of Jesus' utterance, "Give back to Caesar what is Caesar's, and to God what is God's" — including some parallel instruction from the apostle Paul (Romans 13). These themes and passages have unavoidable implications for contemporary Christian attempts to think through the relationships between church and state.

In the following paragraphs I shall try to demonstrate some of the diversity in the ways the New Testament treats the relationships between church and state in the first century — and even some of the

15. For an impressive defense of the nation-state, see Pierre Manent, *A World Beyond Politics? A Defense of the Nation-State,* New French Thought Series (Princeton: Princeton University Press, 2006).

diversity in Old Testament depictions of God's covenant people in exile and the ways these depictions prepare the ground. In an earlier chapter I briefly treated Mark 12:13-17 (which includes "Give back to Caesar what is Caesar's, and to God what is God's") and Romans 13:1-7, and I shall not work through those crucial texts again here. Yet this is a good place to recall that sorting out biblical perspectives on the relationships between church and state is never a mere matter of citing a list of passages, for many of the passages have been interpreted in highly creative ways. A full discussion would require detailed evaluation of the various interpretations. That would turn this book into a work of another sort, so I shall avoid such discussion here, except for mention of two or three aberrant interpretations that deserve brief notice.

A few interpreters have understood the "Give back to Caesar what is Caesar's" passage to be an ironically powerful way of saying that *nothing* belongs to Caesar, so nothing should be paid to him.[16] Everything belongs to God. How could the God of the Bible share his authority with another? This interpretation then becomes the ground for the kingdom of God to become a "pocket of resistance" perpetually on the alert to criticize the Caesars of this world for their abuse of power. Certainly it is right to remember that God and Caesar do not operate in mutually exclusive domains: God remains sovereign, and Caesar, however imperial, is never more than God's vassal. Nevertheless, the interpretation that some propose will not withstand close scrutiny. Jesus does not encourage withholding taxes. The traditional interpretation of Mark 12 is surely the obvious one and is in line with the sweeping New Testament tension between inaugurated eschatology and consummation: Jesus already claims that all authority in heaven and earth is his (Matthew 28), and he is presented as the mediatorial king who exercises all of God's sweeping authority (1 Corinthians 15), and yet that authority is itself mediated and frequently contested until the consummation. Moreover, the traditional interpretation of Mark 12 has rightly understood the seminal significance

16. E.g., Johnny Awwad, "The Kingdom of God and the State: Jesus' Attitude to the Power and Governing Structures of His Day," *Theological Review* 22 (2001): 35-60, esp. 48-52.

of Jesus' words in detaching his followers from a close identification with one nation, whether Israel or any other. To lose that insight is a terrible price that the "ironic" interpretation must pay.

Similarly, Robert Hurley argues that Romans 13:1-7 is intended to be taken ironically.[17] That interpretation enables Hurley to understand the passage to "mean" exactly the opposite of what it actually says. But the literary markers to which Hurley appeals are far from convincing. Moreover, one recalls the consistent pattern of Acts, which not only seeks to record evidence that the Christian movement is not politically dangerous but carefully reports every favorable judicial decision in favor of the nascent Christian church. Further, Hurley's view does not square very well with biblical exhortations to pray for kings and governors.

Initially more impressive is the insistence by some writers that Romans 13 does not so much tell believers how to govern well as how to be governed.[18] In the flow of Paul's argument, that insight is fundamentally right. Nevertheless, in making his argument, Paul tells us at least a little of what he thinks good government looks like: restraining evil, collecting the necessary taxes, and acting as God's servant in ruling (which presumably has some entailments regarding righteousness). After all, Paul is heir to a tradition that insists, "Righteousness exalts a nation, but sin condemns any people" (Proverbs 14:34). These exegetical observations must be combined with four more bits of data: (a) Many Christians in today's world live in democracies or limited democracies where it is possible to do good *within* government in a way not open to most believers in Paul's day. (b) The Old Testament had already established the obligation of God's people to seek the good of the city in which they were exiled, even if it was not their permanent home: "Also, seek the peace and prosperity of the city to which I have carried you into exile. Pray to the LORD for it, because if it prospers, you too will prosper" (Jeremiah 29:7). (c) The prophet Daniel had given a stellar example of faithful government service, estab-

17. "Ironie dramatique dans la mise en intrigue de l'empire en Romains 13,1-7," *Studies in Religion/Sciences Religieuses* 35 (2006): 39-63.

18. For example, Brian J. Lee, "Govern Well or Be Governed? The Christian and the Civil Authorities in Romans 13," *Modern Reformation* 15/6 (November/December 2006): 16-19.

lishing a reputation for integrity within such service while setting boundaries he was not prepared to cross, even if it cost him his life. (d) One of the earliest of the New Testament documents similarly enjoins, "Therefore, as we have opportunity, let us do good to all people, especially to those who belong to the family of believers" (Galatians 6:10). In short, although Romans 13 functions primarily to tell believers how to be governed (even when the governing authority is the Roman Empire), it nevertheless drops a few hints as to what good government looks like, and, combined with other streams of biblical thought, makes its own contribution as to how believers who are active in governance should conduct themselves.

But this is not the only biblical optic on government. Even if we restrict ourselves largely to New Testament Scriptures on the ground that the new covenant people of God, in line with Jesus' instruction, do not constitute a theocratic nation-state (unlike ancient Israel), the diversity of stances is remarkable. A survey of New Testament themes that contribute to a Christian understanding of the relationships between church and state must include the following (in no particular order of importance):

Opposition and Persecution

The beatitudes of the Sermon on the Mount pronounce a blessing on "those who are persecuted because of righteousness, for theirs is the kingdom of heaven" (Matthew 5:10). This beatitude is then expanded as Jesus addresses his followers directly in the second person: "Blessed are you when people insult you, persecute you and falsely say all kinds of evil against you because of me. Rejoice and be glad, because great is your reward in heaven, for in the same way they persecuted the prophets who were before you" (5:11-12). The persecution presupposes a cultural clash: because the followers of Jesus live by a different set of norms, they are distinguishable from and sometimes objectionable to the larger culture in which they are embedded. In this passage, however, nothing is said to suggest that the persecution is state-sponsored. That changes in Matthew 10. There we are told that Jesus' immediate disciples not only will face opposition from local councils and synagogues (10:17), but, Jesus warns, "On my account you will be brought before governors and kings as witnesses to them and to the Gentiles" (10:18).

The expectation that Christ's people will face persecution, at least some of it explicitly state-sponsored, is not rare in the New Testament. Sometimes it is tied to the thought that Jesus' disciples cannot reasonably expect to be treated better than their Master (e.g., John 15:18–16:4). The book of Acts reports local persecution in both Jewish and Gentile contexts, while faithfully reporting every judicial decision *in favor* of Christians — presumably to draw attention to legal precedents that might go some way to mitigating further attacks. Paul's list of his physical sufferings (2 Corinthians 11:21-28) includes not only deprivations such as hunger and thirst, the effects of savage storms at sea, the dangers posed by thugs and brigands, mob violence, and rounds of floggings meted out by the judicial rulings of synagogues on Jewish adherents, but prison and beatings from Roman authorities ("beaten with rods" is certainly Roman). But the New Testament book that most graphically depicts the Roman Empire as the satanic enemy bent on persecuting and destroying the church is Revelation. The seer John is perfectly aware that sometimes the greater danger to believers is being snookered by the idolatries and comforts of the age (many of the dangers faced by the "seven churches" in Revelation 2–3 have little to do with persecution), but much more of his attention is focused on the imperial cult and the dangers arising from state-sponsored brutality. If the second beast, the beast "out of the earth" (Revelation 13:11-18), works toward massive deception, the first beast, the beast "out of the sea" (Revelation 13:1-10), is "given power to make war against the saints and to conquer them" (13:7).

Restricted Confrontation

Not infrequently the tensions between Christians and the state were registered not at the imperial level but at the local level. They could be triggered by a variety of things, with the other side then making use of the (local) instruments of state authority. According to Acts 16, the preaching of Paul and Silas in Philippi, and especially the casting out of a demon from a female slave who was bringing her owners profit from her fortune-telling, generated such resentment that local officials became involved. The owners "seized Paul and Silas and dragged them into the marketplace to face the authorities. They brought them before the magistrates and said, 'These men are Jews, and are throwing our city into an uproar by advocating customs unlawful for us Romans to accept or practice'" (16:19-21). Under additional pressure from the crowd, the magistrates had the two men "severely flogged" and "thrown into prison" (16:23) — and thus local authority has weighed in. At the very least, this implies that the state (in this case, the Roman Empire) is adopting a kind of "hands off" self-distancing from the local problem. If the state in this instance is not the active agent of persecution, neither is it the bulwark of religious freedom.

In some instances we simply do not know enough about the first-century dynamics to detect where, in opposing *religious* dangers, the *political* dangers might lie. According to Revelation 2:6, 14-16, the Nicolaitans' teaching was akin to that of Balaam, "who taught Balak to entice the Israelites to sin so that they ate food sacrificed to idols and committed sexual immorality" (2:14). Eating food that had been offered to idols could easily mean participating in pagan cults (compare 1 Corinthians 8 and 10); the reference to "sexual immorality" may have in view the spiritual apostasy against which the Old Testament so regularly warns, using fornication as a metaphor[19] — though the link between some pagan worship and fertility cults meant that physical fornication and pagan religion were not always completely distinguishable. Such accommodation God reprobates in the strongest terms: the exalted Christ says to those who have stood firm against such idolatry, "But you have this in your favor: You hate the practices of the Nicolaitans, *which I also hate*" (2:6). The strength of such opposition between faithful Christians and the Nicolaitans might have had political ramifications, if the Nicolaitans had the ear of the authorities, but in this case we do not have enough evidence to make a determination.

19. There is no better treatment of that theme than that of Raymond C. Ortlund Jr., *Whoredom: God's Unfaithful Wife in Biblical Theology,* New Studies in Biblical Theology; Leicester: IVP/Grand Rapids: Eerdmans, 1996), recently reprinted as *God's Unfaithful Wife: A Biblical Theology of Spiritual Adultery* (New Studies in Biblical Theology 2; Downers Grove: InterVarsity, 2003).

Of course, Luke carefully records events that turn out another way — when local authority actually restrains mob violence. The city clerk in Ephesus rebukes the mob because he does not want uproar to attract imperial attention and jeopardize the relative independence of the city's government (Acts 19:35-41). Nevertheless, what begins as purely local confrontation can escalate all the way to confrontation with Rome itself — which is exactly what Paul faces in Acts 26–28. The point to make here, however, is that where there is opposition between church and state, the "state" side of the opposition may be as local as the "church" side of the opposition.

Differing Fundamental Allegiances

Although, as we have seen, the Bible encourages Christians to honor political authorities, pay taxes, and obey the laws (Romans 13), there are limits to this encouragement. When the religious and political authorities in Jerusalem order the apostles to stop preaching, Peter and John reply, "Which is right in God's eyes: to listen to you, or to him? You be the judges! As for us, we cannot help speaking about what we have seen and heard" (Acts 4:19-20). That the believers constitute a separate community distinguishable from the common culture is amply evident in Paul's insistence that the rules of conduct he has laid down apply to the church, not to outsiders. The result is that church members can be disciplined, but obviously not the outsiders. "What business is it of mine to judge those outside the church? Are you not to judge those inside?" (1 Corinthians 5:12). Here, then, the apostle is mandating (legislating?) conduct that is differentiable from what is mandated for or expected of other Roman citizens. However much Paul might reprobate the sins of his age, it is no immediate concern of his to pass legislation that would modify those sins. His focus is on the life, faith, and morality of the Christian community, a part of — but highly differentiable from — the larger culture. Small wonder, for, like Abraham who was "looking forward to the city with foundations, whose architect and builder is God" (Hebrews 11:10), so also believers belong to "the Jerusalem that is above" (Galatians 4:26), even if, like Paul, they can also confess to being Roman citizens.

More comprehensively, Paul tells the Philippians, "But our citizenship is in heaven. And we eagerly await a Savior from there, the Lord Jesus Christ, who, by the power that enables him to bring everything under his control, will transform our lowly bodies so that they will be like his glorious body" (Philippians 3:20-21). The word "citizenship" is inevitably political.[20] The first-century Christians may be citizens of the Roman Empire, but they have a more fundamental allegiance: their citizenship is in heaven. Even the title "Savior" had political overtones in the first century: the emperor Augustus was described as "a saviour who put an end to war and established all good things," while the emperor Claudius was reverenced as "saviour of the world" and hailed as "a god who is saviour and benefactor."[21] The same passage about our heavenly citizenship, Philippians 3:20-21, describes Jesus' power as so extensive that it "enables him to bring everything under his control" — a claim that would certainly sound at least partly political.[22] Inevitably, then, thoughtful Christians maintain some fundamental allegiances that set them apart from other citizens in the Empire who feel no loyalty whatsoever to a "citizenship . . . in heaven."

20. Cf. Peter T. O'Brien, *The Epistle to the Philippians: A Commentary on the Greek Text,* New International Greek Text Commentary (Grand Rapids: Eerdmans, 1991), 461: "Most interpreters recognize that πολίτευμα has added significance in a letter sent to Philippi. This is not, however, because the rendering 'colony' fits. Rather, under the provisions of the Roman form of constitutional government conferred on the city by Octavian in 42 B.C., Philippi was 'governed as if it was on Italian soil and its administration reflected that of Rome in almost every respect'. So, writing to Christians in a city proud of its relation to Rome, Paul tells the Philippians that they belong to a heavenly commonwealth, that is, their state and constitutive government is in heaven, and as its citizens they are to reflect its life (cf. also 1:27, where Paul uses the cognate verb πολιτεύομαι)."

21. For discussion of this point, along with relevant inscriptions and references, see Peter Oakes, *Philippians: From People to Letter,* Society for New Testament Studies Monograph Series 110 (Cambridge: Cambridge University Press, 2001), 139.

22. "In the first century AD, the one whom most people would see as saving in accordance with his power to subject all things to himself was the emperor" (Oakes, *Philippians,* 145).

Different Styles of Government, of Reign

The kingdom Jesus introduces projects a style of rule radically different from that in the political world. Nowhere is this made clearer than in the dramatic scene reported in Matthew 20:20-28.

> 20 Then the mother of Zebedee's sons came to Jesus with her sons and, kneeling down, asked a favor of him.
>
> 21 "What is it you want?" he asked.
>
> She said, "Grant that one of these two sons of mine may sit at your right and the other at your left in your kingdom."
>
> 22 "You don't know what you are asking," Jesus said to them. "Can you drink the cup I am going to drink?"
>
> "We can," they answered.
>
> 23 Jesus said to them, "You will indeed drink from my cup, but to sit at my right or left is not for me to grant. These places belong to those for whom they have been prepared by my Father."
>
> 24 When the ten heard about this, they were indignant with the two brothers. 25 Jesus called them together and said, "You know that the rulers of the Gentiles lord it over them, and their high officials exercise authority over them. 26 Not so with you. Instead, whoever wants to become great among you must be your servant, 27 and whoever wants to be first must be your slave — 28 just as the Son of Man did not come to be served, but to serve, and to give his life as a ransom for many."

Clearly the expectation of James and John and their mother is that Jesus' kingdom would be primarily political (however righteous and messianic), and they want primary places in the new administration. When Jesus asks them if they can drink his cup, he is asking if they can share in the experiences and commitments that will befall him — and of course he is thinking primarily of his impending suffering (which is why he asks his Father, in Gethsemane, if "this cup" might be taken from him [26:39]). James and John, awash in overconfidence but not yet having any inkling of Jesus' sufferings, boldly reply that they can indeed drink Jesus' cup. With gentle irony they cannot yet understand, Jesus assures them that they will indeed drink from his cup: they will themselves face more than they can yet imagine. Even so, certain appointments in the kingdom are not his to make, but his Father's. The indignation of the ten toward the two brothers is doubtless motivated by a sense of jealousy and betrayal: the two are trying to get onto an inside track with Jesus that would relegate the others to a second tier. Jesus rebukes the whole lot of them. In doing so he contrasts the pattern of authority in the state with the pattern of authority in the kingdom he is establishing. The one side lords it over others; the other side goes to the ignominy of the cross.

Out of this has come the tendency in many Christian circles to speak of "servant leadership." The expression is open to abuse. For many, it now says much about being a servant and nothing about leadership. Whatever else he was, however, Jesus was not a wimp. He was a leader of matchless authority — and in New Testament documents that describe Christian pastors, they, too, enjoy leadership that is to be obeyed; they exercise an authority to which others are urged to submit (e.g., Hebrews 13:17). What, then, is the nature of the contrast Jesus is drawing in Matthew 20? It is certainly not between exercising authority and exercising none. The difference is this: the world's exercise of authority, commonly exemplified in the state, hungers for prestige and praise; its leaders want to be first, and they end up lording it over others, scrambling up the ladder by crushing the skulls of those they are trampling behind them. By contrast, Jesus comes into the fullness of his royal authority by going to the cross, by serving others even to the point of agonizing suffering and the starkest of deaths, undertaken for the good of the people over whom he will rule. The Son of Man "did not come to be served, but to serve, and to give his life as a ransom for many" (Matthew 20:28). Similarly, Christians who exercise authority in the church do not mark their discipleship to Jesus by abandoning all exercise of authority, but by exercising it within the constraints of a life sacrificially lived for the sake of others.

The contrast is striking. Of course, in the richness of God's common grace, there are governors who genuinely have a servant's heart, governors who are not unduly corrupted by honor and power. Sadly, there are ecclesiastical leaders who take their cue as to what leadership is from the surrounding world, who sell their souls for pomp, flattery, and the lust for ever-increasing manipulative control. Yet if

Christians follow their Master, then as their influence increases in the world, so their conduct shames the rulers of this world. The different styles of rule, of the exercise of authority, prove so divergent that each is aghast at the other.

The same pattern is deeply embedded in the gospel itself. We must learn to adopt "the same attitude of mind Christ Jesus had" (Philippians 2:5) — the attitude of mind that "did not consider equality with God something to be used to his own advantage" (2:6) but led him instead to the incarnation, to servanthood, to death on a cross (2:7-8). If we preach Christ in the public sphere, we proclaim the wisdom of God that the world thinks terribly foolish (1 Corinthians 1:18–2:5). Indeed,

> in order to understand rightly what it means to have the mind of Christ, we must remember who "Christ" is for Paul: the crucified one. To have the mind of the Lord is to participate in the pattern of the cross (cf. Phil. 2:1-11), for the wisdom of God is manifest definitively in the death of Jesus. Consequently, the privileged spiritual knowledge of which Paul speaks should result in the renunciation of all privilege, all boasting and quarreling.[23]

In short, the internal dynamic of authority in the church at its best is so very different from the internal dynamic of authority in the world that the trajectories of church and state under such conditions are bound to be divergent.[24]

---

23. Richard B. Hays, *First Corinthians,* Interpretation (Louisville: Westminster John Knox Press, 1997), 47.

24. Some whose experience and study of government have been restricted to the best of the Western tradition will find my insistence on this divergence overstated. All I can say is that they have not looked closely at governments in, say, East Asia, the Central Asian republics, Africa, Latin America; they have not read widely in history outside the Western canon. Sometimes bullying governments are nothing but the incarnation of thugs, of course. But very often an undergirding philosophical structure shapes the exercise of authority — whether the tribal authority vested in the leader of the clan, or the elitist self-congratulation of Plato's (and Harvard's) philosopher-kings, or the oligarchy of the Marxist *nomenklatura* who alone rightly implement Marxist teachings, or the assumption of Confucian polarities that place rulers "up" and everyone else "down." Rulers in such traditions may be good or bad according to their own lights, of course, but good is never measured simply along Christian axes. The second-century

The Transformation of Life, and Therefore
of Social and Governmental Institutions

The gospel, when believed and obeyed, changes the direction and values of people. "Dear friends," writes the apostle Peter, "I urge you, *as foreigners and exiles,* to abstain from sinful desires, which war against your soul" (1 Peter 2:11). In other words, the moral transformation is self-consciously countercultural. Some Christian belief and behavior will simply seem odd, perhaps slightly antisocial, to many people in the broader Roman culture. But some Christian belief and behavior have the potential for attracting the interest of the state. The exclusiveness of Christian claims will seem both narrow and vaguely threatening in the light of imperial policies designed to accommodate diversity while Romanizing all religions. The absence of images will seem atheistic. And the steadfast refusal of Christians to worship Caesar will appear not only disrespectful but treasonous.

The brilliant little letter to Philemon, though it carefully avoids any hint of advocating the overthrow of slavery, nevertheless lays the groundwork for its destruction. Where such teaching was promoted and in some measure practiced, the social order was being threatened.

In the End, Jesus Wins

The claim that all authority *already* belongs to Jesus (e.g., Matthew 28:18-20), the promise that he will reign until he has destroyed all his enemies (1 Corinthians 15:25) will certainly be offensive to those who believe they owe no allegiance to Jesus, and it may attract the anger of the state. When the apostle insists that the gospel overturns the wisdom of the wise, whether Jew or Greek (1 Corinthians 1:18-25), we sim-

---

emperor Hadrian was a "good" emperor in the sense that he was energetic, well organized, disciplined, and so forth. Had there been trains, he would have made them run on time. He could also be brutal toward Christians, and he listened to pagan voices urging that the Empire was weakening owing to Christian influence. Certainly the West has had its share of awful leaders, but we are blind to our heritage if we fail to observe how many universally admired good leaders have brought into government with them something of the distinctive Christian emphasis on *service.*

ply cannot avoid the conclusion that Paul was not thinking of something like "private religion": what he proclaimed was public truth. "At heart, then, there is a *fundamental contradiction,* even *opposition,* between the Gospel and the world. . . . Hence, the Gospel as public truth, the Gospel in the public sphere, is not an easy word to speak, for it goes against the grain, and operates from a different wisdom, in the light of which human wisdom is shown to be folly."[25] When we recall that Christians in the New Testament look forward to the consummation, when *every* knee will bow and confess that Jesus is Lord (Philippians 2:11), when the kingdom of this world becomes the kingdom of our Lord and of his Messiah (Revelation 11:15; cf. Revelation 19), we perceive that Christian faith in the New Testament, though doubtless highly personal, was never merely private. Inevitably, the larger culture was going to be confronted — and this included the state.

Summary of the Diversity of Biblical Themes

The diversity of stances adopted by various New Testament documents toward the state presupposes some commonalities, while local conditions and complementary theological truths evoke disparate emphases. Owing to the teaching of the Master himself, Christians in the first century understood that the Christian church was not isomorphic with any nation but was a transnational community, and that the sovereign God whom they confessed had ordered the government of the state for good purpose, so that it was incumbent on all Christians to respect and submit to that authority not only in the spirit of good citizenship but out of loyalty to God. Equally, however, the early Christians understood that where the state abused its God-given mandate and commanded believers to do something God had forbidden, or prohibited something God had enjoined on them, they must clash with the state and suffer the consequences, for allegiance to the God who is over both church and state takes absolute priority. And God will be utterly vindicated at the end.

25. Paul Trebilco, "Gospel, Culture, and the Public Sphere: Perspectives from the New Testament," *Evangel* 24/2 (2006): 42.

Once these stable points are established, the New Testament can depict not only the Empire's positive judicial rulings but also the Empire's most brutal persecution. It can work carefully through subtle confrontations and fundamental differences in the way authority is exercised in state and church, and it can anticipate the consummation when all without exception will bow the knee to King Jesus. Taken together, the texts encourage good citizenship within the Empire while insisting on the Christian's primary allegiance to a heavenly citizenship. The proclamation of the gospel transforms people wherever it is believed and received, and sooner or later such transformation will either improve the state or excite its opposition.

These divergent patterns do not constitute differentiable typologies of the relationships between church and state. Rather, the surging commonalities work out in flexible ways depending on the vitality of Christians, the character of local government officials, the "accidents" of mob violence, the precedents of court decisions, the intensity of persecution, and much more. These variations in the relation between church and state become more subtle yet when we recall that, when the state opposes or persecutes believers, it usually focuses on Christian individuals rather than on the church *as church,* while the New Testament documents regularly distinguish between what *Christians* are doing in the outworking of their faith and what *the church as church* is mandated to do.

But before we take the final steps of this chapter and reflect on how these biblical variables speak to us today, we must pause to remind ourselves of some historical and theological matters generated by (a) the development of democracy, which alters what good the Christian might do within the corridors of power in the state;[26] (b) some of the ways in which Jesus' distinction between Christ and Caesar have worked out in highly diverse patterns of separation of

26. I briefly touched on some of these issues in chapter 4 of this book. I have not attempted to say anything about the history of the rise of democracy and its integrated legal tradition: that would require another sort of book well beyond my expertise. For an erudite and provocative analysis, see the first two volumes (a third one is planned) by Harold J. Berman, *Law and Revolution: The Formation of the Western Legal Tradition* (Cambridge: Harvard University Press, repr. 1983); *Law and Revolution II: The Impact of the Protestant Reformations on the Western Legal Traditions* (Cambridge: Belknap, 2006).

church and state; and (c) reflection on the corresponding heritage of other religions, not least Islam.

Historical and Theological Reflections

It might be simplest to take four steps.

(1) For Americans, perhaps no phrase defines the relationship between church and state more comprehensively than "the wall of separation between church and state." But few recognize that "the wall of separation" is not found in the First Amendment; fewer still recognize that, while it is widely used in diverse Western democracies, it carries very different overtones from country to country. A little historical background will not go amiss.

The First Amendment to the United States Constitution says, "Congress shall make no law respecting an establishment of religion, or prohibiting the free exercise thereof; or abridging the freedom of speech, or of the press; or the right of the people peaceably to assemble, and to petition the government for a redress of grievances." Although the matter is disputed, "an establishment of religion" probably had in view, at the time, the fact that some states had an "established" religion: Connecticut, for instance, was tied to the Congregational Church. Congress was not to meddle in such matters, which had the effect of leaving an established church in some states, and leaving other states without an established church, as the states themselves preferred.

In 1779, Thomas Jefferson's Bill for the Establishment of Religious Freedom in Virginia, which Jefferson himself judged to be a novel experiment, made all forms of the Christian faith to stand on the same footing as Islam or Hinduism. True freedom of religion demands both the free exercise of religion and the disestablishment of religion. At about the same time, Jefferson's friend and rival, John Adams, drafting the Massachusetts Constitution, embarked on a rather different vision of religious freedom. He thought that the state served the cause of religious freedom best by balancing the freedom of many private religions with the legal establishment of one public religion, which he wanted to be Christianity. Thus Massachusetts and Virginia headed in different directions, and according to the Bill of Rights (which included the First Amendment), ratified in September 1789 (note the later date!), Congress was not to interfere.

In the bitter election of 1800, Jefferson, whose radical biblical criticism and whose romantic Deism made him anathema to many conservative Christians, nevertheless won the support of some conservative Christians who cherished religious liberty.[27] After receiving a letter from the Baptist Association of Danbury, Connecticut (where, of course, their own religious affiliation was not part of the establishment), congratulating him on his victory and applauding him for his defense of religious liberty, President Jefferson responded on New Year's Day, 1802. In oft-repeated words, Jefferson wrote,

> Believing with you that religion is a matter which lies solely between Man & his God, that he owes account to none other for his faith or his worship, that the legitimate powers of government reach actions only, & not opinions, I contemplate with sovereign reverence that act of the whole American people which declared that *their* legislature should "make no law respecting an establishment of religion, or prohibiting the free exercise thereof," thus building a wall of separation between Church & State.

So there it is: a wall of separation. Although this letter did not become common knowledge until the middle of the nineteenth century, the phrase then took on independent life in many countries. The more secular interpretation was that religion is private and may be protected in that sphere, while the state must be secular. It is at least doubtful that that is quite what Jefferson himself meant. After all, in the context of his letter to the Baptists of Connecticut, the President's purpose was to defend the free exercise of religion, rather than to ban it to the private sphere. Moreover, as is well known, Jefferson ended this missive

---

27. Many of them had of course been influenced by Roger Williams, refugee from Massachusetts and founder of Rhode Island. Recently James Calvin Davis (*The Moral Theology of Roger Williams: Christian Conviction and Public Ethics,* Columbia Series in Reformed Theology [Louisville: Westminster John Knox, 2004]) has argued that although Williams's ecclesiology was distinctive, much of his argumentation derived from his Reformed convictions somewhat modified by his understanding of natural law, rather than from mere pragmatics or moral relativism.

with a prayer, responding in kind to the Baptists' prayers for him. But whatever Jefferson meant, the First Amendment was increasingly seen through the grid of that phrase. It entered the vocabulary of the Supreme Court in 1878 *(Reynolds v. United States),* though probably it played little if any role in the decision. The climax came in the landmark case *Everson v. Board of Education* (1947), in which Justice Hugo L. Black, writing the majority opinion and citing no precedent other than *Reynolds,* famously argued that in the words of Jefferson, the First Amendment *itself* has erected "'a wall of separation between Church and State.' . . . That wall must be kept high and impregnable. We could not approve the slightest breach."[28] This set the stage for the kind of jurisprudence that was strictly separationist in the second half of the twentieth century.[29] Arguably, the Court is backing away slightly from such strict separation now.[30] What is in any case transparent is that the metaphor of the wall in Jefferson's letter to the Danbury Bap-

28. The rhetoric appealed to the role of Jefferson as a leading architect of the First Amendment, with the aim, of course, of interpreting the First Amendment in terms of the (later) "wall of separation" letter. But Jefferson was in France in 1789 when the First Amendment was drafted and ratified.

29. One of the more important histories of the Court is that of James Hitchcock, *The Supreme Court and Religion in American Life,* vol. 1: *The Odyssey of the Religion Clauses;* vol. 2: *From "Higher Law" to "Sectarian Scruples"* (Princeton: Princeton University Press, 2004). One of the things that Hitchcock makes clear is how the later Justices view the state as *over* religion. Even commentators who are a long way from supporting an "originalist" reading of the Constitution and Bill of Rights commonly find the Court's decisions on the relationships between church and state to be a mess of inconsistencies and poor argumentation: see, for instance, Charlie Fried, *Saying What the Law Is: The Constitution in the Supreme Court* (Cambridge: Harvard University Press, 2005).

30. See the compelling essay by John Witte Jr., "Publick Religion: Adams v. Jefferson," *First Things* 141 (March 2004): 29-34. See also Noah Feldman, *Divided by God: America's Church-State Problem — And What We Should Do about It* (New York: Farrar, Straus and Giroux, 2005). Perhaps it should be said that some who think this is the case argue for a modified "originalist" position: Randy E. Barnett (*Restoring the Constitution: The Presumption of Liberty* [Princeton: Princeton University Press, 2004]), for instance, thinks that the controlling "grid" by which the Constitution is to be read and preserved is whatever interpretation of it contributes to liberty, to which, after all, the framers were committed. Yet as soon as one adopts a *selection* of original themes only, one is necessarily adopting a stance that is both uncontrolled and amoral (unless one has made a prior commitment to the view that liberty is the *summum bonum*).

tists has become more central in the mind of the Court, let alone in popular opinion, than the actual wording of the Bill of Rights.

(2) This historical background underlies the plethora of stances adopted by different groups of Americans and other Anglo-Saxons today as to what the relationship between church and state *ought* to be. It would take a very long chapter to survey them all. Nevertheless, by pointing to a handful of books and articles we may sample some of the diversity and attempt some evaluation. Authors in five of the six categories that I now describe clearly do *not* think that the "wall of separation" is absolute. One of these first five categories thinks it shouldn't be there at all. And the sixth wants the wall to be as high and as impregnable as possible.

(a) Sometimes disparate theories of the relationship between church and state are said to be grounded in Augustine, who thus gets blamed (or praised) for slightly conflicting views. Thus the well-researched volume by Robert Dodaro argues that because true *iustitia* (justice) begins and ends with the adoration of God, and God is knowable only through the mystery of the incarnation, therefore ultimately there cannot be true *iustitia* apart from Christ.[31]

By contrast, Robert Markus argues that Augustine conceives of three realms: the sacred, the profane, and, between them, the secular. The sphere of the sacred is bound up with Christian belief and practice; the sphere of the profane concerns itself with beliefs and practices that Christians must repudiate. By contrast, the secular realm occupies neutral space. It is made up of elements from the broader culture that Christians may legitimately adopt or at least adapt.[32] Markus's appeal to an autonomous secular sphere enables him to distance himself both from those who think Augustine ties Christianity irrefragably to public life, and thus to the Constantinian settlement, and from those who think the Constantinian settlement must be rooted out tooth and nail. Christians and non-Christians alike can make use of the goods in this autonomous secular realm, even if they do so with a "different faith" and "different hope." In fairness to

31. Dodaro, *Christ and the Just Society in the Thought of Augustine* (Cambridge: Cambridge University Press, 2004).

32. Markus, *Christianity and the Secular* (Notre Dame: University of Notre Dame Press, 2005).

Markus, it is important to observe how carefully he distinguishes this secular sphere from contemporary secular liberalism. Augustine's secular sphere, Markus argues, unlike secular liberalism, is devoid of moral categories. It is bound up only with meeting material needs, with establishing order and security.

The very recent work by Kristen Deede Johnson[33] appeals to Augustine in a slightly different way. The heritage of liberal democracy has taught people to rank tolerance among the highest of the virtues, while what she calls "post-Nietzschean celebration of difference"[34] sets such a premium on difference that the result is incompatible with liberal democracy. The way ahead, Johnson avers, is *beyond* tolerance and difference (hence her subtitle): we learn from Augustine that there is no ultimate harmonization of differences until the coming of the Heavenly City. But Augustine also taught us that Christianity is "nothing if not a public, social ethic embodied in the life of the Church (not, we are careful to note, embodied in the political realm of the earthly city)."[35] What we must foster, while we wait for the Heavenly City, is integrity of speech and authenticity of expression as different communities converse — not celebrating difference in itself (for eventually there will be unity, even if we have to wait until the Heavenly City to achieve it), and not celebrating the false guise of "neutrality" cherished by liberalism (for ultimately it requires that all sides abandon all or part of their particularity in order to rank "neutrality" more highly).

(b) A recent book by Jeffrey Stout[36] attempts a similar but slightly different mediating position. He insists that liberal secularists think of themselves as administrators or arbiters of the public sphere, while in fact they are simultaneously one of the parties in that sphere — a point they regularly overlook. They are one of the participants in political conversation, not the framers and still less the judges of that con-

---

33. Johnson, *Theology, Political Theory, and Pluralism: Beyond Tolerance and Difference,* Cambridge Studies in Christian Doctrine (Cambridge: Cambridge University Press, 2007).

34. Johnson, *Theology, Political Theory, and Pluralism,* 250 — but the expression recurs frequently in her work.

35. Johnson, *Theology, Political Theory, and Pluralism,* 257.

36. Stout, *Democracy and Tradition,* 2d ed. (Princeton: Princeton University Press, 2005).

versation. On the other hand, Stout wants to remind those he calls "the new traditionalists" (basically those who criticize the liberal sec-ularists) that liberal democracy *itself* is a "thick" tradition, so the tra-ditionalists should not lay claim to it as if it were all theirs. Nominally, then, Stout wants to trace out a path between folk on the left like Rich-ard Rorty (who wants religion purged from public discussion) and John Rawls (who thinks religion should be confined to well-defined and limited private roles) and "new traditionalists" such as John Milbank, Alasdair MacIntyre, and Stanley Hauerwas. Yet the thrust of the book is more sympathetic to liberal democracy (which pretty soon becomes, in Stout's usage, indistinguishable from liberal secularism) in general and to John Rawls in particular than Stout lets on. Stout seems to think that if he can show that liberal democracy is itself a "thick" tradition, the new traditionalists will have to embrace it. But *contra* Stout, democracy is not a conceptual tradition that stands over against Aristotelianism and Augustinianism; rather, it is a form of or-ganizing government that stands over against monarchy, oligarchy, and totalitarianism. Stout offers many helpful insights along the way, but he does not really seem to understand the nature of the religious claims of those he labels "the new traditionalists."

(c) A range of theologians and movements rejects all models of the relationship between church and state of a Constantinian variety. The worst abuses of Christians against the broader culture have taken place when Christians have enjoyed too much power. These thinkers want a "diaspora" model of churchmanship. Christians, they say, are a pilgrim people in a strange land. We should think of ourselves as the new diaspora, still in exile until the dawning of the consummated kingdom.

In one form of this heritage, complete withdrawal, or a with-drawal as complete as possible, is the only solution that makes sense. The Amish win. But there are more attenuated forms of this tradition, one of them scarcely known and the other well known and increas-ingly popular. The one that is still relatively little known is ably de-fended by Darryl G. Hart.[37] He strongly supports the view (espoused

---

37. See especially his *A Secular Faith: Why Christianity Favors the Separation of Church and State* (Chicago: Ivan R. Dee, 2006); or, in briefer compass, his "Christianity

earlier in this chapter) that one must make a distinction between what the church *as church* has to say and the way Christians may be involved in the broader culture, including the state. But he goes further and insists that even *Christians* (as opposed to the church) should not make their political and cultural appeals on *Christian* grounds. In other words, although they should certainly be involved in doing good in and even to the city, Hart is not happy for the good that they do to be identified as a distinctively Christian product or stance.

Even more suspicious of all state power is the better-known alternative represented by the many books of Stanley Hauerwas.[38] The church must be the church — a political body in its own right. If it tries to serve the state, it is soon mired in the compromises of the Constantinian settlement. Christians need to envisage — and advocate — a different form of democracy, one that eschews preeminence and power. Thus instead of ignoring the culture, including the state, we must challenge culture and state utterly and seek to demonstrate a better way by constituting ourselves a Christian culture, a kingdom culture that takes the teaching of Jesus very seriously. If his opponents ask Hauerwas for a theory or justification for the existence of the state, Hauerwas repeatedly insists that he is under no obligation to furnish one. For Hauerwas and most others within this tradition, influenced as it is by the work of the Mennonite scholar John Howard Yoder, this way of living entails a commitment to absolute pacifism. Certainly in recent

---

and Politics: The Difference Between Christians and the Church," *Modern Reformation* 13/5 (September/October 2004): 32-33. See also Willis B. Glover, *Biblical Origins of Modern Secular Culture: An Essay in the Interpretation of Western History* (Macon: Mercer University Press, 1984); Rodney Stark, *The Victory of Reason: How Christianity Led to Freedom, Capitalism, and Western Success* (New York: Random House, 2006).

38. His most important books of political theology include: Stanley Hauerwas and William H. Willimon, *Resident Aliens: Life in the Christian Colony* (Nashville: Abingdon, 1989); Stanley Hauerwas, *The Peaceable Kingdom* (Notre Dame: University of Notre Dame Press, 1991); Hauerwas, *After Christendom? How the Church Is to Behave If Freedom, Justice, and a Christian Nation Are Bad Ideas* (Nashville: Abingdon, 1991); Hauerwas, *Where Resident Aliens Live: Exercises for Christian Practice* (Nashville: Abingdon, 1996); and Hauerwas, *Performing the Faith: Bonhoeffer and the Practice of Nonviolence* (Grand Rapids: Brazos, 2004). See also the essay by Daniel M. Bell Jr., "State and Civil Society," in *The Blackwell Companion to Political Theology,* ed. Peter Scott and William T. Cavanaugh, Blackwell Companions to Religion (Oxford: Blackwell, 2006), 423-38.

years the polarization and debates between pacifists and just war theorists have become both intense and sophisticated.[39]

(d) A slight variation on this sort of approach is nicely represented in the recent book by Glen H. Stassen and David P. Gushee.[40] The book abounds in helpful insights and thoughtful exegeses. Above all, it is characterized by a valiant attempt to bring together positions that many have judged to be disparate. For instance, Stassen and Gushee insist that the pacifist and the just war theorist ought to see themselves as closer than they commonly do. Just war theorists who truly understand the teaching of Jesus will surely want to uphold non-violence and justice, so they should develop their just war theory "as the most effective way to minimize violence and injustice, not merely to rationalize making war."[41] It is entirely wrong to state that the world or government have their own spheres of authority divorced from Jesus and his teaching and then appeal to just war theory *instead* of to the teaching of Jesus. These and other ways

of marginalizing and compartmentalizing Jesus' lordship set up some other lord — the government, the need for retribution or na-

39. The best place to see detailed interaction along these lines is in the pages of *First Things* during the past decade. For further reading in the area (in addition to the works of Hauerwas himself, many of them listed above), see Arthur F. Holmes, ed., *War and Christian Ethics: Classic and Contemporary Readings on the Morality of War*, 2d ed. (Grand Rapids: Baker, 2005); John Howard Yoder, *The Politics of Jesus*, 2d ed. (Grand Rapids: Eerdmans, 1994); Richard A. Horsley, *Jesus and Empire: The Kingdom of God and the New World Disorder* (Minneapolis: Fortress, 2003); Alexander F. C. Webster and Darrell Cole, *The Virtue of War: Reclaiming the Classic Christian Traditions East and West* (Salisbury: Regina Orthodox Press, 2004); Jean Bethke Elshtain, *Just War Against Terror: The Burden of American Power in a Violent World*, 2d ed. (New York: Basic Books, 2004); and, specifically in interaction with Hauerwas, see especially L. Gregory Jones, Reinhard Hütter, and C. Rosalee Velloso Ewell, *God, Truth, and Witness: Essays in Conversation with Stanley Hauerwas* (Grand Rapids: Brazos, 2005). See too the review essay by Burnam W. Reynolds, "The Once and Future Just War — A Review Essay," *Christian Scholar's Review* 35 (2006): 259-74, and the important book by J. Daryl Charles, *Between Pacifism and Jihad: Just War and Christian Tradition* (Downers Grove: InterVarsity Press, 2005).

40. Stassen and Gushee, *Kingdom Ethics: Following Jesus in Contemporary Context* (Downers Grove: InterVarsity Press, 2003). Not far removed from Stassen and Gushee, but more narrowly focused on the political sphere, is the book by Alan Storkey, *Jesus and Politics: Confronting the Powers* (Grand Rapids: Baker, 2005).

41. Stassen and Gushee, *Kingdom Ethics*, 164.

tionalism — as lord over the rest of life. They are therefore idolatry. And they create secularism, because they teach that outside the private realm, or a future realm, or an ideal realm, Jesus is not relevant. Instead what are relevant are secular norms or authorities without critique from Jesus. Thus they remove just war theory from correction by gospel ethics, so that it serves some other lord and gets used dishonestly to justify wars that are not just. We argue that just war theory is not autonomous. Either it serves the purpose of reducing violence and seeking justice under Christ's lordship, or it serves some idolatrous loyalty such as rationalizing a war that we have an urge to make. Either Jesus is Lord over just war theory, or just war theory serves some other lord over Jesus.[42]

What Stassen and Gushee do not probe are some of the other dimensions that properly contribute to the insistence that Jesus must remain Lord of all. For instance, in line with many other just war theorists, Cole argues that *under the conditions and limitations of just war theory* Christians are *morally bound* to engage in just war: that is, not to do so, under those conditions, is a failure to keep what Jesus designates as the second commandment, the commandment to love our neighbors as ourselves. If it is in our capacity to stop a terrible injustice that is taking the lives of many, and we refuse to do so because it might cost us the lives of some of our own people, what is lacking is love.[43] Moreover, others have synthesized the biblical teaching on the kingdom of God in a slightly different way from that espoused by Hauerwas or by Stassen and Gushee[44] or insist that the attempt to unify the pacifist and the just war theorist is more problematic than some think.[45]

A side note: a rather troubling anomaly about the book by

42. Stassen and Gushee, *Kingdom Ethics,* 165.

43. Darrell Cole, "Good Wars," *First Things* 116 (October 2001): 27-34; Cole, *When God Says War Is Right: The Christian's Perspective on When and How to Fight* (Colorado Springs: WaterBrook, 2002).

44. E.g., Russell D. Moore, *The Kingdom of Christ: The New Evangelical Perspective* (Wheaton: Crossway, 2004).

45. E.g., Helmut David Baer and Joseph E. Capizzi, "Just War Theories Reconsidered: Problems with Prima Facie Duties and the Need for a Political Ethic," *Journal of Religion and Ethics* 33 (2005): 119-37.

Stassen and Gushee, and about a great many others that espouse a similar approach to the nature of the kingdom,[46] is the eagerness with which their authors bash the reigning superpower, the United States, for its assorted abuses of power, while arguing that part of the answer lies in strengthening the authority of a really super-superpower, the United Nations. So it turns out that they are not very much afraid of too much power in one place after all; they just don't like the American locus of power. None of these books raises questions about the astonishing degree of nonaccountability in U.N. structures or the U.N.'s demonstrated adeptness at corruption — displayed not least in the spectacular "Oil for Food" scandal. In other words, when they move from theology and exegesis to try to sound prophetic in the contemporary world, they often sound merely faddish and naive.

(e) Far harder to categorize is the independent and subtle work of Oliver O'Donovan.[47] O'Donovan is far from viewing "Constantinianism" as a term of shame or opprobrium. He is in line with the historian Robert Louis Wilken, who argues that, by and large, far from "doing ethics for Caesar" (as is commonly charged), the church after Constantine held Caesar accountable to higher standards — exemplified when, in A.D. 390, Ambrose excommunicated the Christian Theodosius for the massacre he had perpetrated in Thessalonica. Indeed, O'Donovan can go so far as to suggest that the First Amendment to the U.S. Constitution marks the symbolic end of Christendom, when it prohibits Congress from making a law to establish or hinder religion, for it frees the state from all responsibility to recognize God's self-revelation in history. This does not mean that O'Donovan offers an aggressive defense of "Christendom." Rather, he argues that in the wake of Jesus' triumphant resurrection and exaltation, all the political authorities of the world have been made subject to Christ, who has

46. E.g., N. T. Wright, *Evil and the Justice of God* (Downers Grove: InterVarsity Press, 2006).

47. In what follows I refer primarily to his *The Desire of the Nations,* 2d ed. (Cambridge: Cambridge University Press, 2005), and his *The Ways of Judgment,* The Bampton Lectures 2003 (Grand Rapids: Eerdmans, 2005). But see also the extraordinarily useful compendium by Oliver O'Donovan and Joan Lockwood O'Donovan, eds., *From Irenaeus to Grotius: A Sourcebook in Christian Political Thought 100-1625* (Grand Rapids: Eerdmans, 1999).

triumphed over them, so that, at least in principle, they have no power left. Nevertheless, God grants them limited authority to act in this present age, before the ultimate manifestation of Christ's kingdom. The First Amendment, then, actively denies what the Bible teaches: the state has an obligation to recognize God's self-disclosure in history. Within this framework, O'Donovan does not argue that Christians should aggressively pursue the establishment of Christian states but says that they will arise from time to time, even though none of them will be permanently established in this present age.

In *The Ways of Judgment,* O'Donovan asserts that "the authority of secular government resides in the practice of judgment."[48] By "judgment" O'Donovan does not mean to reduce the authority of government to the sphere of the judicial. Rather, judgment is *"an act of moral discrimination that pronounces upon a preceding act or existing state of affairs to establish a new public context."*[49] So if political authorities have been set in place in the wake of Christ's exaltation, they constitute a secondary witness to God's own act of judgment. Using this controlling motif of judgment, much of the rest of the book works through the nature of political authority, the representation of the people, the nature of democracy, and much more. Transparently O'Donovan is in favor of fairly limited government.

O'Donovan's work has been subjected to probing scrutiny.[50] Even if one may criticize some aspects of how he arrives at the point, one of O'Donovan's great strengths is his ability to carve out a theological grounding for the role of government without sliding into many of the traps into which so many theorists tumble.

(f) Various parts of Christianity's spectrum in America are not slow to criticize other parts. The left criticizes the right,[51] and the

48. O'Donovan, *The Ways of Judgment,* 3.

49. O'Donovan, *The Ways of Judgment,* 7 (emphasis his).

50. See especially Craig Bartholomew, Jonathan Chaplin, Robert Song, and Al Wolters, eds., *A Royal Priesthood? The Use of the Bible Ethically and Politically: A Dialogue with Oliver O'Donovan,* Scripture and Hermeneutics Series (Grand Rapids: Zondervan, 2002). Obviously this volume could not take into account O'Donovan's more recent work.

51. E.g., Randall Balmer, *Thy Kingdom Come: How the Religious Right Distorts the Faith and Threatens America: An Evangelical's Lament* (New York: Basic, 2006); Jimmy Carter, *Our Endangered Values* (New York: Simon & Schuster, 2005); Carter, *Palestine:*

right criticizes the left.[52] But all such criticisms are exercises in sedate self-restraint compared with the unrestrained rhetoric of the secular far left. Even their titles say a great deal.

In *American Fascists: The Christian Right and War on America,*[53] Chris Hedges lumps just about anyone who is a Christian into a dark conspiracy largely controlled by theonomists. Perhaps the Presbyterian background of Hedges makes him choose this particular target, but whatever the derivation, Hedges is convinced that Christians are about to do to America what the early Nazis did to Germany.

Michelle Goldberg's *Kingdom Coming: The Rise of Christian Nationalism*[54] is another work that focuses on theonomy (or "reconstruction"). She manages to lump together Timothy McVeigh (a harbinger of "theocratic authoritarianism"), Tim Keller, Marvin Olasky, and D. James Kennedy. She doesn't mention Rick Warren. She has no idea at all about the variations in belief and outlook among these and other evangelicals — or if she does, she certainly does not normally let on. Worse, when she does recognize a difference, her "approach, like that of all the anti-theocrat authors, is to assume that the most extreme manifestation of religious conservatism must, by definition, be its most authentic expression."[55]

In *The Baptizing of America: The Religious Right's Plans for the Rest of Us,*[56] James Rudin foresees ID cards identifying every person's religious faith, compulsory Bible studies in all government departments and big businesses, preferential treatment for Christocrats *(sic),* and so forth.

Kevin Phillips, in *American Theocracy: The Peril and Politics of*

Peace Not Apartheid (New York: Simon & Schuster, 2006). I find it difficult to decide which of the three has the most egregious distortions of both history and theology.

52. Newt Gingrich, *Rediscovering God in America: Reflections on the Role of Faith in Our Nation's History and Future* (Nashville: Integrity, 2006).

53. Hedges, *American Fascists: The Christian Right and War on America* (New York: Free Press, 2007).

54. Goldberg, *Kingdom Coming: The Rise of Christian Nationalism* (New York: Norton, 2006).

55. So Ross Douthat, "Theocracy, Theocracy, Theocracy," *First Things* 165 (August/September 2006): 25.

56. Rudin, *The Baptizing of America: The Religious Right's Plans for the Rest of Us* (New York: Thunder's Mouth, 2006).

Radical Religion, Oil, and Borrowed Money in the 21st Century,[57] ties the dangerous theology rather less to Rushdoony and reconstructionists than to Hal Lindsey and rapture eschatology. Does *anyone* in the Bush cabinet hold to either theological structure? No matter: they've either been snookered or are hiding their real beliefs.

These books reflect almost laughably poor research. Yet in New York City, where these books sell like hot dogs at a baseball game, "evangelicalism" is now a dirty word on a par with "jihadism" or "fascism." Certainly there are as many kooks on the right as on the left. But what we need is a little more care in trying to find out what people really believe and how they really act,[58] and a little less guilt by association and wild extrapolation.

The only reason for bringing these books up here is that most of them appeal to the "wall of separation" as a defense of their position. If we must have conservative Christians in the country, they had better learn that religion is a purely private matter. In other words, Jefferson's wall of separation lies between the state *and all outward expressions of religion that have any bearing on anything in which the state may have a vested interest,* not between the state *and the church as church.* In short, these writers think that the only way the wall of separation can be maintained is by making religion, especially Christianity, as private as possible. Some of these writers feel so much under threat that they think legislation should be passed to ban Christians from public office. How they think the "free exercise" phrase is strengthened by this approach is hard to imagine. In the name of freedom they deeply wish to curtail the freedoms of those who may disagree with them. As America becomes more polarized, issues of the relationship between church and state become more heated and more threatening than ever before.

(3) So far the historical notes in this chapter have focused on America's peculiar experiments with the perennial tensions in the Western world between church and state. The trajectory in the United

57. Phillips, *American Theocracy: The Peril and Politics of Radical Religion, Oil, and Borrowed Money in the 21st Century* (New York: Viking, 2006).

58. One thinks, for instance, of the interesting sociological study of Andrew Greeley and Michael Hout, *The Truth about Conservative Christians: What They Think and What They Believe* (Chicago: University of Chicago Press, 2006).

Kingdom, of course, looks very different. Because England and Scotland both have their own national church, talk of relationships between church and state really do tend to focus on the church *as church,* whereas in America talk of relationships between church and state, as we have seen, tend to drift toward talk of relationships between Christian religion and state. In England, it is highly likely that issues surrounding the possible disestablishment of the national church will receive more attention in years ahead, owing to the decline in its influence (some pollsters say that on any weekend in England there are now more worshipers in mosques than in church buildings), to the incipient breakup of the church over doctrinal and moral issues, and to the public disavowal of any substantive confessionalism on the part of the Prince of Wales, who will be its next Head.[59] Of course, there are many other models of church/state relations. Some countries (e.g., Hungary), concerned that morals be taught in the public school system, have in recent years invited Christian leaders to teach the Bible within the system. It is not at all clear how long this invitation will stand, but from this side of Hungary's experience in the Eastern bloc this is perceived to be a wonderful expression of *freedom.*

The point to observe is that just as democracy has many shapes (as the beginning of this chapter tries to make clear), and just as the concept of the nation-state has several shapes, so the notion of freedom of religion has followed different trajectories. Inevitably these variations change the relationships between church and state. The American Revolution and the French Revolution were not far apart in history, but in some ways they headed in opposite directions. In substantial measure, the origin of the U.S. Constitution (including the Bill of Rights) aimed to protect (the Christian) religion from the state; the French Revolution was much more interested in protecting the state from religion. In its wake, the value of *la laïcité* (which variously means something of a cross between laicization and secularization) was unquestioned — and still is.

Comparison of the trajectories from the American and the French revolutions has often been attempted. Results have been

---

59. As has been widely reported, at his coronation he would prefer to be designated "Defender of faith" rather than "Defender of the faith."

mixed. It is worth reporting two of them here. The first is from Dietrich Bonhoeffer, who spent a little time in America before World War II and left with a certain ambivalence over the interplay between religion and democracy in the United States. American Christians of the "free church" tradition (since there is no state church) feel free to challenge and thus curb the ambitions and pretensions of the state; on the other hand, they also seem too ready to identify the respective roles of church and state, or at least conflate them. In the following quotation, it is important to remember that Bonhoeffer always calls these American "free church" Christians spiritualists or enthusiasts:

> At this point some thought must be given to the special develop-
> ments in the Anglo-Saxon countries and particularly in America.
> The American Revolution was almost contemporary with the
> French one, and politically the two were not unconnected; yet they
> were profoundly different in character. The American democracy
> is not founded upon the emancipated man but, quite on the con-
> trary, upon the kingdom of God and the limitation of all earthly
> powers by the sovereignty of God. It is indeed significant when, in
> contrast to the Declaration of the Rights of Man, American histori-
> ans can say that the federal constitution was written by men who
> were conscious of original sin and of the wickedness of the hu-
> man heart. Earthly wielders of authority, and also the people, are
> directed in their proper bounds, in due consideration of man's in-
> nate longing for power and of the fact that power pertains only to
> God. With these ideas, which derive from Calvinism, there is com-
> bined the essentially contrary idea which comes from the spiritu-
> alism of the dissenters who took refuge in America, the idea that
> the kingdom of God on earth cannot be built by the authority of
> the state but only by the congregation of the faithful. The Church
> proclaims the principles of the social and political order, and the
> state makes available the technical means for putting them into
> effect. These two quite alien lines of thought converge in the de-
> mand for democracy, and it is enthusiastic spiritualism that be-
> comes the determining factor in American thought. This explains
> the remarkable fact that on the European continent it has never
> been possible to find a Christian basis for democracy, while in the

Anglo-Saxon countries democracy and democracy alone is regarded as the Christian form of the state. The persecution and expulsion of the spiritualists from the Continent has in this respect been fraught with the most far-reaching political consequences. If in spite of this the Anglo-Saxon countries, too, are suffering from severe symptoms of secularization, the cause does not lie in the misinterpretation of the distinction between the two offices or kingdoms, but rather in the reverse of this, in the failure of the enthusiasts to distinguish at all between the office or kingdom of the state and the office or kingdom of the Church. The claim of the congregation of the faithful to build the world with Christian principles ends only with the total capitulation of the Church to the world, as can be seen clearly enough by a glance at the New York church registers. If this does not involve a radical hostility to the Church, that is only because no real distinction has ever been drawn here between the offices of Church and state. Godlessness remains more covert. And indeed in this way it deprives the Church even of the blessing of suffering and of the possible rebirth which suffering may engender.[60]

One can quibble with quite a few of the details. Bonhoeffer's analysis depends more than a little on his Lutheran background with its "two kingdoms" theology, and even more on his deep awareness of the vaulting, limitless ambitions of the German state in which he is living. Certainly one may take exception to some of his historical analysis, which in any case now sounds rather dated. Nevertheless it is an excellent reminder of how the relationship between church and state varies enormously from country to country in the Western world, and from period to period within any one country.

Or again, here is Jacques Maritain, writing shortly after World War II when he had moved from France to the United States:

[A] European who comes to America is struck by the fact that the expression "separation between Church and State," which is in itself a misleading expression, does not have the same meaning here and in Europe. In Europe it means, or it meant, that complete

60. Dietrich Bonhoeffer, *Ethics* (1955; New York: Touchstone, 1995), 104-6.

isolation which derives from century-old misunderstandings and struggles, and which has produced most unfortunate results. Here it means, as a matter of fact, together with a refusal to grant any privilege to one religious denomination in preference to others and to have a State established religion, a distinction between the State and the Churches which is compatible with good feeling and mutual cooperation. Sharp distinction *and* actual cooperation, that's an historical treasure, the value of which a European is perhaps more prepared to appreciate, because of his own bitter experiences. Please to God that you keep it carefully, and do not let your concept of separation veer round to the European one.[61]

Once more one could quibble over details. The contrast Maritain perceives is not really between America and Europe but between America and France: when Maritain penned these lines, more than one nation in Europe still boasted a state church (e.g., England) or churches (e.g., Germany), generating patterns of relationships between church and state different both from those of America and from those of France. Clearly, Maritain is describing an America of more than half a century ago. Since then, processes of secularization and backlash have generated a rather different temper in church/state relations in the United States. Moreover, while intellectual and media elites in America adopt many of the stances of (the American version of) postmodernism, elites in France are still deeply committed to structural modernism. Not long ago, President Chirac spoke warmly of the universal project of humanism and of France's role in propagating it. Yet even after these and other caveats have been entered, Maritain's observations strike today's reader as shrewd. At least in part, the American Revolution and its aftermath were designed to support freedom *for* religion; at least in part, the French Revolution and its aftermath were designed to support freedom *from* religion. To this day, there are many Europeans who dismiss overt Christian appeal in matters of public policy to the curse of "civil religion."[62]

61. Jacques Maritain, *Man and the State* (1951; Washington: Catholic University Press of America, 1998), 182-83.
62. E.g., Geiko Müller-Fahrenholz, *America's Battle for God: A European Christian Looks at Civil Religion* (Grand Rapids: Eerdmans, 2007).

This means that when it comes to freedom of religion, what Christians look for in France is rather different from what they look for in Europe. Some French universities, for instance, prohibit all Christian (or other religious) gatherings on their premises. Where a similar prohibition has been attempted in the United States (sometimes on the ground that Christian groups are intolerant since they will not appoint to office those who are practicing homosexuals), Christians respond by appealing to the First Amendment and, so far at least, have prevailed in court. In France, much more authority rests with the university authorities themselves than is the case in the United States, so what is or is not permitted can appear a little more arbitrary. But the nature of the Christian appeal for use of public university premises is very different. Provided Christians are using their group time for study of the Bible and Christian teachings, the French commitment to academic freedom may respond favorably. Where Christians want to include corporate worship, the French commitment to *la laïcité* may forbid the meetings altogether.[63] So Christians shape their meetings and their appeals around study and teaching. I am not arguing that one heritage or another has all the answers. I am merely pointing out that the shape of the relationships between church and state (including state-sponsored institutions, like universities) can vary enormously, and it is difficult to affix normative status, or even long-term stability, to any one of them. Such differences in outlook account for at least some part of France's antipathy toward the United States.[64]

63. I am grateful to David Brown of Groupes Bibliques Universitaires de France (the French equivalent of IVCF/IFES) for talking these matters over with me. See the little booklet that GBU produced: *Liberté de conscience, Liberté d'expression: Communiquer l'Évangile en France aujourd'hui: est-ce légitime?* (Juillan: Fédération Évangélique de France, 2004). Perhaps this is also the place to mention that the cultural (including intellectual) differences between French and American universities extends to multiple related domains. It is difficult to imagine on American campuses a book like that of Luc Ferry, *Apprendre à vivre: Traité de philosophie à l'usage des jeunes générations* (Paris: Plon, 2006). The book is serious popular philosophy and is selling extraordinarily well. Ferry's thesis is that, rightly understood, philosophy does not so much teach you how to think as how to live. Ferry then works through five major "philosophies" and evaluates each in turn. One of these is Christianity, and his treatment is remarkably fair and shrewd. His only significant criticism is that it is too good to be true.

64. This is not the whole of the matter, of course, but it is part of it. See Roger

(4) It is time to look outside the world that is historically, by heritage, Christian. Not a few historians and social scientists have assumed that modernity would cause religion to wither on the vine. Transparently, there are so many exceptions to that thesis that new studies are appearing to challenge the old assumptions. One of the most interesting is that of David Herbert,[65] who traces out some of the complex ways in which religion may interact with "civil society" (his expression). One of the strengths of his book is its four case studies: the role of Islam in Britain this side of *The Satanic Verses,* the role of Catholicism in Poland, the role of various religions in Bosnia, and the role of the Islamization (again, his expression) of Egypt this side of Nasser.

This is not the place to review again the fact that Islam has (a) no heritage of "Give back to Caesar the things that are Caesar's, and to God the things that are God's," (b) a rather different view of the nation-state, which is clearly secondary to the *ummah,* the people of Islam, (c) nothing quite like a national church, still less a denomination, such that discussion of the relationships between church and state, in some Western categories, makes much sense,[66] (d) a sense of historical grievance stemming from the decline of its own influence during the past century and a half or so, and (e) a rising sense of power stemming from the "successes" of its own radical elements, from the fiscal power it exerts because of rising oil revenues, and from its demographic advantages in Europe and elsewhere (a birthrate of about 3.5 while Europe as a whole is under 1.4).

There are so many possible directions that developments in the Muslim world could go that prognostication can be little more than speculation. Many writers have charted examples of the growing strength of more militant strands of Islam — whether Wahaabis in Saudi Arabia, increasing Islamicist rhetoric and education in Egypt

---

Scruton, *The West and the Rest: Globalization and the Terrorist Threat* (Wilmington: ISI Books, 2002).

65. Herbert, *Religion and Civil Society: Rethinking Public Religion in the Contemporary World,* Ashgate Religion, Culture & Society Series (Aldershot: Ashgate, 2003).

66. This point, however, is sometimes overstated. Some Muslim states have a grand mufti, a renowned Muslim teacher who is qualified to make rulings that are binding on the people.

during the last three or four decades, or small indices like the fact that fifteen years ago a Muslim in Malaysia could convert to another religion without going before a *Shari'a* court, but now that small liberty has been taken away and the customary court sentence is punishment. On the other hand, some writers argue that Islam has internal resources to develop its own appreciation for and defense of democracy.[67] One watches with interest the competing forces within a country like Turkey, forces that are set out with rare power in Orhan Pamuk's remarkable novel, *Snow*.[68] The Muslim world is full of ironies and may yet see some remarkable backlashes. Some have argued that Muslims tend to be most open to the West in those countries in which the governments are most vehemently opposed to the West, such as Iran. There is at least some evidence that many ordinary Muslims in some parts of the world are fed up with the violence of their own jihadists, who, far from winning the hearts of the people on the long haul, may end up alienating a lot of them. Or will they constantly find an adequate number of young recruits in countries whose birthrate provides a seemingly endless supply?

In any dispute, personal or national, perception is not everything, but it plays a very big part. Devout Muslims whose only detailed conversation with Westerners has been with those in the liberal heritage are unlikely to be attracted by what they see and hear. The liberal's elevation of the value of religious tolerance to the highest place in the order of virtues will, to a devout Muslim, appear to be a form of functional atheism. Allah brooks no rivals. If the choice is between Islam and profound espousal of religious pluralism as a good in itself, then to the devout Muslim Islam wins, hands down. Even if that Muslim wants to disavow the violence of the jihadists, he or she will not want to embrace the religious pluralism that characterizes so much of the West.

If that Muslim then meets conservative, confessional Christians, a startlingly new conversation takes place. Now the Muslim

67. E.g., M. A. Muqtedar Khan, "American Muslims and the Rediscovery of America's Sacred Ground," in *Taking Religious Pluralism Seriously: Spiritual Politics on America's Sacred Ground,* ed. Barbara A. McGraw and Jo Renee Formicola (Waco: Baylor University Press, 2005), 127-47.

68. Pamuk, *Snow* (2002; New York: Vintage Books, 2004).

meets Christians every bit as committed to confessing the universal sweep of God's sovereignty as do Muslims. These Christians insist every knee will one day bow to King Jesus. They reject, on a deeply principled basis, the religious pluralism that characterizes much Western thought, if that religious pluralism is presented as the ideal. Yet on the other hand, they equally reject violence as a way of advancing the gospel and delight in the empirical pluralism of most Western democracies, not as an absolute good, nor as the highest of moral virtues, but as the best way forward in a fallen and broken world full of idolatries and errors (including our own). Religious pluralism cannot be an ultimate good, for it will not be found in the new heaven and the new earth, toward which we press; but if in this broken world it curbs violence and coercion, if it promotes relative freedom among those who (whether they recognize it or not) bear God's image, then we thank God for the gifts of common grace and for the wisdom of the Master who insisted on some kind of distinction, no matter how complex and how little absolute, between the sphere of Caesar and the sphere of God. We reserve the right to proclaim Christ, and we will give our lives to maintain that right; but we have no interest in ostensible "conversions" achieved at sword-tip, and we distance ourselves from forebears who did not see that point clearly.

As for democracy, if we promote it, we do so not because we take it to be an absolute good, still less as the solution to all political problems, and not even because it is an ideal form of government, but because, granted that the world is fallen and all of us prone to the most grotesque evils, it appears to be the least objectionable option. Our eschatology teaches us that the game isn't over. The way we get to the end is not by military conquest, and not even by the ballot box, but by our Lord's return — and meanwhile we engage in the proclamation of the good news about Jesus in word and deed and remember that he himself taught us that Caesar has a sphere, under God, that is to be respected, an authority that is to be obeyed.

As I say, when devout Muslims meet Christians of that ilk, the conversation over vision and political ends and means may not be quite as antithetical. But whether Islam can develop the resources to produce its own *modus vivendi* with a Caesar detached from promoting Islam as part of governmental policy is still far from certain.

We must look at Muslim states from yet another perspective: How do Christian churches fare under Muslim governments? In other words, if we are asking questions about church and state, what is the nature of the relationship when the state is Muslim? Here there is considerable variation. During the last five years in Indonesia, close to four thousand Christians have been martyred and many church buildings burned to the ground. This is not the result of the policy of central government, but local governments have certainly looked the other way. In Malaysia, Christian churches have substantial liberty, provided the Christian community maintains its locus primarily among the Chinese segment of the population. Even so, to build a church building with a steeple and cross, even for the Chinese Christian population, is forbidden, for such accoutrements are judged too provocative. Malay churches in Malaysia do not officially exist, and Malays (most of whom are Muslim) who convert to Christianity face enormous difficulties.

Open churches among the Saudi population do not exist, and a Saudi who converts publicly from Islam to Christianity is unlikely to survive. It is illegal to build any religious building other than a mosque. In Turkey the official public policy favors more freedom, but there are many local variations, and many common irritations: for example, it is difficult to get a government job if you are a Christian, and in some areas any open witness like passing out free New Testaments risks a severe beating. In Iran there are sporadic outbreaks of violence against Christian church leaders. So the question must be asked: How will churches in the more restricted Muslim countries view their governments?

Of course, the same question could be asked of non-Muslim persecuting regimes. A recent survey by Open Doors assigns the title "worst country for Christian persecution" to North Korea. Where such persecution is more-or-less unremitting and frequently violent, the more benign of Niebuhr's models will seem simply irrelevant to most Christians living there. Where opposition, persecution, and even martyrdom await Christians with any public face, expansive chatter about theoretically ideal models of possible relations between Christ and culture is little more than speculative farce.

Concluding Reflections

It is time to draw some strands together.

(1) Our survey, though far from comprehensive, shows how difficult it is to talk about the relations between church and state without addressing the broader topic of the relations between Christians and the state, and the still broader topic of the relations between religion and the state. The interplay of these polarities is extraordinarily complicated, owing not only to different histories in different countries but also to different understandings of democracy, different assumptions about secularism, different visions of God and of faithfulness, very different religions, and so forth.

From a Christian point of view, it is unhelpful to speak of "the Christian West" or of "our Christian nation" or the like.[69] In America, this is not only because of the legal force of the First Amendment (however it is interpreted) but also because nowadays the numeric shift in numbers of Christians, from West to East and from North to South, is so dramatic that such expressions sound increasingly parochial and out of date. Still more important, talk of "the Christian West" actually stifles the advance of the gospel in parts of the world where countervailing religions and ideologies want people to believe in the stereotype of the Christian West so that Christian claims can be dismissed as merely Western. Above all, Christians who wish to be faithful to the Bible will remind themselves of their heavenly citizenship. Not to understand this is to identify too closely with the kingdoms and orders of this world, with disastrous results both materially and spiritually. As Peter Swift has put it, "If a Muslim becomes a Christian, the civilizational cost is self-evident; he becomes estranged from his roots, and those he leaves behind are dismayed at the civilizational defection their loved one has undergone. The cost of becoming a disciple of Jesus is to leave behind the civilizations of this world and find one's identity within the Kingdom of God. What a tragedy if that cost is cheapened by being perceived as a move westward rather than heavenward!"[70] Of course, the

---

69. Cf. Mark Weldon Whitten, *The Myth of Christian America: What You Need to Know about the Separation of Church and State* (Macon: Smyth & Helwys, 1999).

70. Swift, "The Clash of Civilizations and the Kingdom of God," *The Briefing* 329 (January 2006): 11.

complementary truth is that we *do* live here and now in some *particular* country, and as Paul can declare himself to be a Roman, so I may declare myself to be Ugandan, or Canadian, or Australian, or French, or Japanese. Certainly there ought to be no confusion for Christians as to where their *primary* identity lies, even while they remember that the Christian Scriptures themselves enjoin us to submit to the authority of the state except where doing so involves the believer in disobedience to the God in whom all authority is finally grounded.

(2) Most who read these pages live in democracies. Compared with Christians of the first century living under the Roman Empire, this reality brings new freedoms and new responsibilities. On the side of freedom, it is difficult to imagine a Christian in Judea about A.D. 65 singing, "And I'm proud to be a Judean man/For at least I know I'm free."[71] Yet on the other hand, the biblical injunctions to submit to the state as to God means, in our context, that we *must* take our obligations toward a *participatory* democracy seriously. This, combined with the moral obligation to "do good to the city," involves believers in matters of government at *some* level (all the way from voting to influencing government to legislating and governing) in ways impossible for Paul or Luke — and this means that today it is more difficult to develop a "them" versus "us" mentality typical of believers under totalitarian regimes. While that may improve our sense of participation, doubtless it also increases the possibility of being snookered into confusing the kingdom of God with our own government or party.

(3) The subtlety of these dangers demands more attention. Consider, for example, the oft-repeated advice that if we wish to influence the broader culture through the media and in the corridors of power we must translate our Christian values and priorities into secular categories. Is this good advice? Yes and no. Clearly, the advice reflects pragmatic wisdom. On issues from race to abortion to poverty to homosexuality, we are likely to appeal to a broader range of people if our arguments are not couched in Christian categories and if we manage to form "co-belligerencies" on some strategic issues. Yet we would be naive not to perceive that that is precisely where the danger lies. If all

---

71. If a Jew could say something like this (John 8:33), it was apparently in the heat of debate rather than a well-considered judgment.

of our energy is devoted to making our stances acceptably popular by appealing to goals that are broadly secular, it is a short step to enabling those secular values to take precedence over a Christian frame of reference that bows in principle to the Lordship of Christ.[72] In other words, we ourselves may come to put such stock in our clever adaptations that they mean more to us than the biblical frame of reference that generated the stances in the first place. Moreover, because politics is regularly a pretty vicious form of interchange, our opponents are likely to sniff out our Christian beliefs anyway, and then they will blast us for hiding them and trying to appear secular when we are in reality religious wolves in secular sheep's clothing. Then we will be damned not only for our views but also for our dissembling.

Worse still, our form of discourse may be signaling that we think the secularists are *right:* we *ought* to avoid making any appeal to our "religious" convictions because we support the separation of church and state. That public stance gives subtle advantage to the extraordinarily dangerous view that "the wall of separation" prohibits Christians — or Muslims or Hindus or Buddhists or animists — from participating in the shaping of public policy, instead of defending the view that the wall of separation prohibits entangling the government with the establishment of the church *as church.* If Christians are not allowed to argue in the public arena *as Christians,* then implicitly we are supporting the contentions of Pete Singer and Richard Dawkins and their friends, to the effect that atheistic secularists are the only people who are arguing their case from a "neutral" position.

Five further layers of subtlety call for attention.

(a) When the government hands out money for community benefit — for a job creation program, say, or to help AIDS sufferers — should any of that money go to non-ecclesiastical Christian (or other religious) organizations that try to serve the community in these ways? In many democracies, that is what happens; in some democracies, that is precisely what does not happen. In the United States, it is one of the things that is currently being tested. One might have

72. A number of folk in the tradition of liberal Christianity have warned conservative Christians of this point: e.g., "We mainliners were once offered social action in exchange for faithfulness, and we bit hard" (Jason Byassee, "The Almost Formerly Important," *Christianity Today* 50/3 [March 2006]: 72).

thought that such indiscriminate largesse is no breach of the First Amendment provided different religious organizations similarly organized receive equal benefit, for then it is hard to see how there is "establishment" of any one religion. But that, of course, is an "originalist" reading of the Constitution. For some decades, courts have tended to limit such distribution of funds if any part of them goes to a distinctively religious component (e.g., teaching the Bible as well as distributing food to the poor). In many ministries, however, it is almost impossible to separate "religious" and "secular" components. From a Christian perspective, it is highly undesirable to do so. I would have thought that there is no breach of the First Amendment if there is a substantial state interest in the ministry and if the support provided by the state is happily distributed to similar ministries of various denominations and religions when citizens of those denominations and religions are similarly organized — but of course, one must deal with the courts and their decisions as they are, not as one wishes they were.

(b) At the local level, the impact of demography, working out in democracy, must surely come into play. Where a neighborhood is predominantly Muslim, or Christian, or whatever, there should be no pressure on government to provide equal support *at the local level* to all religion-ministries that may be supported *elsewhere in the country.* In other words, as unreasonable as it sounds to some, a little common sense in these discussions would be a good thing.

(c) Much more so than in any other Western democracy, America has developed the fine art of individual whining. If a school that receives state dollars puts on a Christmas play with a Christmas theme, all it takes is one vociferous atheist or vociferous Muslim to complain about his or her child feeling alienated or wounded, and school administrators are likely to shut down the Christian traditions and resort to a bland "Season's Greetings" presentation, usually involving Martians or others of indeterminate race, culture, gender, or creed who cannot be in competition with our convictions. Of course, if the school is located in a neighborhood where many religious traditions compete, then a great deal can be said for celebrations that inform the entire community of those different traditions. But where there is one whiner worried about loss of self-esteem, one begins to wonder why there is little concern for *community* self-esteem, for forbearance *within* the community, for community pleasure at supporting the *majority* tradition.[73]

(d) More complicated yet is the broadly moral arena. Some American states, not to mention Canadian courts, have legalized "marriage" between homosexuals. Most Western democracies run or sanction large gambling establishments. Confessional Catholics and Protestants alike will be displeased with the former, and confessional Protestants will be displeased with the latter. Their own liberties are not curtailed by such legislation or judicial decisions, of course: they are not forced (at least, not yet!) to sanction homosexual marriage or to gamble. But many Christians will see such steps not only as contrary to the "norming norm" of Scripture but also as deeply harmful to society. Whether they think the harm comes in the social categories of deteriorating families and desperate addictions and bankruptcies, or in the theological category of the threat of God's wrath on the nation, or some combination of the two, they feel morally constrained, not only out of loyalty to God but out of concern for the nation, to influence policy in another direction. In other words, we would prefer to see laws in place that forbid certain conduct because we are convinced that such conduct is bad — bad both theologically and socially. Secularists will view this as religious meddling; we view it as the entailment of love for our neighbor and as inescapably tied to our confession that Jesus is Lord. Secularists may well view Christian political efforts along these lines as frightening examples of theocracy; Christians may well view secularist rhetoric as an attempt to stifle Christian efforts to pass laws they judge to be moral — indeed, as a sign of desperate moral decay that does not care for the well-being of the nation, let alone for the glory of God.

It is unclear how far such polarities can go without democracy itself changing its shape. Indeed, most efforts to point the way forward implicitly adopt either a Christian or a secularist stance. For example, Winnifred Fallers Sullivan clearly understands that all religions im-

---

73. One of the dangerous implications of these developments is that the government takes on the monopolistic power of deciding which speech is permitted because it is protected under the First Amendment, and which speech is prohibited because it offends some other party.

plicitly challenge the state's monopoly on law. Their appeal to transcendent authority challenges the exclusive claims of the state and insists, in effect, on the right to "a life outside the state."[74] With remarkable optimism, Sullivan thinks she can meet this need by passing laws that guarantee equality. But this of course means that the secular view of the state is basically correct, and that such a state, wisely operating, wishes merely to protect the (implicitly erroneous) views of religious citizens.

(e) All of the reasoning of these last few paragraphs is nothing other than an attempt at prudential wisdom as we try to work out, in the light of current social and political conditions, a handful of entailments to Jesus' "Give back to Caesar the things that are Caesar's, and to God the things that are God's." If the developing tension is not between secularists and Christians, however, but between secularists and deeply committed Marxists or devout Muslims, the roiling outcome may be quite different. We return to the fact that neither of these traditions has within its respective heritage a component of thought that *expects* the Marxist or Muslim community to be *distinguishable* from the state or that feels under mandate of its founder to preserve that distinction.

(4) The consequence, then, is that we have additional reasons for thinking that Niebuhr's fivefold typology, as influential as it has been, simply will not do. It will not do because, as we saw in earlier chapters, it offers us alternative ways of thinking about Christ and culture, whereas one of his types cannot be justified by Scripture, and the other four can all be found in Scripture, prompting questions about whether they are alternatives or components of a bigger pattern — a pattern that begins to emerge when we follow the Bible's story line in the categories of biblical theology. Moreover, the fivefold typology is not very effective at interacting with current discussions over postmodernism. And now we find it lacking in an age when notions like "the Christian west" cannot really be sustained, when multiculturalism has shaped many decisions of the Supreme Court, and when immigration patterns force us to think about the way non-Christian reli-

74. Sullivan, *The Impossibility of Religious Freedom* (Princeton: Princeton University Press, 2005), 158.

gions, notably Islam, are likely to view the typologies Niebuhr proposes. In short, as influential as it has been in the past, Niebuhr's fivefold typology now seems parochial.[75]

(5) Two of the elements of religious liberty that Christians espouse are freedom to convert from one religion to another (or to none) and freedom to evangelize. Most Muslim countries will happily allow non-Muslims to become Muslims, but not the reverse. Part of the reason lies with the imperialist expectations of Islam, but part lies in quite a different understanding of "conversion" as compared with the notion of conversion espoused by Christians. To become a Muslim, one need only confess that there is no God but Allah and that Muhammad is his messenger. One is supposed to commit oneself to the five fundamental *practices* of Islam, but plenty of nominal Muslims don't bother. Becoming a Muslim, then, means coming to adopt a position and perform certain practices. This is not normally thought of as coming to know God: such talk is presumptuous, for God is so transcendent that we cannot know him directly. Becoming a Muslim means submitting to the will of God as revealed in the Qur'an, more than coming to know the God of the Qur'an. By contrast, Christian conversion, though it includes changing an allegiance and adopting some practices, is understood to be connected with the work of the Spirit of God in one's life. Regeneration transforms one's life, and the walk of faith in Jesus Christ enables us to speak of knowing God in a way quite different from our life before conversion. A child who grows up in a Christian home may well speak of the moment of his or her "conversion" at, say, age 8 or 15, or after attaining adulthood; a child growing up in a Muslim home would never speak of being converted to Islam. Islam demands conformity to the system; Christianity demands the internal transformation sometimes called regeneration. A person contemplating changing to Islam must simply exercise an act of will — of willed commitment to a new allegiance. Enormous social pressure

75. The same problem touches many contemporary discussions of the relationships between church and state — discussions that work through the possibilities without any recognition of the powerful voices of other religious *within Western democracies,* let alone elsewhere. See, for instance, A. T. B. McGowan, "Church and State: The Contribution of Church History to Evangelical Models for Public Theology," *European Journal of Theology* 14 (2005): 5-16.

may be applied to keep that person aligned with these new-found Muslim commitments. According to Paul, a person contemplating Christ must be enlightened by the Spirit or remain merely "natural" (1 Corinthians 2:14). In short, we have a high stake in preserving a place for "conversion" that is intrinsically supernatural (however much it involves the human will), that demands what some traditions call "soul liberty," and that certainly extends beyond mere practice.

Philip Yancey reports a conversation with a Muslim who told him, "I find no guidance in the Qur'an on how Muslims should live as a minority in a society and no guidance in the New Testament on how Christians should live as a majority."[76] That may not be quite true, but, as Yancey points out, it does highlight "a central difference between the two faiths. One, born at Pentecost, tends to thrive cross-culturally and even counter-culturally, often coexisting with oppressive governments. The other, geographically anchored in Mecca, was founded simultaneously as a religion and a state."[77]

(6) Perhaps this is the place to affirm that, however complicated the theoretical discussion becomes over the relationships between church and state, the most attractive outworking by far is found in the individual Christian or group of Christians who, precisely because they live out their faith, become involved not only in bold witness but also in ways of helping others in the community that cross many thresholds normally controlled by government agencies. A church starts a center in its poor area of town to mentor kids without dads, to help kids to read, to look after some of the sick and the elderly, to start a school that has far more care, discipline, Christian influence, and rigor than in the available options, and so forth. Let the critics cry "Foul!" and demand that religion be private. We serve a Lord who will not allow us to be silent and retreat.

(7) Finally, in all Christian reflection on these matters, however much we wrestle with the complications arising from Jesus' utterance, "Give back to Caesar what is Caesar's, and to God what is God's," we cannot forget, not for a moment, that Jesus is Lord of all, yet at the same time the end is not yet. I know of no finer brief state-

---

76. Yancey, "The Lure of Theocracy," *Christianity Today* 50/7 (July 2006): 64.
77. Yancey, "The Lure of Theocracy," 64.

ment of the resulting eschatological tensions than that written by Richard John Neuhaus in the 1981 founding statement of the Institute on Religion and Democracy:

> Jesus Christ is Lord. That is the first and final assertion Christians make about all of reality, including politics. Believers now assert by faith what one day will be manifest to the sight of all: every earthly sovereignty is subordinate to the sovereignty of Jesus Christ. The Church is the bearer of that claim. Because the Church is pledged to the Kingdom proclaimed by Jesus, it must maintain a critical distance from all the kingdoms of the world, whether actual or proposed. Christians betray their Lord if, in theory or practice, they equate the Kingdom of God with any political, social or economic order of this passing time. At best, such orders permit the proclamation of the gospel of the Kingdom and approximate, in small part, the freedom, peace, and justice for which we hope.

SIX

On Disputed Agendas, Frustrated Utopias, and Ongoing Tensions

—⟨⟨⟨⟨⟩⟩⟩⟩—

Summaries

The first chapter began by setting out a little of the current debate over the meaning of culture. It rejected the older concept of "high" culture in favor of Clifford Geertz's approach: "[T]he culture concept . . . denotes an historically transmitted pattern of meanings embodied in symbols, a system of inherited conceptions expressed in symbolic form by means of which men communicate, perpetuate, and develop their knowledge about and attitudes towards life."[1] That set the stage for surveying the very substantial number of issues Christians face when they ask questions about how they and the Christian subculture to which they belong relate to the larger culture in which they are embedded. This is something Christians face alike in southern Sudan, North Korea, Western Europe, East Asia, and everywhere else. In the English-speaking world, the controlling discussion is still that of H. Richard Niebuhr and his fivefold typology: Christ against culture, the Christ of culture, Christ above culture, Christ and culture in paradox, and Christ the transformer of culture.

The second chapter offered a preliminary critique of Niebuhr. It is difficult to find any biblical warrant for the second entry in his fivefold template. Niebuhr himself concedes that his own reading of the

---

1. Geertz, *The Interpretation of Cultures* (New York: Basic Books, 1973), 89.

fifth option, "Christ the transformer of culture," demands more of a universalistic hope than the biblical texts actually warrant. Above all, however, Niebuhr's typology offers his five types as slightly idealized competing options. Yet this emphasis on choosing from among the options does not square with the canonical function of Scripture. Insofar as at least four of Niebuhr's options can claim some biblical warrant, the question that must be asked is this: Do the biblical texts offer these types as alternatives that believers are welcome to choose or reject? Or are they embedded in a still larger and more cohesive understanding of the relationship between Christ and culture, such that the four or five options of Niebuhr's typology should be thought of as nothing more than possible emphases within a more comprehensive integrated whole? If the latter, then Christians do not have the right to choose one of the options in the fivefold typology as if it were the whole. The name of that game is reductionism.

Much of the rest of the second chapter is devoted to another way of getting at the same question of integration. Instead of focusing on the possible ways to think about the relationship between Christ and culture, this section focuses on some of the great turning points in biblical theology, including creation, the fall, the call of Israel, the coming of Jesus Christ and the onset of an international community that is not itself a nation complete with geographical borders and a political system, and the prospect of a new heaven and a new earth and resurrection existence. It can be shown that Niebuhr's five options tend to emphasize a selection of these biblical-theological turning points and downplay others. For example, the second option, "the Christ of culture," talks happily about the goodness of creation but seriously downplays the fall and its entailments. On the whole, Niebuhr's discussion is thin with respect to the fact that *current* relations between Christ and the church can be properly perceived only in the light of eternity, of a hell to be feared and a new heaven and new earth to be gained. *All* of these turning points must be held together *all* of the time as we try to think constructively and holistically about the relation between Christ and culture.

Some critics, however, will object that the entire discussion up to this point is far too dependent on unsophisticated approaches to "culture" and on a barely hidden modernist epistemology. The third chapter goes some way to address both of those concerns, ending with a discussion of James K. A. Smith's *Who's Afraid of Postmodernism? Taking Derrida, Lyotard, and Foucault to Church.*[2]

What, then, are some of the pressures that force thoughtful Christians to wrestle with how we ought to relate to the broader culture of which we are a part, even if we are a distinguishable part? Many things might have been chosen, but the fourth chapter focuses on secularism, democracy, freedom, and power. In each case, we are dealing with something that can be an enormous force for good, *if firmly embedded within the normative structure of the Bible's story line and priorities,* but which can be both dangerous and idolatrous when it assumes independent value and constructs a frame of reference in flat contravention of Scripture's norms. Inevitably Christians find themselves squeezed between the claims and obligations of the broader culture and their allegiance to Christ. The tensions between Christ and culture are both diverse and complex, but from a Christian perspective they find their origin in the stubborn refusal of human beings, made in God's image, to acknowledge their creaturely dependence on their Maker.

The fifth chapter focuses on one particular element of the relationship between Christ and culture, namely, church and state. The aim of the chapter is to clarify a few of the terms and issues that surround the subject, survey some of the relevant biblical passages, and show how the sometimes competing claims of church and state have evolved in different places. Although there are better and worse examples of how these tensions might play out, there is no ideal stable paradigm that can be transported to other times and places: every culture is perpetually in flux, ensuring that no political structure is a permanent "solution" to the tension.

And so at last this final brief chapter. My aim here is to survey a handful of common treatments of Christ and culture,[3] to show why

---

2. Smith, *Who's Afraid of Postmodernism? Taking Derrida, Lyotard, and Foucault to Church* (Grand Rapids: Baker, 2006).

3. I shall not reiterate again how the simple binary "Christ" and "culture" is in some ways misleading, since every manifestation of Christ is enculturated (see, for example, Graham Ward, *Christ and Culture,* Challenges in Contemporary Theology [Oxford: Blackwell, 2005], 21-22), nor the reasons already provided why the opposed categories nevertheless remain useful.

none of them, even the most insightful, should be allowed to control the discussion, and then to return to a comprehensive approach that allows a great deal of variation in emphasis.

Disputed Agendas and Frustrated Utopias

Perhaps the most seminal evangelical thinkers on this topic during the last century and a half are Abraham Kuyper, Carl F. H. Henry, Francis Schaeffer, and John Howard Yoder. Apparently that is what J. Budziszewski thinks, as he has written a book to evaluate their thought.[4] But of course there are many other leading lights who have written seminal books and articles on the relationship between Christ and culture — for instance, J. Gresham Machen a century ago[5] and I. Howard Marshall at a recent conference of the Fellowship of European Evangelical Theologians.[6] We may have begun our inquiry with Niebuhr, but it is important to remember that Christians have always wrestled with these matters. It is easy to find many relevant passages in Puritan books.[7] One cannot forget, at the time of the English Reformation, Bishop Hugh Latimer's sermon before King Henry VIII, in which he soliloquized, "Latimer! Latimer! Latimer! Be careful what you say. The King of England is here. . . . Latimer! Latimer! Latimer! Be careful what you say. The King of Kings is here."[8] Time and space fail to survey the relevant passages in Calvin's *Institutes* or Augustine's probing reflections on what is distinctive about the City of God, writ-

4. J. Budziszewski, *Evangelicals in the Public Square: Four Formative Voices on Political Thought and Action* (Grand Rapids: Baker, 2006).

5. Machen, "Christianity and Culture," available at http://homepage.mac.com/shanerosenthal/reformationink/jgmculture.htm, accessed October 10, 2006. This is an adaptation of "The Scientific Preparation of the Minister," *The Princeton Theological Review* 11 (1913): 1-15.

6. Marshall, "Biblical Patterns for Public Theology," *European Journal of Theology* 14 (2005): 73-86, expounding 1 Samuel 12; Jeremiah 29:1-14; 1 Timothy 2:1-10; 2 Chronicles 28:1-15.

7. A useful place to begin is Leland Ryken, *Worldly Saints: The Puritans as They Really Were* (Grand Rapids: Zondervan, 1986).

8. Christopher Bryan, *Render to Caesar: Jesus, the Early Church, and the Roman Superpower* (Oxford: Oxford University Press, 2005), 126.

ten after Alaric sacked Rome, or to trace these and other strands back to the seminal thought of the New Testament itself.

Until the final resolution in the culture of the new heaven and the new earth, challenging and sometimes painful tensions will afflict us in these domains. Christians living under one particular model of how these matters should be worked out may labor under a too-limited vision of what might be, of what should be attempted, of what can be achieved. To think our way rapidly through a handful of diverse patterns or experiences of Christ/culture relationships may prove enriching while bringing to light how much these patterns and experiences have in common.

The Fundamentalist Option

If the fundamentalists of the last quarter of the nineteenth century and the first half of the twentieth tended to withdraw from serious engagement with the broader culture,[9] at least some of their heirs have tended to swing the pendulum pretty hard the other way. In some ways this is preferable to the isolationism that preceded it. Yet much of this cultural engagement is reactive: fundamentalists spot directions being taken by the broader culture that they feel are immoral or dangerous and adopt strategies to confront them and if possible overturn them. At the risk of generalization, they are reasonably effective at combating what they do not like in the culture even while exhibiting relatively little interest in the ways one should support the culture, working into the worlds of art and music. A substantial part of the appeal is to tradition: America may not be a Christian nation, they say, but it was founded on Christian principles — and the movement itself is an appeal to return to such Christian principles. It would be more realistic to acknowledge that the founding of the nation was borne along by adherence to some Christian principles and not others. After all, there cannot be many today from any camp who want to return to slavery.

---

9. The book to read is George M. Marsden, *Fundamentalism and American Culture,* 2d ed. (Oxford: Oxford University Press, 2006).

In the long haul, Christians have to appeal farther back than to the middle of the eighteenth century — to the Scriptures themselves, and the events to which they attest — and think through where we are today and will be tomorrow. To learn from history is one thing; to make constant appeal to yesteryear is to support rather too much of the nostalgic and rather too little of the prophetic. Moreover, fundamentalists tend to address a select list of evils — abortion, homosexuality, secularism working its way into school curriculum, and the like — and ignore a much broader list of social evils. Most frightening to their opponents is the transparent triumphalism they display when they gain some victory. The advance of the kingdom of God seems to be substantially aligned with certain political goals, and when those goals seem within reach, the euphoria in the fundamentalist camp is unmistakable.

In their defense, however, especially against those who charge them with veering toward theocracy that would destroy democratic principles, most of what they are calling for is not more dangerous than a sort of 1950s conservative America. That might strike opponents as a bit old-fashioned, but the most sober of these opponents would not argue that in the 1950s America was not democratic.[10] And when the opponents charge fundamentalists with being enslaved by consumerism and other elements of the American dream, it is worth recalling that several important studies have shown that, while the American left is happy to vote for higher taxes, the American right is usually far more generous with its own pocketbooks (even if we all agree that the generosity is far too limited). Still, none but some of the fundamentalists themselves, and some of their opponents who demonize them and yell "Theocrat!" at them, believe that the future lies with them.

Luther and His Heirs

The two kingdoms theory has become highly sophisticated and is interpreted by Lutherans themselves in fairly disparate ways. One erudite summary is offered by John Witte Jr.:

10. See chapter 4, above, nn. 28-29.

> The earthly kingdom is distorted by sin and governed by the Law. The Heavenly kingdom is renewed by grace and guided by the Gospel. A Christian is a citizen of both kingdoms at once and invariably comes under the distinctive government of each. As a heavenly citizen, the Christian remains free in his or her conscience, called to live fully by the light of the Word of God. But as an earthly citizen, the Christian is bound by law, and called to obey the natural orders and offices that God has ordained and maintained for the Governments of this earthly kingdom.[11]

What this vision rightly captures is the tension. On the one hand, whether we call them two kingdoms or two sources of authority, we implicitly recognize that the kingdoms of this world do not acknowledge the Lordship of Christ. There is little point in constantly reasserting that we are all part of the same culture, when one substantial segment of the culture acknowledges an ultimate authority unrecognized by the rest of the culture. On the other hand, by insisting that Christians are simultaneously citizens of the earthly kingdom and of the heavenly kingdom, the Lutheran vision allows no easy escape from unavoidable tensions between the paired and competing allegiances.

But it is easy so to polarize the two kingdoms that we forget that one God stands over all. Worse, if we then apply such a polarized two kingdoms theory to every domain of human endeavor, we shall not even attempt a unifying approach to knowledge: there will be knowledge grounded in human reason, and knowledge grounded in revelation and faith, and the two will not meet. In some ultimate sense, of course, such a unified vision awaits the new heaven and the new earth. But not even to attempt to move in that direction here and now is to repeat the disastrous error into which believers fell when the medieval synthesis collapsed. Thomas Aquinas had divided secular work and religious activities; correspondingly, he distinguished between truth grounded in reason and truth grounded in revelation. How should we attempt to stop these polarities from flying apart? Here the church made the wrong choice: the spiritual truths would simply trump the other truths. The long-term effect has been to marginalize

---

11. John Witte Jr., *Law and Protestantism: The Legal Teachings of the Lutheran Reformation* (Cambridge: Cambridge University Press, 2002), 5-6.

211

Christian teaching as being detached from the broader world of day-to-day existence.[12] To quote Lutheran Robert Benne,

> Were this version of Lutheran theology taken to its logical conclusion it would deprive the gospel of any intellectual content and the law of any moral content. The biblical narrative and theological reflection on it would not be given any epistemological status to engage secular learning. It would champion a form of Lutheran quietism in the realm of education. Much as German Lutherans in the 1930s separated the two kingdoms (government under law separated from Christianity under the gospel) and allowed the Nazi movement to go unchecked by appeal to the intellectual and moral content of the Christian vision, so this approach would allow modern secular learning to go unchallenged by that vision.[13]

More broadly, Lutherans, as I've said, have differed among themselves as to how the two kingdoms should relate to each other. Should civil law, for instance, preserve spiritual morality by forbidding blasphemy and imposing sanctions on those who breach the law? Luther did not think so; Melanchthon did. The ruler of the earthly kingdom ought to uphold spiritual morality (involving the relations between God and human beings) as well as personal morality (involving human-to-human relations). Push Melanchthon hard enough and it is difficult to see how one can avoid ending up with an established church; push Luther hard enough and it is difficult to see how one can avoid marginalizing from the public square Christians and their views on almost everything.

Abraham Kuyper

The year 1998 marked the centenary of Kuyper's 1898 celebrated Stone Lectures, delivered at Princeton Theological Seminary. The

---

12. See especially Arnold S. Nash, *The University and the Modern World: An Essay in the Social Philosophy of University Education* (London: SCM, 1945), 181-82; see also Duane Litfin, *Conceiving the Christian College* (Grand Rapids: Eerdmans, 2004), 144-45.

13. Robert Benne, *Quality with Soul: How Six Premier Colleges and Universities Keep Faith with Their Religious Traditions* (Grand Rapids: Eerdmans, 2001), 133; cited also by Litfin, *Conceiving the Christian College,* 145.

event was celebrated by special conferences at Princeton Seminary, the Free University of Amsterdam, and Calvin Theological Seminary.[14] The best of Kuyper's work that has been translated into English appeared in a convenient *Reader,* and a probing analysis of Kuyper's Stone Lectures was published.[15] Shortly after the centenary, a biography of Kuyper was published, followed by a long and detailed analysis of Kuyper's public theology.[16] Since then, a number of specialized studies have appeared.[17]

At least part of the reason why Kuyper still elicits so much attention is that he was a Christian thinker who was spectacularly successful at putting his ideas into practice. His theological vision led directly to the founding of Christian trade unions and other Christian organizations, a Christian university, a Christian political party, and ultimately to his own role in government. Others with minds just as fecund as his, theologians who in fact developed ideas very similar to his, have proved far less influential, for the sufficient reason that their ideas on public theology never led to similar public success. Sean Michael Lucas shrewdly observes how similar are the theological stances and public visions of Abraham Kuyper and Robert L. Dabney, who died at the age of seventy-seven in 1898 — but no group celebrated the centenary of his passing in 1998.[18] Situated on the losing side of the American Civil War, Dabney found himself in an essentially defensive posture, while Kuyper was aggressively building new institutions. Small wonder that many Christian leaders at the beginning of the

14. The papers for these conferences appeared, respectively, in Luis E. Lugo, ed., *Religion, Pluralism, and Public Life: Abraham Kuyper's Legacy for the Twenty-first Century* (Grand Rapids: Eerdmans, 2000); Cornelis van der Kooi and Jan de Bruijn, eds., *Kuyper Reconsidered: Aspects of His Life and Work* (Amsterdam: VU Uitgeverij, 1999); and *Markets and Morality* 5/1 (2001).

15. James D. Bratt, ed., *Abraham Kuyper: A Centennial Reader* (Grand Rapids: Eerdmans, 1998); Peter S. Heslam, *Creating a Christian Worldview: Abraham Kuyper's Lectures on Calvinism* (Grand Rapids: Eerdmans, 1998).

16. James E. McGoldrick, *Abraham Kuyper: God's Renaissance Man* (Darlington: Evangelical Press, 2000); John Bolt, *A Free Church, A Holy Nation: Abraham Kuyper's American Public Theology* (Grand Rapids: Eerdmans, 2001).

17. E.g., Vincent Bacote, *The Spirit in Public Theology: Appropriating the Legacy of Abraham Kuyper* (Grand Rapids: Baker, 2005).

18. "Southern-Fried Kuyper? Robert Lewis Dabney, Abraham Kuyper, and the Limitations of Public Theology," *Westminster Theological Journal* 66 (2004): 179-201.

twenty-first century turn to Kuyper and not to Dabney as a guide for their own efforts.

Doubtless the passage from Kuyper most frequently quoted is this: "Oh, no single piece of our mental world is to be hermetically sealed off from the rest, and there is not a square inch in the whole domain of our human existence over which Christ, who is sovereign over *all,* does not cry, 'Mine!'"[19] Yet that truth, which all thoughtful Christians will confess, must be integrated with other truths — for example, that Christ's sovereignty is widely contested now as it will not be in the new heaven and the new earth; that until the end an unavoidable tension exists between the covenant community of God's people and those who, on Christian terms, do not know him; that there is an epistemological chasm between those who accept God's revelation in Jesus Christ and those who do not. Kuyper's distinctiveness lies in how he puts these and related matters together. Because all truth is God's truth, because nothing we legitimately study is unrelated to Christ, Kuyper felt compelled to demonstrate how Christ's sovereignty operates in every sphere. At least during the first half of his career, Kuyper pursued these lines while insisting on the distinctiveness of the church, on the uniqueness of the special grace that Christians alone have received. By setting up a *Christian* university and by establishing a *Christian* trade union and a *Christian* political party, all the while underlining that Christ is Lord of *all,* he was simultaneously insisting that there is unique insight in the *Christian* revelation and that Christians are mandated to affirm Christ's Lordship in *every* sphere. The result is a vision that emphasizes the uniqueness of the church[20] and of what is now often called special revelation, while equally underscoring the importance of what was later called the cultural mandate. Add this synthesis to the remarkable success he achieved in his lifetime, and Abraham Kuyper's almost iconic influence is understandable.

Yet once Kuyper achieved political power, his thinking underwent a subtle shift in emphasis. Eventually three major problems developed

---

19. Bratt, ed., *Abraham Kuyper: A Centennial Reader,* 488.

20. And even, as we saw in chapter 5, the distinction between what the church *as church* legitimately does and what *Christians* ought to be doing.

— embedded to some extent in his own thought, and occasionally noto-
rious in the thought of his followers. (a) The antithesis between belief
and unbelief, between redeeming grace and common grace, waned. A
Kuyper scholar like James Bratt applauds the development;[21] with
more discernment, Klaas Schilder bemoans the development. Schilder's rather dense little book, *Christ and Culture*,[22] makes the point
powerfully. When Kuyper puts disproportionate emphasis on creation
at the expense of redemption, on common grace at the expense of redeeming grace, Schilder asserts, he is moving away from Reformed orthodoxy. Richard Mouw rather cheekily calls this Schilder's "Anabaptist
corrective" of Kuyper — admitting, of course, that Schilder himself
would not have acknowledged Anabaptist influence.[23] In any case, it
seems pretty clear that the second half of Kuyper's career sees him
gently moving away from what is *central* in the driving force of the Bible's story line.[24] (b) A second element that contributed, after Kuyper's

21. James D. Bratt, *Dutch Calvinism in Modern America: A History of a Conservative Subculture* (Grand Rapids: Eerdmans, 1984), 19.

22. Most easily accessed on the web at http://www.reformed.org/webfiles/cc/christ_and_culture.pdf (most recently accessed 18 February 2007) under the copyright of G. van Rongen and W. Helder (1977).

23. Richard J. Mouw, "Klaas Schilder as Public Theologian," *Calvin Theological Journal* 38 (2003): 281-98. Similarly, Lucas, "Southern-Fried Kuyper?" 200, argues that "the limitation of public theologies such as Dabney's and Kuyper's can be traced to their failure, oddly enough, to maintain the antithesis between church and world." Another way of getting at the same problem is the suggestion of Henry R. Van Til, *The Cal-
vinistic Concept of Culture* (Grand Rapids: Baker, 1959), 244, that the expression "common grace" should always be put in quotation marks so that it does not stand on an
equal footing with redeeming grace — a point Mouw (p. 297) also picks up.

24. The same is true, I think, of some who have tried to develop Kuyper's
thought. Bacote's book, *The Spirit in Public Theology: Appropriating the Legacy of Abraham Kuyper,* referred to above, attempts to develop the doctrine of the Spirit, the Spirit
in creation and mediating common grace, to buoy up and enrich Kuyper's vision. The
effort is stimulating in many ways, but it depends too much on merely possible infer-
ences. Worse, it keeps insisting, without evidence, that this aspect of the doctrine of
the Spirit is as important as the Spirit's role in redemption. Quite apart from doubtful
claims about equal importance, it is surely necessary, if Schilder's criticism is to be
avoided (Bacote does not refer to Schilder), to show how these complementary roles of
the Spirit are properly related to each other. More careful, and more theologically comprehensive, is T. M. Moore, *Consider the Lilies: A Plea for Creational Theology*
(Phillipsburg: P & R, 2005).

departure from the scene, to the extraordinarily rapid decline of Christian influence in the government and culture of the Netherlands was the heavy emphasis within Kuyperianism on presumptive regeneration. This is not to argue that dramatic, still less traumatic, conversion of children reared in Christian homes is necessary; nor is there a biblically mandated need for certainty about the moment of one's conversion. Rather, it is to assert that theologically and biblically, presumptive regeneration is not well grounded, and pragmatically, it has led, in the Netherlands and South Africa (where the doctrine has most frequently been defended), to churches with very substantial numbers of unregenerate people (however culturally conservative they are) whose children then simply walk away from the faith.[25] (c) Not entirely unrelated to the previous two points is a third: Kuyperianism is most attractive when Kuyper's personal piety is in play (in exactly the same way that the reforming zeal of Wilberforce is attractive because of his commitment to the gospel and his transparent evangelical piety). When Kuyperianism, a branch of European Reformed theology, becomes the intellectual structure on which we ground our attempts to influence the culture, yet cuts itself loose from, say, the piety of the Heidelberg Confession, the price is sudden death.

Minimalist Expectations

In the last chapter I mentioned the approach of Darryl G. Hart, who exemplifies one form of a stance that advocates minimal hope of Christian influence in the broader culture. For instance, in the domain of the academic world, Hart argues that Christian academics ought to abandon Kuyperian attempts to integrate their faith and their scholarship.[26] They ought to recognize that the rules of scholarship are estab-

25. For a defense of presumptive regeneration, see Lewis Bevens Schenck, *The Presbyterian Doctrine of Children in the Covenant* (1940; Phillipsburg: P & R, repr. 2003); Douglas Wilson, *Standing on the Promises: A Handbook of Biblical Childrearing* (Moscow: Canon, 1997). The former is critically reviewed by Maurice J. Roberts, "Children in the Covenant," *Banner of Truth* 501 (June 2005): 20-24.

26. Darryl G. Hart, "Christian Scholars, Secular Universities and the Problem of Antithesis," *Christian Scholar's Review* 30 (2001): 383-402.

lished by the modern academy, and simply play by those rules — a kind of "Lutheran" (as he takes it) submission to the kingdom of this world, the authority of this world, that cannot come to terms with the kingdom of God. Somewhat similarly, Frederica Mathewes-Green likens culture to the weather and thinks we have about as much influence over culture as we do over the weather (well, yes, we can seed some clouds now and then, she avers).[27] We simply live in it, and we must learn to live faithfully in it. Whatever minor positive changes we bring about will simultaneously bring about a "downturn in a different corner," and in any case the changes will not be permanent. "The culture will always be shifting, and it will always be with us."[28] In other words, our task is not to change the weather but "to care for *individuals* [my emphasis] caught up in the pounding storm."[29]

If the only thing these and similar authors were warning us against were utopianism and the crushing disappointment that inevitably follows when the utopian ideal fails, they would be rendering stellar service.[30] We need to be reminded that the only human organization that continues into eternity is the church; we need to remember that even cultural gains are often followed by losses, that sin rears its head sometimes in violent persecution and sometimes in subtle deception (Revelation 13!), that biblical narrative itself shows us how often a good king is followed by a bad king and vice versa. It is unwise to speak of "redeeming culture": if we lose the unique significance bound up with the *redemption* secured by Christ in his death and resurrection, we lose the ongoing tension between Christ and culture that must subsist until the end.

Yet it is possible so to focus on the rescue and regeneration of *individuals* that we fail to see the temporally good things we can do to

---

27. Frederica Mathewes-Green, "Loving the Storm-Drenched," *Christianity Today* 50/3 (March 2006): 36-39.

28. Mathewes-Green, "Loving the Storm-Drenched," 38.

29. Mathewes-Green, "Loving the Storm-Drenched," 38.

30. A similar cycle of hyped utopianism often attends proposals for dealing with world poverty and the like, with almost no lessons learned from the past: see the devastating detail compiled by William Easterly, *The White Man's Burden: Why the West's Efforts to Aid the Rest Have Done So Much Ill and So Little Good* (New York: Penguin, 2006). This is not to say that nothing useful can be done, as even Easterly makes clear.

improve and even transform some social *structures.* One does not abolish slavery by doing nothing more than helping individual slaves.[31] Christian educational and academic structures *may* help countless thousands develop a countercultural way of looking at all reality under the Lordship of Christ.[32] Sometimes a disease *can* be knocked out; sometimes sex traffic *can* be considerably reduced; sometimes slavery *can* be abolished in a region; sometimes more equitable laws *can* foster justice and reduce corruption; sometimes engagement in the arts *can* produce wonderful work that inspires a new generation. When such things become part of an inherited set of assumptions passed on to the next generation, they have become part of the culture; they have effected some cultural change. Of course, none of these good things is guaranteed to be enduring; none brings in the consummated kingdom. Yet in these and countless other ways cultural change is possible. More importantly, doing good to the city, doing good to all people (even if we have special responsibility for the household of faith), is part of our responsibility as God's redeemed people in this time of tension between the "already" and the "not yet."[33]

Post-Christendom Perspectives

Here the premier book, for our purposes, is the recent publication by Craig A. Carter, *Rethinking Christ and Culture: A Post-Christendom Perspective.*[34] This useful and well-written work combines a critique of the Niebuhr typology with an affirmation of an Anabaptist/Yoder/Hauerwas approach to culture.[35] It is easy to see how the two — the

31. See Deann Alford, "Free at Last: How Christians Worldwide Are Sabotaging the Modern Slave Trade," posted at http://www.christianitytoday.com/40851, accessed 21 February 2007.

32. Cf. William C. Davis, "Contra Hart: Christian Scholars Should Not Throw in the Towel," *Christian Scholar's Review* 34 (2005): 187-200.

33. See the helpfully provocative book by Paul F. M. Zahl, *Grace in Practice: A Theology of Everyday Life* (Grand Rapids: Eerdmans, 2007).

34. Grand Rapids: Brazos, 2007.

35. Carter himself is careful not to lump people together in such a way that distinctions among them are obliterated.

critique of Niebuhr and the affirmation of Yoder — are linked in Carter's mind. Niebuhr's typology is possible only on the assumption of the fundamental legitimacy of the Constantinian settlement.[36] Substantial chunks of it have to change once we perceive "why Christendom was a bad idea."[37] Weigh in the massive decline of Christian influence in most of those parts of the world once thought of as constituting Christendom, and the urgency of the need to rethink Niebuhr becomes transparent. Moreover, some of Niebuhr's categories are far too antithetical. For instance: Carter follows Yoder in seeing how following Jesus entails being a part of a countercultural community. Loyalty to Jesus within this community means being opposed to the totalizing claims of the nation-state, of modernity, autonomous reason, and consumerism. This sounds a bit like Niebuhr's "Christ against culture" option. Carter insists, however, that following Jesus does not mean that we stand against classical music, family farms, and medicine. Christ does not stand against culture in every respect. Niebuhr's antitheses need to be moderated.

In the second half of his book, Carter proposes his own typology. He makes a fundamental divide between, on the one hand, three Christendom types and, on the other, three non-Christendom types. All three of the Christendom types accept violent coercion. The three are:

(a) Type 1: Christ legitimizing culture
(b) Type 2: Christ humanizing culture
(c) Type 3: Christ transforming culture

In Type 1, the examples include the Crusades and German Christians during World War II; the Christology of this model is fundamentally docetic. Type 2 includes Luther and Billy Graham, while the Christology remains partially docetic. Type 3 embraces Augustine and Cromwell; appeal is made to the Old Testament theocracy, and the Christology is "inconsistently Nicene."

36. This point is constantly made in the literature and right across the theological spectrum. See, for instance, the editorial by James F. Kay, "Overture," *Theology Today* 63 (2006): 1-4.

37. This is the title to Carter's fifth chapter.

By contrast, all three of the *non*-Christendom types reject violent coercion. Two of the three in this new list bear a formal resemblance to two of the three above, but their fundamental difference is bound up with the principled rejection of violent coercion. The three are:

(a) Type 4: Christ transforming culture
(b) Type 5: Christ humanizing culture
(c) Type 6: Christ separating from culture

In Type 4, the examples include William Penn, Martin Luther King Jr., and Desmond Tutu; the Christology in all three of these types is fully Nicene. Type 5 embraces Mother Teresa and the Mennonite Central Committee; Type 6, supported by the Apocalypse, includes the Benedictines and the Anabaptists.

Thus the fundamental distinction, in Carter's mind, between the first three types, compromised by adhering to Christendom, and the last three, which are Nicene and are unwilling to be aligned with Christendom, is the latter's rejection of the use of force (though Carter slightly loads the issue by referring to "violent coercion" rather than to force, thereby refusing to acknowledge distinctions in kind and use of force).

There is much that is attractive in Carter's passionate voice. What genuine Christian will not admire Carter's desire to follow Christ wholly, to ensure that following Jesus does not degenerate into an ostensible spirituality that is abstracted from life in the here and now? Moreover, Carter is part of a larger heritage that asks not only what the individual *Christian's* relationship with the broader culture ought to be but what the *Christian community's* relationship with the culture ought to be, if that community rightly displays the counter-cultural commitments demanded by allegiance to Jesus. We can understand why, as Mouw puts it, Schilder's critique of Kuyper can be thought of as "the Anabaptist corrective." Moreover, at the level of concrete decisions regarding how Christians should be concerned for the poor, for instance, or should stand against the great god consumerism, Carter has many useful things to say, and on such matters he and his followers will surely join hands with many Christians in other traditions.

Yet however acute his criticism of Niebuhr, and however thought-provoking his own schema, Carter's thesis raises problems that will not go away. Most of them I have already addressed, in greater or lesser detail, earlier in this book, but it will not hurt to highlight three of them in summary form here.

First, the dividing line in Carter's thought is "violent coercion" — whether one thinks there is any place for it or not. Historically, this is, more or less, the adoption of pacifism as the dividing line. Even if one thinks Carter's interpretation of the Scriptures and scriptural themes he references is correct — and rather often I do not — it is difficult to see why one should make pacifism the dividing line. He grants a subsidiary role to the Nicene Creed but manages to argue, against considerable evidence, that those who adopt any form of "violent coercion" have a flawed Christology from the perspective of Nicea, while those on the pacifist side fully embrace the Christology of Nicea. I heartily concur that there are "orthopraxy" components in authentic Christianity (though I may not always agree with Carter what they are), but surely there is more to the orthodoxy components than the Christology of Nicea. Paul, for instance, can say some pretty trenchant things about the difference between authentic Christianity and inauthentic Christianity and those who espouse either (Galatians 1:8-9), and can make the dividing line rather different from either Nicea or pacifism. There is little in Carter's work that reflects on what the gospel *is,* how it is tied not only to Christology but also to sin and judgment, to mercy, and to the cross and resurrection of Jesus. It is not that Carter wishes to deny, say, the resurrection of Jesus. Far from it: he affirms it. But there is little in his argument that convincingly puts together the entire story line of the Bible, including the great turning points in redemptive history. He is tired, he avers, of the old divisions between liberalism and conservatism, both of which are dead ends, both reflecting a secularized kind of faith that is nothing less than "a heretical deviation from Christianity, and it is dying."[38] Certainly Christianity has too often been domesticated by modernism, yet Carter, it appears, wishes to domesticate it by his post-Christian pacifist ideals. One does not sense here a careful submis-

---

38. Carter, *Rethinking Christ and Culture,* preface.

sion to Scripture and an evenhanded learning from Christians throughout history. Rather, this is a raw championing of pacifism to which every other consideration must bend, all in the name of following Jesus.

Second, this leads to a string of omissions or distortions — I do not know what else to call them — that finally make readers wonder if they are being had. For instance, Carter can pass on the famous remark of Agricola, a chief speaking to his fellow Britons, as recorded by Tacitus: "[The Romans] rob, butcher, plunder, and call it empire; and where they make a desolation, they call it 'peace.'" But he does not discuss the *pax Romana,* odd instances where old nations sued to come under the Roman authority (e.g., King Eumenes II bequeathing the ancient kingdom of Pergamum to Rome, such that it became the Roman province of Asia Minor), or the manner in which anarchy often proves at least as vile as corrupt imperialism, such that Scripture can speak with every bit as much condemnation against the one as against the other. There is little probing of "common grace" (whether it is called that or not). The commitment to pacifism, that is, his absolute rejection of "violent coercion," leads him to devote several pages to defending the view that the Crusades and World War II are moral equivalents, both equally morally indefensible.

Third, one comes away from Carter's book without any estimate of the complexities of getting issues about Christ and culture right. Very remarkably for someone who sees himself in the post-Christian era, Carter paints only in white and black. Both in the New Testament and in great swaths of the church's history, Christians have wrestled with what it means to live faithfully between the "already" and the "not yet." Carter's book tells you, in effect, to reject "violent coercion," and the problem is solved. Yet I come away unconvinced by his reading of the parable of the sheep and the goats, unpersuaded by some of his occasional forays into exegesis, painfully convinced that the Bible leaves a lot of loose ends bound up with the fact that Paul (for instance) was simultaneously a citizen of heaven and of the Roman Empire. In short, despite its many invaluable insights, Carter's book comes across as not only mistaken on some crucial points but sadly reductionistic.

Persecution

Although it would be possible to list a substantial number of other developing patterns between Christ and culture, it would be a sad betrayal of our brothers and sisters in Christ in more oppressive parts of the world if we gave no thought at all to this category. Some Christians live under regimes, whether local or national, that are brutally repressive — whether systemically or sporadically. When I was a boy, Christians still read Foxe's *Book of Martyrs*. It is still worth reading. But today it needs to be supplemented. One thinks, for instance, of Don Cormack's moving and probing account of Christian sacrifice and martyrdom in Cambodia, especially under Pol Pot.[39] The two million killed in southern Sudan during the past two decades are still awaiting a suitable chronicler and historian.

The obvious thing to say is that Christians in such environments do not spend a lot of time contemplating Niebuhr's typology. But that does not mean that Christians in such situations think only in terms of "Christ against culture." The reality turns out to be more complex.

We are often told that the blood of the martyrs is the seed of the church. That is not true when the violent persecution is so complete that the church is either completely or almost entirely wiped out (e.g., Albania under the Communists, Turkmenistan today). But where persecution is not complete, or comes in waves with times of relative peace between the waves, there the old saying often demonstrates its insight. The persecution tends to reduce the number of spurious converts and "Christians" who are not serious, so that when some measure of freedom, however limited, is restored, the church may grow very rapidly.

Certainly in such situations Christians cannot help but see themselves as "other" than the dominant culture in many respects. When threats and brutality go on for many decades, the Christian community sometimes ends up bruised and discouraged. But sometimes Christians are the ones who prove to be most hopeful and helpful under the dynamics of a brutal regime, precisely because they live with eternity not far away.

Sometimes Christians in such difficult places long to emigrate

39. *Killing Fields, Living Fields* (London: Monarch, 1997).

to an easier part of the world, and they do so if they have the opportunity. We have witnessed the emigration of Christians from numerous dominantly Muslim countries as the mood of Islam has become more militant. But sometimes they choose to stay because they want to help where the need is greatest. Without wishing to criticize either side, we cannot help but see that these two groups have a slightly different perception of their place in and interaction with the surrounding culture.

But the chief point to observe is that choices of entire paradigms as to what we think the relationship between Christ and culture *ought* to be — or, more narrowly, what the relationship between the church and the state ought to be — is a luxury reserved for those who have options. Those of us who live in relative security must learn this lesson in humility.

Conclusion

What this potted survey ought to tell us is that none of the powerfully advanced theories commonly put forward to explain the relationships between Christ and culture or to implement an improved dynamic is very compelling as a total explanation or an unambiguous mandate. Each has decided strengths; some are better at drawing in the highly diverse and complementary strands of Scripture and historical interpretation than others whose coinage is reductionism. Moreover, as empirically useful as certain grids may be, thoughtful Christians need to adopt an extra degree of hesitation about canonizing any of them in an age in which we are learning the extent to which our own cultural location contributes, for better and for worse, to our understanding of these theological matters, as of all theological matters.[40] Above all, we must grasp that even the most intellectually robust theory of how things work, or ought to work, falters in practice within a generation or two, because human beings falter: we overlook something, or we distort the balance of things, or, because this is a fallen and broken world, our well-intentioned actions invite a nasty reaction on the part

40. Cf. Craig Ott and Harold A. Netland, eds., *Globalizing Theology: Belief and Practice in an Era of World Christianity* (Grand Rapids: Baker, 2006).

of unbelievers, and the tension between Christ and culture spins off in some new direction. One recalls the wisdom of C. S. Lewis:

> What is the good of telling the ships how to steer so as to avoid collisions if, in fact, they are such crazy old tubs that they cannot be steered at all? What is the good of drawing up, on paper, rules for social behaviour, if we know that, in fact, our greed, cowardice, ill temper, and self-conceit are going to prevent us from keeping them? I do not mean for a moment that we ought not to think, and think hard, about improvements in our social and economic systems. What I do mean is that all that thinking will be mere moonshine unless we realise that nothing but the courage and unselfishness of individuals is ever going to make any system work properly. It is easy enough to remove the particular kinds of graft or bullying that go on under the present system: but as long as men are twisters or bullies they will find some new way of carrying on the old game under the new system. You cannot make men good by law: and without good men you cannot have a good society.[41]

Ongoing Tensions

In one of the most attention-getting introductions he has ever managed, Michael Horton begins an essay with the lines:

> It was confusing to grow up singing both "This World Is Not My Home" and "This Is My Father's World." Those hymns embody two common and seemingly contradictory Christian responses to culture. One sees this world as a wasteland of godlessness, with which the Christian should have as little as possible to do. The other regards cultural transformation as virtually identical to "kingdom activity."[42]

One of the important points of this book is that both of these options, and a lot of others as well, are, in the light of Scripture, painfully

41. *Mere Christianity* (1952; San Francisco: HarperSanFrancisco, 2001), 73.
42. Michael S. Horton, "How the Kingdom Comes," *Christianity Today* 50/1 (January 2006): 42-46.

reductionistic. With appropriate caveats, it is easy to find some biblical warrant for both of these songs, and for a few others with apparently competing messages as well. That, however, is simply another way of saying that each is built on too selective a reading of biblical themes.

Sociologists will develop their own grids for analyzing complex movements, of course, and find ways to categorize diverging Christian responses to the broader culture. The descriptive power of such grids may be insightful in various ways, and of course they can also be challenged on assorted grounds. But once grids like those proposed by Niebuhr or Carter (or anyone else) claim some measure of *prescriptive* power, they must be tested by Scripture. One of the things I have tried to show is that the ostensible test of Scripture is inadequate if it turns on a convenient arrangement of proof-texts and biblical precedents. In addition to close exegesis of a wide range of biblical texts, we need to think through how they fit into the great turning points of redemptive history, into the massive movement from creation to the new heaven and the new earth, with critical stops along the way for the fall, the call of Abraham, the rise and fall and rise again of Israel, the coming of the promised Messiah, his teaching, ministry, death, and resurrection, the gift of the Spirit and the birth of the church. Nor can we ignore great theological structures, including the Trinitarian nature of the Godhead, all that the cross achieves, and the unavoidable implications of New Testament eschatology with its unyielding combination of inaugurated and future eschatology.

If such massive biblical and theological structures control our thinking on these matters, and such revelatory categories are worked out in our lives in adoration and action, then various ways of thinking about the relationship between Christ and Caesar may prove heuristically helpful but will not assume canonical force. We will be much better able to be as flexible in this regard as are the New Testament documents, without undermining such absolutes as "Jesus is Lord!" The same fundamental structure of biblical theology will speak as powerfully to Christians under persecution who cry for release and for the dawning of the consummated kingdom as to Christians whose love for their neighbors drives them toward heroic efforts on behalf of AIDS sufferers. It will embrace the exclusive claims of Christ and the uniqueness of the church as the locus of redeeming grace, and yet it will demand of believers that they recognize their creaturely existence in this old, fallen creation and reflect on the ubiquitous commands not only to love God but also to love their neighbors as themselves. Instead of imagining that Christ *against* culture and Christ *transforming* culture are two mutually exclusive stances, the rich complexity of biblical norms, worked out in the Bible's story line, tells us that these two often operate simultaneously.

> As a stand-alone posture, *against* too often turns into brittle condemnation, a stance of haughty (presumed) moral superiority, wagons circled. *Transform* on its own may degenerate into naïve idealism, even utopianism, a stance concerning which Dietrich Bonhoeffer reserved some of his most severe words. The radical begrudges God his creation, Bonhoeffer insists, for the radical seeks a self-sovereignty incompatible with recognition of our indebtedness to others in the past as well as the present. The radical is all ultimacy, prepared to sacrifice the penultimate, the here and now, for some eschatological goal.
>
> Avoiding these extremes, we must see Christ against *and* for, agonistic *and* affirming, arguing *and* embracing. This is complex but, then, Christianity is no stranger to complexity.[43]

To pursue with a passion the robust and nourishing wholeness of biblical theology as the controlling matrix for our reflection on the relations between Christ and culture will, ironically, help us to be far more flexible than the inflexible grids that are often made to stand in the Bible's place. Scripture will mandate that we think holistically and subtly, wisely and penetratingly, under the Lordship of Christ — utterly dissatisfied with the anesthetic of the culture.[44] The complexity will mandate our service, without insisting that things turn out a certain way: we learn to trust and obey and leave the results to God, for we learn from both Scripture and history that sometimes faithfulness

---

43. Jean Bethke Elshtain, "With or Against Culture?" *Books & Culture* 12/5 (September/October 2006): 30.

44. The metaphor is that of Thomas de Zengotita, "The Numbing of the American Mind: Culture as Anesthetic," *Harper's Magazine* (April 2002): 33-40.

leads to awakening and reformation, sometimes to persecution and violence, and sometimes to both. Because creation gave us embodied existence, and because our ultimate hope is resurrection life in the new heaven and the new earth, we will understand that being reconciled to God and bowing to the Lordship of King Jesus cannot possibly be reduced to privatized religion or a form of ostensible spirituality abstracted from full-orbed bodily existence now.

Such rich reading of Scripture will achieve two more things. To a generation that scrambles for the top and then looks around and asks, "Is this all there is?" a biblical vision that focuses on Christ and his cross, on the links between this world and the next, on bold Christian living and faithful witness, and on a large-scale vision that makes the world our parish while loving the neighbor next door, raises our eyes above ourselves, and delights in the glory of God. When churches so taught thrust their members into engagement with the wider world, their members are far less likely to be snookered by the world to which they are to bear witness and in which they are to do good. We will avoid the trap aptly described by Horton: "Instead of being in the world but not of it, we easily become of the world but not in it."[45] Instead, we will live in the tension of claiming every square inch for King Jesus, even while we know full well that the consummation is not yet, that we walk by faith and not by sight, and that the weapons with which we fight are not the weapons of the world (2 Corinthians 10:4).

45. Horton, "How the Kingdom Comes," 46.

Index of Subjects

Index of Names

Abélard, Pierre, 17, 34, 62
Adams, John, 173
Ahmadinejad, Mahmoud, 125
Alexander, T. D., 44n.22
Alford, Deann, 218n.31
Allah, 35, 53
Alston, William, 91n.38
Ambler, Eric, 1
Ambrose, 182
Aristippus, 19
Aristotle, 10
Ataturk (Mustafa Kemal), 138
Audi, Robert, 91n.38
Augustine, 24, 25, 27, 28, 38, 40, 59, 106, 108-12, 176-77, 208, 219
Augustus, 166
Avram, Wes, 8n.14
Awwad, Johnny, 160n.16

Bach, J. S., 1
Bacote, Vincent, 213n.17, 215n.24
Baer, Helmut David, 181n.45
Bailey, D. Jeffrey, 155n.9
Bailyn, Bernard, 124n.19
Ball, David T., 57
Balmer, Randall, 183-84n.51
Barnett, Randy E., 175n.30

Barr, James, 44n.22
Bartholomew, Craig, 183n.50
Bauckham, Richard, 7-8, 39n.17, 138n.38
Bauer, Walter, 32-33
Bell, Daniel M., Jr., 179n.38
Benedict XVI, 119
Benne, Robert, 212
Berger, Peter L., 116
Berman, Harold J., 172n.26
Birkett, Kirsten, 119n.11
Bismarck, Otto von, 157-58
Black, Hugo L., 175
Blake, William, 29
Blocher, Henri, x, 34, 51n.25, 68, 74
Bloesch, Donald, 97n.56
Bockmuehl, Markus, 42n.20
Bolt, John, 213n.16
Bonhoeffer, Dietrich, ix, 187-88, 227
Bonjour, Laurence, 91n.38
Bottum, Joseph, 85n.24
Bouchard, Donald F., 104n.64
Boulton, David, 116n.3
Bratt, James D., 81n.19, 213n.15, 214n.19, 215n.21
Brault, Pascale-Anne, 106n.67
Bright, Bill, ix

235

Index of Scripture References

241